W9-AEX-406

PROPHETIC WOMAN

Anne Hutchinson. Given to the Commonwealth by the Anne Hutchinson Memorial Association and Massachusetts State Federation of Women's Clubs. Cyrus E. Dallin, A.N.A., Sc. Courtesy of Massachusetts State Library.

PROPHETIC WOMAN

ANNE HUTCHINSON AND
THE PROBLEM OF DISSENT
IN THE LITERATURE
OF NEW ENGLAND

AMY SCHRAGER LANG

University of California Press
Berkeley · Los Angeles · London

University of California Press
Berkeley and Los Angeles, California

University of California Press, Ltd.
London, England

©1987 by
The Regents of the University of California

This book has been published with the assistance of a grant
from the Andrew W. Mellon Foundation.

Portions of this book have appeared in *ESQ: A Journal of the
American Renaissance, New England Quarterly, Prospects,* and
Women's Studies.

Library of Congress Cataloging-in-Publication Data
Lang, Amy Schrager.
  Prophetic woman.

  Bibliography: p.
  Includes index.
  1. American literature—New England—History and
criticism. 2. Hutchinson, Anne Marbury, 1591–1643,
in fiction, drama, poetry, etc. 3. Antinomianism in
literature. 4. Prophecy (Christianity) in literature.
5. Women in literature. 6. Dissenters, Religious, in
literature. 7. New England in literature. 8. Puritans
in literature. 9. Feminism and literature—New
England. I. Title.
PS243.L28   1987   810'.9'974   86-11214
ISBN 0-520-05598-5 (alk. paper)

Printed in the United States of America

1   2   3   4   5   6   7   8   9

*To Peter
and to Daniel and Emma*

Contents

Acknowledgments

Many people have offered their support, criticism, and encouragement in the course of this study. I am particularly grateful to Sacvan Bercovitch, whose rigor as a teacher and generosity as a critic have been invaluable. I owe a special debt to Myra Jehlen and Cecelia Tichi, who contributed their critical insight, their valuable time, and their friendship to this project. I am indebted as well to Susan Dickman, Michael T. Gilmore, Leo Marx, Ruth Perry, Stephen J. Tapscott, and my colleagues at the Massachusetts Institute of Technology for their continuing interest and support. Monica Kearney gave me much-needed assistance in preparing this manuscript for publication.

The Irene C. Cuneo Fellowship of the American Association of University Women, the Research Fellowship for Recent Recipients of the Ph.D. of the American Academy of Learned Societies, and the Massachusetts Institute of Technology's Old Dominion Fellowship provided crucial support during the early phases of this project. As a Rockefeller Research Associate in the Women's Studies in Religion Program at Harvard Divinity School, I received generous financial assistance and much encouragement during its completion.

My greatest debts are, of course, personal ones. To Peter Lang, without whose help this work could not possibly have been done, to Daniel and Emma, who suffered through it and made it better, and to Jules and Jeanne Schrager, I can only offer my thanks.

Abbreviations

AC David D. Hall, ed., *The Antinomian Controversy, 1636–1638*: A Documentary History, (Middletown, Conn.: Wesleyan University Press, 1968).

CW Robert E. Spiller and Alfred R. Ferguson et al., eds., *The Collected Works of Ralph Waldo Emerson* (Cambridge: Belknap of Harvard University Press, 1971–).

HS William Emerson, *An Historical Sketch of the First Church of Boston from its Formation to the Present Period* (Boston, 1812).

JMN William H. Gilman et al., eds., *Journals and Miscellaneous Notebooks of Ralph Waldo Emerson* (Cambridge: Belknap of Harvard University Press, 1960–82), 16 vols.

N Eliza Buckminster Lee, *Naomi, or Boston, Two Hundred Years Ago* (Boston, 1848).

SL Nathaniel Hawthorne, *The Scarlet Letter* (New York: Library of America, 1983).

ST Jonathan Edwards, *Some Thoughts Concerning the Revival of Religion*, in *The Great Awakening*, ed. C. C. Goen, vol. 4 of *Works of Jonathan Edwards* (New Haven: Yale University Press, 1957–).

STS Charles Chauncy, *Seasonable Thoughts on the State of Religion in New England: A Treatise in Five Parts* (Boston, 1743).

TS Nathaniel Hawthorne, *Tales and Sketches* (New York: Library of America, 1982).

US   George Bancroft, *History of the United States of America*, Centenary Edition (Boston: Little, Brown, 1879), 6 vols.

UTC   Harriet Beecher Stowe, *Uncle Tom's Cabin or, Life Among the Lowly* (Cambridge: Harvard University Press, 1962).

W   Ralph Waldo Emerson, "Woman," in *Complete Works of Ralph Waldo Emerson* (Cambridge: Riverside Press, 1884).

WE   Jonathan Edwards, *The Works of President Edwards* (New York, 1843), 4 vols.

WWP   J. Franklin Jameson, ed., *Johnson's Wonder-working Providence, 1628–51*, in *Original Narratives of Early American History* (New York: Scribners, 1910), 19 vols.

1

Introduction

In 1830 the Salem *Gazette* printed a biographical sketch of Anne Hutchinson written by Nathaniel Hawthorne, native son and aspiring young author. The sketch, entitled "Mrs. Hutchinson," is a curious one. Not only does Hawthorne assume that his readers will recognize his Mrs. Hutchinson and remember her history but he assumes as well the immediacy of her story. Nowhere in the sketch does he detail the story of Hutchinson's excommunication from the First Church of Boston or her banishment from Massachusetts Bay in 1638. Instead, "Mrs. Hutchinson," ostensibly a portrait of the seventeenth-century heretic, begins with an attack on the "public women" of the nineteenth century, in whose ranks one might, Hawthorne suggests, find Hutchinson's "living resemblance." Hawthorne acknowledges the peculiarity of this opening—excusing "any want of present applicability" by the "general soundness of the moral"—but insists nonetheless on the aptness of his comparison. Hutchinson, that public woman of the past "whereof one was a burthen too grievous for our fathers,"[1] has been succeeded by a new breed of woman no less burdensome and far more numerous. Paradoxically, the religious heretic of the 1630s is reincarnated in the female sentimental novelist of the 1830s.

Twenty-five years before writing his famous letter to William Ticknor bemoaning the domination of the literary marketplace by the "d——d mob of scribbling women," Hawthorne introduces his reader to Anne Hutchinson by deploring the "irregularity" of the "ink-stained Amazons" who present themselves at the bar of literary criticism. In Hawthorne's estimation the "false liberality and . . . courtesy" accorded these women by their reviewers combine to "add a girlish feebleness to the tottering infancy of [American] literature" (*TS*, 18). All too clearly,

1

the Amazons will "expel their rivals . . . and petticoats [will] wave triumphantly over all the field" (*TS*, 18).

Hawthorne himself realized that the juxtaposition of seven-teenth-century antinomian and nineteenth-century author de-manded explanation, particularly since the latter, rather than promulgating "strange and dangerous opinions," consistently urged the virtues of home and hearth. What links these dispa-rate figures is "feminine ambition." Both Hutchinson and her literary counterpart of the nineteenth century have abandoned their embroidery for careers as public speakers. As prophetess in one case and novelist in the other, each has stepped out of her appointed place and indelicately displayed her "naked mind to the gaze of the world, with indications by which its inmost secrets may be searched out" (*TS*, 19). This unseemly exposure of a private self to the public gaze—indecorous at best and at worst positively lewd—is urged on antinomian and sen-timental author alike by an apparently irresistible "inward voice." Like the errant Anne Hutchinson, who, according to Hawthorne, confused "carnal pride" with the gift of prophecy, so the misguided author yields to the "impulse of genius like a command of Heaven within her" (*TS*, 19).

The similarity between antinomian and sentimentalist, both of whom appeal to an inner voice to rationalize their intrusion into the public arena, casts the literary critic in the role of the Puritan magistrate. The court of literary opinion must, Haw-thorne insists, "examine with a stricter . . . eye the merits of females at its bar, because they are to justify themselves for an irregularity which men do not commit in appearing there" (*TS*, 19). Likewise, Hawthorne refuses to dismiss the Puritan's judg-ment against Anne Hutchinson as the action of an "illiberal age." On the contrary, "worldly policy and enlightened wis-dom" would also dictate her banishment (*TS*, 21). In the inter-est of the rising culture, the literary critics of the nineteenth century would do well to banish from the American literary scene those whose "slender fingers" enfeeble it.

The energy of Hawthorne's sketch comes from his intuitive recognition of a resemblance between Anne Hutchinson and the scribbling women. The story of "the Woman," as Hawthorne invariably calls Hutchinson, is offered as the quintessential story of female empowerment—of its origin in an erroneous "inward voice," its unseemly public expression, and its disastrous social effect. Inevitably, that story is fraught with tension. In fact, insofar as one term points toward the broad masculine realm of autonomous action in the world while the other calls us home again, the phrase "public women" captures a crucial contradiction. This contradiction is similarly reflected in the competing images of unnatural strength and equally unnatural weakness in Hawthorne's sketch. The female author, with an Amazon-like disregard for feminine decorum, expels her male rivals from the literary field, but the flag her "slender fingers" hoist over that field is only, after all, a "petticoat": the woman warrior writes domestic fiction.

On the one hand, the act of female authorship constitutes an assertion of autonomy and, thus, a challenge to authority as dramatic as Hutchinson's antinomianism. By choosing "the path of feverish hope, of tremulous success, of bitter and ignominious disappointment" (*TS*, 19), the woman writer defies her place. On the other hand, it is not strength but rather the "girlish feebleness" of the sentimental domestic novel penned by the Amazon that threatens to undermine the national literature. In other words, the trouble with the Amazon, ink-stained or otherwise, is that she remains a woman and, as Woman, implies an order that, as Amazon, she violates. Insofar as Woman contains in herself the possibility of Amazonian defiance, she suggests the further—and more frightening—possibility that men too might step out of their places.

In this sense the gender-specific problem of the public woman figures the larger dilemma of maintaining the law in a culture that simultaneously celebrates and fears the authority of the individual. That dilemma has long been identified with antinomianism, but Hawthorne's sketch calls our attention to the fact that the problem of individual autonomy is especially problematic when the individual is female. The fact that Anne Hutchinson, the classic American representative of a radical and socially destructive self-trust, is a woman compounds and complicates her heresy. In "Mrs. Hutchinson" the problem of

antinomianism is propounded as the problem of Anne Hutchinson, which is, in turn, the problem of the public woman.

It is precisely this sequence in which I am interested. What
little information exists about the historical Anne Hutchinson
has long since been unearthed; likewise, the term *antinomian*
has been appropriated by scholars in a wide variety of disci-
plines to mark the outer limits of American individualism. But
in all the work that has been done on antinomianism, both as
Puritan and as American heresy, the fact that the antinomian is
embodied as a woman has received scant attention. Another
history of antinomianism needs to be written, one focusing
on the special relevance of "the Woman" to the nature of antinomian heresy and depending less on the historical record
than on the "literary" one. In the context of this history, Hawthorne's sketch seems less odd than inevitable.

The contours of Hutchinson's story are familiar. In 1634 Anne
Hutchinson, a woman in middle age, left England with her
large family to follow the much-admired Reverend John Cotton to New England. Admitted to the church, her husband
elected to the high office of deputy to the Massachusetts General Court, Hutchinson set about establishing herself in her
new home. Her first prominence was as a nurse-midwife and
spiritual adviser to women, but sometime during her first two
years in Boston she began to hold weekly gatherings for the
purpose of reviewing and commenting on the sermon of the
previous Sunday. These meetings, first attended exclusively by
women, quickly grew to include men and soon drew a regular
attendance of sixty or more of the town's inhabitants, including
the young governor, Henry Vane, and a number of other men of
power and prominence. As her following changed in both size
and prestige, so too, apparently, did Hutchinson's message.
Rather than simply recapitulating the weekly sermon, she undertook to reproach the Massachusetts clergy. The leaders of
the church, she claimed, had fallen into a covenant of works.
"Legalists" all, they mistakenly took sanctification—the successful struggle of the saint against sin—as evidence of elec-

tion, failing to understand that works and redemption bear no necessary connection. In essence Hutchinson spoke for a doctrine of free grace, characterized by the inefficacy of works and the absolute assurance of the saint. Until the arrival in 1636 of her brother-in-law and supporter, the Reverend John Wheelwright, John Cotton alone was exempt from her criticism.

Hutchinson's followers, convinced that the Massachusetts Bay ministers were guilty of preaching a covenant of works, were moved to action. Efforts were made to replace the Reverend John Wilson, then pastor of the Boston church, with John Wheelwright. The animosity between Hutchinson's supporters and her opponents grew until, in January 1637, a Fast Day was set aside in an effort to restore the peace. In a conciliatory move John Wheelwright was asked to deliver the Fast Day sermon. His sermon provoked a charge of sedition, and this charge, in turn, brought petitions on his behalf to the General Court. Accusations of antinomianism from one side were met with thinly veiled charges of papism from the other. Between the two the errand of the New Israel seemed doomed. As disruption and contention spread, affecting participation in colonial elections and the conduct of the Pequot War, not even the prominence of Hutchinson's followers could protect her. The authorities of the Bay moved into action, first meeting privately with Hutchinson, Cotton, and Wheelwright to inquire into their difference with the orthodox ministers. Discontented with the answers they received, the ministers convened a synod—the first in the colonies—for the purpose of formulating and responding to the errors of the antinomians. The General Court followed suit with sterner measures: the leaders among the antinomians were variously disenfranchised and banished, their male supporters disarmed. Considered by most the ringleader, Hutchinson was herself brought to trial by the Court in the fall of 1637 and by the church the following spring. Exiled and excommunicated, she fled to Rhode Island in 1638, moving five years later to New York, where, apparently in providential vindication of her judges, she and all but one member of her family were killed in an Indian raid.

The rapidity with which the Massachusetts Bay community fell into dissension has captured the interest of a wide range of modern scholars. In a period in which scarcity and inflation were intensified by a steady increase in population, the disproportionate affiliation of merchants with the "Hutchinsonians" has been explained as a response to the "insupportable pressures" suffered by those who would be both pious and successful in commerce. The merchants, it is claimed, used antinomianism as their way to rebel against an authoritarian Puritan regime, which tended to constrain their economic behavior.[2] The special appeal of Hutchinson's "primitive feminism" to women has also been explored. In her "new theology," one scholar argues, "*both* men and women were relegated, vis-à-vis God, to the status that women occupied in Puritan society vis-à-vis men."[3] Social and intellectual historians have mined the antinomian controversy for information about the limits of Puritan orthodoxy, social "boundary-marking" in the colonies, Puritan attitudes toward dissent, and the status of women in early New England. Literary critics have adopted the term *antinomian* to describe the oppositional quality they find in the classic literature of the American Renaissance and have taken the antinomian impulse to enable literary production in a Puritan culture. Important as it is, however, this wealth of historical data and literary conjecture does relatively little to advance our understanding of the symbolic value of the story of Anne Hutchinson beyond reinforcing what the early narratives tell us more forcefully—that is, that antinomianism represented a rejected alternative to the New England Way.

While the orthodox struggled to bring together citizen and saint, to establish a connection between private and public realms of experience, the antinomian, building on the ambiguous status of the individual in Reformed theology, proposed a new relationship between the two central facts of Christianity—the unmerited redemption of mankind by Christ and the continued existence of sin and misery in the world. Justification, the antinomian claimed, is a gift freely given to fallen man without which all his pious endeavor is to no purpose. At the moment of conversion, the saint, like an empty vessel, is cleansed and filled with Christ's love, and by this motion of the divine, the chosen are at once freed from accountability under the Law and assured of election. Individual identity is subsumed in divinity; the works of the saint are one with Christ's. As one English antinomian explained it, "in all your acts Christ acts, and in all Christ acts within you, you act . . . and in your lowest acts Christ acts as well as in your highest."[4] Man's sinful nature remains unaltered by the influx of grace, but the antinomian's perception of his sinfulness is radically changed. Secure in his election, the antinomian ascribes neither real nor symbolic value to deeds: sin exists only "that there may be a place for faith." Instead of the orthodox notion of "visible sainthood," which proposed that grace would emanate in good works and which thus nicely accommodated the exigencies of community, antinomianism offered a perfectionist theology wherein election is witnessed and sealed by the spirit and cannot be tested by outward means.

Even in this brief description of the heresy, it is possible to discern both the paradoxical nature of the antinomian as he presents himself to the world and the larger problem of authority that antinomianism engages. The antinomian regards the saint as indissolubly joined with Christ. Individuality is merely the medium through which God exerts himself. Because this is equally true of all the saints and because the nature of divinity is necessarily constant, the experiences of the saints answer one another "as face answers face in a glass."[5] Thus, those who "belong to God" are able to distinguish between God's people and the reprobate. On these grounds the American antinomians rejected the colonists' view of themselves as a chosen people, bound by covenant to fulfill God's work in the New World, and offered in its place the notion of a mystical community of the elect. The system of rewards and punishments adduced from the Law and embodied in temporal authority is, for the antinomian, irrelevant. Sin and sanctity alike are transient, inconsequential events, their significance lost in the very moment of the Spirit's invisible witness to election.

From this moment forward, the antinomian lives in a world free of the sometimes productive, sometimes disabling anxiety

characteristic of the Puritan saint. Election is, for him, a condition of self-abnegation, his individuality no longer individual,
his labors at an end, his destiny secure. In this sense, as the
Puritans were wont to point out, antinomianism "quenches all
endeavor." Yet rather than appearing passive, the antinomian
seemed, even to the Puritans, to indulge the furthest extremes
of self-assertion. For those who did not share their belief in the
immediate union of the elect with Christ, the antinomian's
claim to invisible witness, absolute assurance, and exemption
from the Law could only seem like sheer arrogance. Abandoning the social for the teleological, then, the antinomian elevates
the self to a new status precisely by insisting on the dissolution
of the self in Christ.

The theological idea that the covenant of grace releases the elect
from accountability under the Law is not indigenous to the
United States. The idea is generally traced back to Paul's epis-
tles, while the term *antinomian* is said to have been coined by
Luther, who used it in reference to the German Johannes Agric-
ola.[6] The charge of antinomianism was leveled against John of
Leyden and the Anabaptist leaders of the Münster Rebellion in
1533, and concern with the heresy burgeoned during the English Civil War as writers like John Eaton, the "father of English
antinomianism," produced tract after tract with titles like *The
Honey-combe of free Justification by Christ Alone.* The persistence of
the term into the nineteenth century likewise is not peculiar to
America, nor is its appearance in literary guise. James Hogg's
1824 *Confessions of a Justified Sinner* relates the fall into antinomianism of the unrepentant Robert Colwan; Mike Hartley, the
"Antinomian weaver," makes his appearance twenty-five years
later in Charlotte Brontë's *Shirley.* Yet there is reason to speak of
American antinomianism as a separate phenomenon, for here
the heresy is encoded in the story of Anne Hutchinson's conflict with the authorities of the Massachusetts Bay as this was
repeated and elaborated from one generation to the next. Tied
to the figure-legend of Anne Hutchinson, the local history of
antinomianism is distinct from its universal one. Moreover, it is
gendered female from the outset.

New World antinomianism was suppressed in 1638 and the authority of the ministers and magistrates restored. Yet the recurrent and pejorative use of both the figure of Anne Hutchinson and the term *antinomian* into the nineteenth century suggests that the tensions ostensibly resolved at the time lingered on, transformed. Celebratory or even apologetic accounts of the antinomian controversy are rare even though precedents exist for the celebration of if not heresy then at least certain heretics. The Romantic historian George Bancroft reconstructed Roger Williams, for example, as a "lark" giving voice to the "clear carols" of intellectual liberty, thus suggesting that some forms of Puritan heresy could be absorbed into a future consensus. Hutchinson resists just such renovation. Arrogant, rebellious, enthusiastic, the American Jezebel remains "tinged with fanaticism" throughout her history.[7] She is striking largely for her ability to rouse anxiety. If only because it remained so disturbing to Americans for so long, Hutchinson's story tells us a great deal about the unspoken concerns of her countrymen. But to account for its longevity and its force, we will need terms other than those commonly used. Most crucially, we must distinguish between the antinomian controversy itself—a historical event important largely because it sheds light on the social reality of the early colonies—and the narrative accounts of that controversy—the stories told about it (or more loosely, drawn from it), sometimes in self-defense, sometimes in indignation, but always to caution against present or future danger. While representing themselves for the most part as "histories," these narratives contribute less to our knowledge of the "real" controversy than they do to our understanding of how Americans have formulated and lent meaning to a series of events, local in nature and removed in time.

John Winthrop, for instance, goes to some lengths to insist that the Hutchinsonians were summoned before the Court not as heretics but because they "disturb[ed] the Churches . . . interrupt[ed] the civill Peace . . . and began to raise sedition amongst us, to the indangering of the Commonwealth." "Hereupon for these grounds named, (and not for their opinion . . .)," he goes on, "for these reasons (I say) being civill disturbances, the Magistrate convents . . . and censures them."[8] Winthrop's vehemence on this point has quite reasonably been taken as a response to English accusations that the colonists prosecuted cases of conscience as civil crimes, accusations he feared would be politically damaging to the Bay colony. Like his ministerial colleagues, the official historian of the controversy knew that in antinomianism he was faced with an interpretation of doctrine that proposed not only an alternative conception of the self but also, by implication at least, a radically different order of society.

It would seem that gender is of no concern here, but the immediate political motive and the larger ideological one do not entirely explain Winthrop's narrative. They fail to account for the zeal with which Winthrop details such matters as the physical deformities of Hutchinson's friend Mary Dyer's stillborn child or Hutchinson's own "misconceptions." In order to talk about these elements of Winthrop's narrative, we must think not of history but of story, not of the heretic but of the woman who promises a stable, familial community yet remains capable of producing monsters.

Even in Winthrop's narrative, the historical Anne Hutchinson is swallowed up in the monitory figure of the American Jezebel as narrative history is overwhelmed by cautionary tale. Much as the accounts of the antinomian controversy respond to changes in political climate, shift in their emphasis, and vary in their form, they nonetheless document an urgent and continuing need to choose against antinomianism that can best be understood if we consider the evolution and the place of Hutchinson's story in an American pattern of meaning. Like that story, this study begins with history and ends with literature. It does not treat every account of the antinomian controversy, nor does it trace all representations of the antinomian impulse in the literature of the United States. It focuses instead on the cautionary tale of Anne Hutchinson, a tale that does not simply recast the past for the purposes of the present but continually reenlivens the female heretic only to banish her once again. As an exploration of the strategies Americans used to contain antinomianism, this study is designed not to move away from the larger issues of American individualism engaged by the antinomian controversy but to ground these in a specific story. Insofar as antinomianism presumes, as one scholar has put it, "that social benefit [can] arise from an a-social orientation of the component parts of . . . society,"[9] the story of Anne Hutchinson sets in relief a continuing tension in American culture over the relationship between private and public realms of experience expressed concurrently in the figure of the antinomian and that of "the Woman."

The concurrence of these figures is particularly apparent in Hawthorne's "Mrs. Hutchinson." Hawthorne organizes his sketch into two vignettes, one centering on Hutchinson's crime, the other on her punishment. The first vignette is set at dusk in the Hutchinsons' crude house, newly built at the "extremity of the village," on a street "yet roughened by the roots of the trees, as if the forest . . . had left its reluctant footprints behind" (*TS*, 20). As we enter the "thronged doorway," we sense that everything about this scene is wrong. Positioned at the furthest margin of the settlement where the wilderness still encroaches, "the Woman" faces her distinguished and predominantly male audience: Governor Henry Vane, in whose eyes Hutchinson's "dark enthusiasm" is mirrored; John Cotton, "no young and hot enthusiast" but nonetheless "deceived by the strange fire now laid upon the altar"; the Reverend Hugh Peters, "full of holy wrath"; the "shuddering and weeping" women, and the young men, "fiery and impatient, fit instruments for whatever rash deed may be suggested" (*TS*, 20–21). No one, Hawthorne emphasizes, is indifferent to Hutchinson's words, yet the meeting proceeds in utter silence as far as the reader is concerned. This silencing of Hutchinson measures the tension in Hawthorne's sketch.

The threat of an Anne Hutchinson is captured not in overt statement but in the small disjunctive elements that fill the scene. Hutchinson's proper attire, for example, is belied by the inappropriateness of her preaching. Likewise, her eloquence stands in sharp contrast to the "quiet voice of prayer" we overhear elsewhere in the settlement. Her house is thronged with disciples but devoid of domestic comforts. The household hearth has been supplanted by a "strange fire" that inflames rather than warms; the family board is replaced by an altar. Instead of offering maternal reassurance to the "infant colony," Hutchinson reduces her audience to frightened "children who . . . enticed far from home . . . see the features of their guides . . . assuming a fiendish shape" (*TS*, 21). The woman of this house is no Daughter of Zion but instead a "disturber of Israel" unfolding "seditious doctrines" designed to persuade her neighbors that "they have put their trust in unregenerate and uncommissioned men, and have followed them into the wilderness for naught" (*TS*, 21).

Like the first vignette, the second one begins not with Hutchinson but with another audience, this one sitting in judgment, not in awe. Once again the mood is ominous: a "sleety shower beats fitfully against the windows, driven by the November blast, which comes howling onward from the northern desert" (*TS*, 22). And once again the events of the controversy are associated with that threatening wilderness against which the Puritan community did constant battle. Before us are ranged those "blessed fathers of the land" whom we Americans, Hawthorne reminds us with characteristic irony, rank next only to the "Evangelists of Holy Writ" (*TS*, 22). Hutchinson faces this venerable company with "a flash of carnal pride half hidden in her eye, as she surveys the many learned and famous men whom her doctrines have put in fear" (*TS*, 23). Hutchinson's eloquence is, in some sense, the subject of the first vignette; her arrogance is the theme of the second. We watch first as Hutchinson exults in her contest with the "deepest controversialists" of the day and then as exultation leads inevitably to self-incrimination. With victory in sight, she arrogates to herself the role of judge, claiming "the peculiar power of distinguishing between the chosen of man and the Sealed of Heaven. . . . She declares herself commissioned to separate the true shepherds from the false, and denounces present and future judgments on the land, if she be disturbed in her celestial errand. Thus," says Hawthorne, "the accusations are proved from her own mouth" (*TS*, 23). He means, of course, that Hutchinson's words reveal her antinomian tendencies, but the impact of the vignette depends heavily on the Woman's usurpation of man's place as judge and on her arrogant assertion of a superior knowledge of God's will.

Like the words that inspire her audience to turn against minister and magistrate, the theological demonstration that stands behind Hutchinson's condemnation of the Bay leaders—that is, antinomianism as the Puritans understood it—is absent from Hawthorne's sketch. Both omissions work to define Hutchinson's crime as social rather than theological and, in this way, to broaden its relevance. She is guilty of resistance to lawful authority, on the one hand, and of refusing to play the part of woman, on the other. The failure of domesticity that Hawthorne associates with the eloquence of "the Woman," because he regards it as a violation of the law that governs her nature, points inevitably to heresy and sedition. In Hawthorne's sketch, then, antinomianism names a pattern of opposition shared by the "public woman" of the nineteenth century and the heretic of the seventeenth.

The antinomian lays claim to an unassailable inner knowledge, and the moment when Hutchinson alleges her peculiar powers is both the moment of her condemnation and the dramatic climax of Hawthorne's sketch. As Hawthorne understood, knowledge of the kind Hutchinson claimed respects no authority outside itself and is susceptible to no proof. Witnessed by an invisible spirit taken to be divine, it supersedes all other forms of knowledge. The antinomian regards this knowledge as a product of the influx of divinity and herself merely as the organ of its expression. Potentially, at least, the inner certainty this knowledge lends empowers the individual to act without reference to external authority or even against it. But the antinomian's knowledge transcends her condition. She must continue to live in the world and act the part of the sinner. Having relinquished the old natural self to God, however, she no longer attributes the usual significance to her words and deeds, for these cannot adequately represent the new self that belongs to God. Her deeds are hers only in the most provisional sense.

The uncomfortable resemblance between the language of antinomianism and a dominant American rhetoric committed to the values of individualism and the unfettered expression of the self in the political and economic arenas as well as the private one has encouraged scholars to generalize the problem of antinomianism into one simply of authority, of how the claims of the individual are to be balanced against those of the community. And, in fact, translated into the secular language of self and community, the problem of antinomianism might be said to stand at the heart of liberal ideology. But this shift in terms suppresses the role of gender in our formulation of the heresy and, in this way, replicates earlier versions of Hutchinson's story in which gender is likewise the suppressed issue. In other words, by generalizing the problem of antinomianism, we set aside the very story that has defined antinomianism for Americans. By placing "the Woman" in the "centre of all eyes" (*TS*, 23), Hawthorne's sketch recalls us to that story. It reminds us that the problem of antinomianism and the problem of female empowerment are entwined from the very beginning.

2

Disturber in Israel

In the last decades of the nineteenth century, Charles Francis Adams wrote what served for many years as the definitive history of the antinomian controversy. Framing his account of the controversy on one side with a chronicle of the first settlement and on the other with a study of town and church government, Adams made clear the importance he thought ought to be accorded it. "From a theological point of view," he wrote, the conflict "is now devoid of interest. . . . But the, so-called, Antinomian controversy was in reality not a religious dispute. . . . It was the first of many New England quickenings in the direction of social, intellectual, and political developments,—New England's first protest against formulas."[1] As far as Adams was concerned, antinomianism was "the refuge of the libertine," and since not even the general court of Massachusetts had found the Hutchinsonians guilty of outright immorality, Adams found it easy to set antinomianism aside in interpreting the events of the 1630s. In his view Anne Hutchinson was less important as a heretic than as the "great prototype" of those harmless, if "misty," Transcendentalists for whom New England would later become famous. But even in this role, Hutchinson was not very important. The real controversy, Adams claimed, was not over minute and "unintelligible" differences in doctrine, however interesting the later history of New England might make these. Nor was Anne Hutchinson, accidentally pushed into the limelight as she was, essential to its meaning. The important history of the antinomian controversy was neither Puritan nor female but American and male. The antinomian controversy was neither more nor less than "a struggle for civil power and ecclesiastical supremacy in a small village community": the question it raised was "whether Massachusetts was to be radical and doctrinaire, or conservative and practical."[2]

Naive though Adams may seem in some respects, his view of the controversy is not, at base, so different from that of modern historians. Believing with Adams that social conflict frequently has its origins in questions other than those identified by the stressed community, they have directed their efforts, in large measure, at penetrating the accounts of the antinomian controversy to uncover its underlying (and, for them, more authentic) causes. If they do not dismiss the theological problem as "devoid of interest," historians nonetheless approach contemporary explanations of the controversy with a certain legitimate skepticism. They find in the class composition of the Hutchinsonians evidence of a clash between a rising but as yet powerless group of merchants and a land-wealthy elite led by John Winthrop. Likewise, they struggle to account for Hutchinson's appeal to women in terms that have less to do with theology or gender than politics. The economic condition of the colonies, the status of the ministers, the political posture of the nonseparating faction that controlled the Bay, the extent of congregational control of the churches, the authority of the colonial magistracy all garner their attention.

In a sense, then, modern historiography supports, if not the specific analysis of the controversy offered by Adams, at least a version of this. But antinomianism cannot be written out of our interpretation of the conflict between "orthodox" and "heretic" any more than Anne Hutchinson can be written out of her own story. The period from 1636 to 1638 was an extraordinary one in the history of colonial New England, extraordinary not only because the colony was at once so new and so deeply divided[3] but also because in the resolution of the antinomian controversy we can find the seeds of a cultural consensus that some argue has not yet lost its force. That consensus, from the first, declared Americans a peculiar people inhabiting a wilderness theirs by promise in which "to assert oneself in the right way . . . was to embody the goals of New England," a New England which was itself "a 'way' . . . into the future."[4]

The antinomian controversy describes a crucial moment in the evolution of this consensus. The Puritans represented Anne Hutchinson as the epitome of what the New World saints should not become. The questions she raised, as woman and as antinomian, forced the Puritans to articulate the terms of membership in their venture. Locating in Hutchinson a whole configuration of threats, both social and doctrinal, they clarified the communal borders. Antinomianism and the images of individual license, social disruption, and a communal fall from grace that accompanied it helped to define a pattern of "deviant" individualism.[5] To make sense of Hutchinson's presence in their midst—in fact, to tell her story—the Puritans had to locate her in the larger myth that shaped the Great Migration. From the outset Hutchinson was not merely a middle-aged troublemaker, a woman of "haughty carriage," but the American Jezebel, the woman in whom immorality and false prophecy were combined. And like her prototype, the wife of the evil King Ahab, this Jezebel threatened to bring down the wrath of God on the New Israel. In this guise Anne Hutchinson served as a symbolic locus for a broad spectrum of fears about self-assertion and individual autonomy, about the relationship between the public and the private self, and about the reliability of the visible world. To understand the evolution of the figure of Anne Hutchinson, then, we must begin with those remote, but not really "unintelligible," religious ideas that were the avowed cause of her troubles.

Anne Hutchinson and the Puritan authorities began their thinking from the same premise. As they understood it, God had made a covenant with Adam—a covenant demanding that Adam perfectly obey the laws of God, in return for which God would grant salvation. But God gave Adam free will and, as a result, he was capable of disobedience. When Adam failed to fulfill his part of the agreement, God cast him out of Eden and the covenant of works ended. Thereafter, man's will was directed toward evil. But God, in His mercy, made another covenant with man. Since fallen man was no longer capable of perfect obedience, the covenant of grace "freely [offered] unto sinners life and salvation by Jesus Christ, requiring of them faith in him, that they may be saved, and promising to give unto all those that are ordained unto life, his Holy Spirit to make them willing and able to believe."[6]

Both Anne Hutchinson and the ministers understood this new dispensation to have certain corollaries. The elect were chosen by God, "ordained unto life," for reasons known only to God; who they were only He could tell. The invisible, true church was composed of all the elect—dead, living, and yet to come. Just as one of the effects of the Fall was a loss of the "will to do any spiritual good," the coming of grace involved a similar alteration of the will. Natural man is "altogether averse from . . . good, and dead in sin." But the new man, created in grace, is translated: God "freeth him from his natural bondage under sin, and by his grace alone enables him freely to will and do that which is spiritually good."[7] The new man cannot attain the perfect obedience of an Adam, but neither is he doomed to live wholly in sin. On all of this the Puritans and Anne Hutchinson agreed. They diverged sharply, however, in their understanding of the implications of the covenant of grace in the world.

The leaders of Massachusetts Bay envisioned a commonwealth in which civil and religious institutions would work harmoniously to uphold the special covenant between God and the New Israel. Full participation in the affairs of the community was, therefore, contingent upon church membership, and full involvement in the church depended on a demonstration of sainthood. The fulfillment of the covenant required that the invisible status of men be determined, not surely—for the Puritans understood that certain knowledge of election was God's alone—but with as much accuracy as possible. In their desire to keep the visible church as much like the invisible as possible, they evolved the paradox of "visible sainthood." Admission to full membership in the church depended on the "relation" of a private experience of conversion, and this account of the influx of grace, if judged authentic by the congregation, served as one basis for identifying the regenerate. But further evidence was to be found in the public acts of the saint. If one of the effects of justification, or salvation, is the potential for willing the good, the ministers reasoned, then election should be evidenced by sanctification, the doing of good. They did not expect full compliance with the Law: rather, they assumed that if the motion of grace is accompanied by the will to do good, a saint ought to be identifiable by his deeds. By using sanctification as one evidence of justification, by associating human behavior with the extent of a man's "interest in Christ," the Puritans thought they had made the invisible virtually visible.[8]

The ministers, of course, recognized man's ultimate dependence on Christ. Nevertheless, they assumed that the saint differed fundamentally from the "natural" man by virtue of his ability to perform "gracious workes." They did not ignore the problem of hypocrisy, maintaining, rather, that "even Eagle-eyed Christians will have much adoe so to discerne of sanctification in themselves, before they see their justification, as to cut off all hypocrites from having the like in them." But they found comfort in the belief that "hypocrites are melted as iron, which will returne again to his former hardness," while God's "owne people are melted into flesh, which will never returne to his hardness more . . . so that the one is a temporary faith, and the other persevereth."[9] The perseverance of the saints was not sufficient to reassure Anne Hutchinson. If, as the ministers themselves claimed, Christ's grace alone enables men to do good, then, she reasoned, "there is no inherent righteousnesse in the Saints . . . but in Christ only" (*AC*, 223). This initial "error" gave rise to an irresistible chain of logic. Given her assumption that Christ's grace at work in man and not man's own will produces good behavior, it followed that man's unaltered sinfulness should be no cause for distress. There is no point in appealing to God for gifts and graces, "but only for Christ." In fact, to exhort a man to "any duty" is foolish because he "hath no power to do it" (*AC*, 235). The distinction between the graces of hypocrites and believers is obliterated once neither is capable of independently willing the good, and "all the activity of a beleever is to act in sinne" (*AC*, 228). Since the "Devill and nature," as well as Christ, "may be cause of gracious workes" (*AC*, 240), any attempt to group men on the basis of their behavior is futile. The outcome of this reasoning is clear: if all activity initiated by the believer is sinful, then presumably "the Spirit acts most in the Saints when they indeavor least" (*AC,* 231). Sanctification cannot, therefore, demonstrate justification.

Anne Hutchinson, having begun with the same covenant of grace as the Puritans, argued the case literally. If the grace of God "flows from Christ" into the hearts of men, then none can truly know its presence but the saint himself. Moreover, since obedience to the Law can be simulated by the worst of hypocrites, not even the righteousness of a new Adam can be taken as evidence of salvation. As Edward Johnson disdainfully put it, Hutchinson claimed that "because Felons and Traytors coyne counterfeit Gold, therefore true Gold should not pass for current."[10] To her way of thinking, the "witness of the spirit" was the only testimony to a state of grace. The invisible, in other words, was invisible. In the ministers' position Hutchinson saw clear equivocation—and in that equivocation their doom.

The Hutchinsonian position on works radically alters the characteristics of the saint. Working, struggling, striving for grace is all for naught. The Christian is but an empty vessel which Christ may or may not fill up; the acts of the saint on earth are at once his own and Christ's and are wholly unrelated to his eternal fate. The only important distinction between men —the distinction between regenerate and reprobate—is invisible. The perfect Christian is, in these terms, the one who, emptied of self and confident in Christ, waits passively for the moment when his dependence is rewarded with sure knowledge of salvation.

The dangerous implications of such a literal interpretation of the covenant of grace were obvious to the ministers and magistrates. What is more, in antinomianism they had a ready label for such heretical maunderings. The contention that Christians, under a covenant of grace, are freed from the Law might have been taken as a simple restatement of the orthodox notion that the new dispensation allows a greater latitude in matters of behavior than the old. The Puritans, however, like most Protestants, assumed that it posited a complete rejection of legal authority and a concomitant lack of restraint in human behavior. Debauchery, dishonesty, licentiousness were, they were sure, its issue. Antinomianism was seen as "extending the principle of perfectionism so as to hold that actions normally regarded as sinful are not sinful in the perfect."[11] It was, as one modern historian has put it, a "sort of metaphysical synonym for anarchy,"[12] at least insofar as it seemed to imply that the well-being of the community was best guaranteed by the unhindered submission of the individual to Christ. Antinomianism, then, collapsed the system that the ministers had been at such pains to construct. If sanctified behavior could not be taken as validating a confession of regeneration, then church membership must rest solely on the applicant's own testimony regarding the state of his soul.

In fact, antinomianism pointed directly to an exclusive, non-evangelical church in which the congregation would be fully empowered. Challenging the visible foundation of the church, Hutchinson laid the groundwork for a full-scale battle over church membership and government. The ministers had adopted a method of admission to the church according to which candidates were examined for right knowledge, right conduct, and experienced grace. If, however, as the antinomians contended, "none are to be exhorted to beleeve, but such who we know to be the elect of God" (*AC*, 225), and if only "he that hath the seale of the Spirit may certainly judge of any person, whether he be elected or no" (*AC*, 226), these tests are fruitless and the church, as it was constituted in New England, false. Rightly organized, the antinomians intimated, the church would be composed of self-proclaimed saints having mystical knowledge of one another's election. All members would be "sealed" and each would confirm the sainthood of his fellows. In the view of the antinomians, these "children of God" form the only true congregation, a congregation which, given the temporal and spatial limitations of human existence, is as like as possible to the invisible church. Assuming that no minister can "convey more of Christ, than hee by his own experience hath come into" and that none "can teach one that is anoynted by the Spirit of Christ" (*AC*, 233–34) more than he already knows, ministerial function would be greatly reduced. The evangelical role of the minister would be denied by the closed system of admission, and his didactic one by the very nature of crucial knowledge. The minister, no longer taken to be specially attuned to the state of men's souls, would be subject to the same scrutiny as any other purported child of God. His authority would be severely limited, and his status—higher in the New World than it had ever been in the Old—would be greatly diminished. The function of the minister in such a scheme is, as John Wheelwright put it, to call the children of God to battle against "the Antichristian, and those that run under a covenant of works" (*AC*, 163)—not to save the unregenerate from the flames but, on the contrary, to "purge the Church," "to [burn] up all unbeleevers, and all under a Covenant of works" with the "very fire of the word" (*AC*, 166). In the church imagined by Wheelwright and Hutchinson, "such as see any grace of God in themselves, before they have the assurance of God's love sealed to them are not to be received members" (*AC*, 227).

The antinomians' concept of congregational authority was, then, as extreme and as literal as their understanding of the covenant. And just as their insistence on the invisibility of grace called forth a stream of rhetoric in defense of visible sainthood, so their conception of a fully empowered church composed of warranted saints elicited an explication of ministerial authority. During the 1630s, in an effort to institutionalize the congregational ideal for which they had been persecuted in England, the Puritans granted the brethren of the churches enormous power. Full members of the church were given a mandate to try candidates for the ministry and to elect clergymen to office; they held the power of dismissal, which, albeit rarely used, gave them an important check on the conduct of the ministers; they decided matters of church discipline by vote. This arrangement, although it undoubtedly reinforced the congregation's sense of itself as a community with joint responsibility for the conformity of its members, carried with it certain difficulties. Because it conformed to separatist practice, the relegation of power to the "people" compromised the Bay's claim of nonseparation. Further, it seemed to deplete the power of the ministers over their congregations. In response to this latter problem, the ministers began to search for a middle way that would simultaneously ensure their authority and support congregationalism.

The central question was where the power of the ministers originated: did the office carry with it special authority, or was authority delegated by the particular congregation to a particular pastor? For the clergy the answer to this question meant addressing the distinction between a sacerdotal and a contractual ministry. On the one hand, if the clergyman received his power solely and directly from Christ, then congregationalism made no sense. Congregational independence would have no expression in reality, ordination by the membership would be meaningless, no claim could be made of free consent to ministerial ascendancy, and the difference between Puritan and Anglican would, in large measure, be lost. On the other hand, if the minister's power arose purely from his contractual relation to his congregation, not only would it be difficult to maintain that the Massachusetts churches were nonseparating, but the clergyman would be forever at the mercy of his flock as well.

The ministers found their way out of this classic Protestant dilemma through a crucial rhetorical distinction: "Though the brethren of the church received the power of the keys from Christ, this power was theirs . . . in such a manner that they could not exercise the keys without electing officers. Church members held the keys 'virtually,' the ministers 'formally,' by virtue of the power inherent in their office. There was nothing, therefore, that the congregation could delegate to them."[13] Thus, the ministers retained sacerdotal power without denying the contractual basis of congregationalism. This hedging of the contradiction intrinsic to their position allowed them their independence. They escaped subjection to the whims of the people and reserved for themselves the highest authority in matters of doctrine and discipline.

But the presence of the Hutchinsonians highlighted the vulnerability of this "middle way." The antinomians' commitment to what might be called perfect congregationalism carried the early ministerial position to its logical extreme and, in this way, made conspicuous the limitations placed on congregational power by the ministers' argument. Their actual challenge to the ministry—the attempt to replace John Wilson with John Wheelwright as pastor of the Boston church—made this even clearer. In the abstract such a move on the part of the membership should have been possible. But, in fact, the ministers' reassertion of control over disciplinary actions, their closing of the ranks in the face of congregational defiance, and their close alliance with secular leadership guaranteed the Hutchinsonians' failure. The battle over the pulpit initiated by Hutchinson and her allies did, however, call public attention to the equivocal nature of the ministerial position on matters of doctrine and church polity.

The problem of assurance, to which both antinomian and orthodox had carefully attended, likewise prompted equivocation and was similarly resolved by rhetorical means. Just as election, even when taken to be manifest after the fact, is itself invisible, so too is assurance. The ministers dealt with this problem by adopting a morphology of conversion in which the steps of both preparation for election and assurance of it were outlined in visible terms. The saint could gain assurance by passing through carefully marked stages of grief, despair, and faith. More important, he could describe these to demonstrate his election. The difficulty with such a scheme is obvious: since all men do not experience regeneration in exactly the same way, how identify a true progress through the stages of conversion? On the one hand, the ministers were forced to see the saints as separate, unique individuals; on the other hand, they believed that selflessness, the obliteration of this very uniqueness, was one image of salvation. One way to cope with this apparent contradiction was proposed by Thomas Shepard, who distinguished between "substantial" and "circumstantial" works of the Spirit: "Do not think the Lord works compunction in all the elect in the same circumstantial work of the Spirit, but only in the same substantial work; the Lord works a true sense of sin for substance and truth of it, yet there are many circumstantial works, like so many enlargements and comments upon one and the same text."[14]

In other words, although all men would not experience the

stages of conversion in the same way, the morphology of conversion isolated the substance that would be reflected "circum-
stantially" in each man's conversion. This nicely contained idiosyncrasy by simultaneously anticipating it and denying it
significance. That each man will manifest compunction in his
own way is only to be expected, Shepard suggests, but these
differences are not important. In one breath, Shepard both allows individuality and directs its thrust away from disorganization and toward a community of faith. Just as commentary on a
text may contain truths, so the various human expressions of
the movement of the Spirit within are true; but Truth lies only at
the source. This solution gave the morphology of conversion
renewed validity by making room in it for the actual differences
between men. Moreover, Shepard's insistence on a shared
"substance" provided the spiritual basis for a fellowship of the
elect despite individual variation in the manifestation of grace.
Like the difference between "formal" and "virtual" possession
of the keys to heaven and hell, the difference between "substantial" and "circumstantial" works of the Spirit sounded cautiously noncommittal to the Hutchinsonians. It seemed to
them not just a haphazard basis for fellowship but an open denial of God's freedom to work in mysterious ways. Shepard
might concern himself with the commentary, but they were interested only in the text.

The debate that Hutchinson's doctrines sparked among the
ministers centered on where exactly faith fit into the orthodox
design. To most of the ministers, as to Thomas Shepard and
Thomas Hooker, faith followed attendance upon the Word and
obedience to the Commandments in the stages of conversion,
but Hutchinson's mentor, John Cotton, disagreed. To see faith
as simply another step in a scale of visible acts and religious emotions such as the morphology of conversion outlined
seemed to him inadequate. When, in examining Cotton about
his influence on the antinomians, the ministers inquired as to
his difference with them on this point, he replied: "A Christian
man's first Assurance doth arise from the Spirit of God apply-
ing God's free grace in an absolute promise; or if in a conditional . . . it is not to Works but to Faith, and to faith not as it is a

work but as it receiveth the free grace of God offered in Christ Jesus" (*AC*, 94). The question was whether faith antedates or postdates the moment of assurance. To represent faith as following upon obedience to the Law could be taken, as Cotton saw, to imply that justification is grounded in sanctification. If the will of the man without Christ is turned toward evil, faith cannot flow from obedience. To posit the opposite, however, is to presume man capable of faith without the intervention of Christ. Cotton's solution was to compress all into one moment:

> the great disputes of late have been, Whether Sanctification may be discerned by any properties in itself. Whether Justification may be seen in the evidence of faith. And whether Sanctification may be seen before Justification. All these have been in vain; and all are taken up in this one conclusion, That we can see neither Sanctification nor faith no nor Justification, before the witness of the spirit, but all at once by it. And whereas it hath been wont to be argued thus, He that believeth shall be saved, He that is justified shall be saved, He that is sanctified shall be saved. Now it is thus, He that shall be saved is justified is sanctified hath faith. viz. He first seeth his good Estate in Gods thoughts of peace, (or in Election) testified to him, and therein reads himself a believer, justified, sanctified; and this is the only way, all others going on in or aside to a Covenant of Works.
>
> (*AC*, 75)

Anne Hutchinson followed suit. She similarly resolved all the important stages in the conventional morphology of conversion into one moment witnessed by the spirit, but she went further. Refusing to see any visible signs as efficacious, she regarded union with Christ as its own evidence and man's only assurance. For a saint to question his assurance (as all the ministers insisted he would) was to cast doubt on his election. In her view "a man is not effectually converted till hee hath full assurance" (*AC*, 234) and "there is no assurance true or right, unless it bee without feare and doubting" (*AC*, 230). Not the ploys of the devil, much less the acts of man, can call into doubt the saint's assurance of salvation. As she so dramatically put it during her trial, "To question my assurance, though I fall into Murther or Adultery, proves that I never had true Assurance" (*AC*, 202). In the case of assurance, as in that of sanctification, the Law has little weight. Faith, like honesty or charity, is but another "work." The circle is closed; one's assurance is one's assurance.

While Hutchinson did not repudiate the Law during her examination, the orthodox claimed that she taught "that we are not bound to the Law, not as a Rule of Life" (*AC*, 352) and that, therefore, no transgression of the Law is sinful. The seeds of such an opinion are present not only in her denial of visible signs but also in her fatal description of her revelations. The Puritans, like other Protestants, assumed that the age of revelations had passed and that man was left with the Word as guidance. They, therefore, sought their doctrine in Scripture. When Anne Hutchinson claimed, in the course of her trial, that the Lord "hath let me see which was the clear ministry and which the wrong" by "an immediate revelation," she exempted herself from the rule of Scripture. For, clearly, if Scripture itself is based on revelation, revelation must supersede it. That she meant revelation of a biblical sort is unquestionable: she claimed to "know" as "Abraham [knew] that it was God that bid him offer his son" (*AC*, 336–37). Ironically, Hutchinson freed herself from the Law by identifying herself with the endlessly obedient Abraham. Her revelations constituted a final repudiation of all efforts to make the invisible visible. The witness of the spirit, prophecy, revelation are not demonstrable events. And election, if it is revealed only by the spirit, cannot be tested outwardly—and need not be; assurance is gratuitous, immediate, and final; God speaks directly to his children.

Excepting her claims to revelation, there is little in what we know of Hutchinson's theological position that constitutes a rejection of the basic assumptions of Calvinist doctrine. Instead, what she questioned was the accommodation of that doctrine to the exigencies of colonial life. It was the "Americanization" of Puritan doctrine, the forms of institutional Puritanism in the New World, that distressed her. The clergy seemed to her to speak out of both sides of their mouth: they rejected all legal schemes for salvation and admitted their insufficiency as judges of election, but in the same breath they insisted on their right to judge and used as the basis for their judgments visible signs that they themselves, when pressed, conceded were fallible. This seemed to Hutchinson an abandonment of the true way, a remaking of God in the image of the ministers. That the Bible, rightly construed, taught free grace and predestination both she and the ministers admitted. Why, then, she asked, did the ministers retreat from the implications of their doctrine? In the end Anne Hutchinson's heresy lay in her rejection of the paradoxes generated out of the orthodoxy's need to reconcile scriptural truth with the requirements of an ordered society.

The Puritan reconciliation of doctrine to social fact was accomplished by means of the myth of the New Israel, the idea of America as a nation bound by special covenant to God. This myth finds one of its first expressions in "A Modell of Christian Charity," John Winthrop's discourse on Christian community in the American wilderness written on board the Arabella as she set sail from England. Winthrop's subject is human interdependence; his purpose, to elucidate the forms of interdependence appropriate to the Puritan venture. He begins by distinguishing between isolated works of charity, prompted by a rational acknowledgment of necessity, and charity as a "habit of the soul." Works if they are only works are of little value, Winthrop makes clear. But works may also be signs. Habitual charity, for example, though it is made evident through works, signifies "love in the heart." This love Winthrop proposes as the "bond of perfection" that knits Christians together in community. Just as the ligaments join the disproportionate members of the physical body and lend it perfect proportion, so, in the Pauline image, the church is made one body by Christ. And so, Winthrop says, extending the analogy, love unites the social body. There would be nothing especially novel in this if Winthrop did not go on to make the capacity for love an outcome of new birth, thereby making election the condition for true community.

Love, Winthrop explains, originates in the new covenant:

> Adam in his first estate was a perfect modell of mankinde . . . and in him this love was perfected . . . but Adam Rent in himselfe from his Creator, rent all his posterity allsoe one from another, whence it comes that every man is borne with this princi-

ple in him, to love and seeke himselfe onely and thus a man
continueth till Christ comes and takes possession of the soule,
and infuseth another principle love to God and our brother.
. . . this love is the fruite of the new birthe, and none can have it
but the new Creature.[15]

Not only does Christ knit together the invisible church; but the
influx of his spirit allows as well for that perfect love out of
which true community is born. Election defines membership in
the visible church, but, as Winthrop sees it, it also identifies
members of the secular community. For the antinomian controversy the crucial import of this conflation of election and social
membership is that it provides a way to allow works to evidence
election in the terms of the covenant of grace. Justification is by
faith alone, and only the elect are capable of the habitual love
that should unite temporal communities. This love is expressed
through works of mercy, justice, and charity. If habitual, those
works truly denote election.

Winthrop lays the groundwork for visible sainthood, but his
final application of the lesson of the sermon goes even further.
He demonstrates that sainthood *must* be visible if the federal
covenant is to be fulfilled. He begins cautiously, saying of his
listeners not that they are saints but that they profess to be "fellow members of Christ." As presumptive members of the invisible church, the colonists are united by the bond of perfection.
But now, as they seek "a place of Cohabitation . . . under a due
forme of government," their love for one another must be made
manifest in their day-to-day dealings. Like other Puritan ex-
egetes, Winthrop understood the migration as a special commission from God. Having discovered both America and themselves in the Bible, the Puritans regarded themselves as a New
Israel crossing the Atlantic just as the original Israelites had
crossed the Red Sea. Like them, the Puritans were embarked on
an errand into the wilderness, and that errand was a preparation for the sight of Christ at the end of time. The compact into which they had entered for the completion of this errand,
the federal covenant, was a conditional one. No absolute promise like the covenant of grace, the federal covenant demanded
works for its fulfillment.

Thus stands the cause betweene God and us, wee are entered
into Covenant with him for this worke, wee have taken out a
Commission, the Lord hath given us leave to drawe our owne
Articles . . . Now if the Lord shall please to heare us, and bring
us in peace to the place wee desire, then hath hee ratified this
Covenant . . . [and] will expect a strikt performance of the Articles contained in it, but if we shall neglect the observacion of
these Articles . . . [if we] shall fall to embrace this present world
and prosecute our carnall intencions . . . the Lord will surely
breake out in wrathe against us . . . and make us knowe the
price of the breache of such a Covenant.[16]

The implied threat masks an assertion of specialness, and
both lend themselves to social ends. The works demanded by
the covenant are no mystery. In fact, Winthrop names them.
But as he does so, it becomes clear that they are the very works
made possible only by love—they are the works of the new
creature:

Now the only way to avoyde this shipwracke . . . is . . . to doe
Justly, to love mercy, to walke humbly with our God, for this
end, wee must be knitt together in this worke as one man, wee
must entertaine each other in brotherly Affeccion, wee must be
willing to abridge our selves . . . for the supply of others neces-
sities, wee must uphold a familiar Commerce together in all
meeknes, gentlenes, patience and liberallity, wee must . . . re-
joyce together, mourne together, labour, and suffer together
. . . in the worke, our Community as members of the same
body, soe . . . the Lord will be our God and delight to dwell
among us, as his owne people . . . wee shall finde that the God
of Israell is among us.[17]

Lest there be any doubt that these are the works of the graceful,
Winthrop once again exploits the metaphor of the body "knitt"
together. What Winthrop has done is to make the conditions of
the federal covenant possible largely by means of the covenant
of grace. Works undertaken to fulfill the secular commission
become themselves evidence of salvation.

The relationship Winthrop draws between the private experience of conversion and the public errand of the New Israel
allows, as others have pointed out, for the conflation of spiritual
autobiography and corporate history.[18] But further, it brings

into being a rhetoric in which public and private become one, in which the calling of the saint and the calling of the community coincide. Social facts are signs of spiritual facts. The public and the private, like the secular and the spiritual, flow into one another. By making election and good citizenship mutually reflexive, Winthrop accommodates a doctrine that denies the efficacy of works to the exigencies of community. He demonstrates that fulfillment of the conditions of the federal covenant is tantamount to a demonstration of election. The orthodox preacher could then be a preacher of works, and thus an evangelist, without denying the invisibility of grace.

When one turns from Winthrop's sermon on Christian polity to John Wheelwright's Fast Day sermon, preached seven years later at the height of the antinomian controversy, the difference between orthodox and heretic becomes apparent. The doctrine of Wheelwright's sermon—"That the only cause of fasting of true beleevers is the absence of Christ"—is itself unorthodox. It was not because Christ had withdrawn from them that the Puritans fasted but so that he would not. The fast was a form of public, collective self-denial undertaken, in this case, in hopes of restoring the peace. That, in the view of Wheelwright, was to seek after the gifts of the spirit rather than the Lord himself. It was to use the fast as a work. For Wheelwright, fasting presented itself as an either-or proposition: "Either Christ he is present with his people, or els absent from his people; if he be present . . . then they have no cause to fast: therefore it must be his absence that is the true cause of fasting" (*AC,* 154). To the ears of the orthodox, embroiled in controversy with Wheelwright and Hutchinson and standing accused by them of preaching a covenant of works, this must have sounded like a taunt. When Wheelwright goes on to point out that "those that are least acquainted with the Lord Jesus are given most of all to fasting" (*AC,* 157) and then offers the papists as an example, the insult is obvious. The Puritans might well have reason to fast, having lost the spirit of Christ. If Christ is with them still, then the fast itself convicts them of error.

The argument over the fast—and the offense the Puritans took at Wheelwright's exposition of it (they later charged him with sedition)—centers on a sermon that admits only invisible, interior evidence of grace. What the antinomians in general and Wheelwright in this sermon argued for was a literal and exclusive interpretation of the covenant of grace. This interpretation, as the authorities were quick to point out to Anne Hutchinson, not only denied the efficacy of works but "quenched all endeavor." And, indeed, Wheelwright's exposition of the gospel attests to the utter powerlessness of man to alter his condition:

> the Gospell is such a doctrine as doth hold forth Jesus Christ and nothing but Christ . . . as doth reveale Jesus Christ to be our wisdome, our righteousnes, our sanctification, and our redemption . . . when all is taken away from the creature, and all given to Christ, so that neither before our conversion nor after, we are able to put forth one act of true saving spirituall wisdome, but we must have it put forth from the Lord Jesus Christ, with whom we are made one . . . we are not able to do any worke of sanctification, further then we are acted by the Lord, nor able to procure our justification, but it must be the Lord Jesus Christ that must apply himselfe and his righteousnes to us; and we are not able to redeeme our selves from the least evill, but he is our redemption.
>
> (*AC,* 160)

As Wheelwright describes conversion, the self is wholly absorbed in Christ. The saint does not act; he is simply the medium through which Christ acts. Grace is invisible, and assurance absolute in the moment of conversion.

Wheelwright's assertion of the helplessness of man proceeds from the perfectly orthodox premise that justification is by faith alone. The absolute promise is taken absolutely; fallen man has no capacity to turn his will to the good without the gratuitous intervention of Christ. The law is not binding, because man has utterly forfeited his power not only to act but even to obey. Orthodox and antinomian agreed that the Fall had resulted in a kind of cosmic stalemate which could be ended only by way of a mediator and that God in his mercy had sent Christ to seal the new covenant of grace. Unlike the Puritans, however, the antinomians thought the implications of this new covenant perfectly clear. "Therefore," Wheelwright declaims, referring to the origins of the covenant, "ought no works of sanctification to be urged upon the servants of God, so as if they had a power to do them, it will kill the soule of a man, and it oppresseth the poor soules of the saynts of God" (*AC*, 162).

It is not difficult to comprehend the magistrates' dismay. This doctrine was fundamentally inimical to the formation of community. The colonists needed an interpretation of the covenant that would allow for the invisibility of grace while providing external tests of election. They needed to validate works not only because they believed that they had contracted with God to fulfill his commission but also because they needed to rationalize the power of the ministers and magistrates. All this the antinomians' literal interpretation of the covenant effectively precluded. If the Law is not binding, what then is to restrain behavior? If the gifts and effects of the Lord are not to be sought but only the Lord himself, how then guarantee the outcome of justification much less the fulfillment of the federal covenant? The antinomians believed these were the wrong questions to ask. They saw the Puritans' concern with the American community as misplaced. The only true community they believed to be the community of saints, exempt from the Law and certain of their election. Winthrop's description of the bond of perfection invisibly uniting the saints in England when they were "absent from eache other many miles" comes closer to Wheelwright's understanding of community than does any description of the close-knit American colony. For Wheelwright, as for Hutchinson, the bond of perfection joins the invisible church, made visible only to the individual saints through the private revelation of their election, through the witness of the spirit.

The antinomians, in other words, rejected the idea of a federal covenant. When Wheelwright speaks of Israel, he speaks historically of a people chosen by God, the type of the invisible church. He uses the Israelites as an example of those who by their "fastings and dayes of humiliation" procured "unto themselves things from God and the blessing of God; but . . . not the Lord himself, they had the Angell of Gods presence to go before them, but they had not the Lord Jesus Christ in them, they had the spiritt to instruct them, but they had not the spirit to dwell in them" (*AC*, 169). In short, they were not saved. John Wheelwright's sermon narrowly limits the meaning of all external phenomena. Just as the commission of murder does not call into doubt membership in the invisible church, so God's special providences need not signify the choosing of a people or the indwelling of the spirit. Outward sign and inner conviction have no bearing on one another. Like the Israelites, the New England settlers might receive the blessings of the Lord, might even have given to them extraordinary signs, but to take this to mean that they are a chosen people is to confuse the works of the Lord with his spirit, to confuse visible community and invisible church. This denial of the meaning of signs must have seemed not merely a corrective but a direct assault on the authority of the fathers. Having distinguished his company of saints from the New Israel of Winthrop and the orthodoxy, Wheelwright concludes his sermon with a consolation to the elect:

> seeing the Lord Jesus Christ his absence is the cause of fasting and mourning, this is a comfort to the children of God, that come what will come they shall be in a happy estate, they shall be blessed: suppose those that are Gods children should loose their houses and lands and wives and freinds, and loose the acting of the guifts of grace, and loose the ordinances, yet they can never loose the Lord Jesus Christ . . . suppose [he goes on, in a moment of foresight] the saynts of God should be banished and deprived of all the ordinances of God, that were a hard case (in some respect) for we had better part with all, then the ordinances; but if the ordinances should be taken away, yet Christ cannot.

> (*AC*, 172)

What served Wheelwright and the antinomians as consolation looked to the orthodox like a sweeping denial of the whole New England venture. Without visible tests of election, with no special covenant binding the immigrants one to another, the city on the hill could not be built. The antinomian's belief in absolute assurance and invisible grace led inexorably to the repudiation of all institutional forms that characterizes Wheelwright's sermon. Wheelwright stands in direct opposition to Winthrop with his concern for demonstrating the organic connection between New World citizenship and sainthood. God's people, Wheelwright insists, may be few, but by comparison "all the Nations are nothing": true community is associated with election, but the saints are scattered like chaff in the wind. There is nothing in what we know of the antinomians to suggest that they concurred with the orthodox in their assumption that God had "sifted a whole Nation that he might send choice Grain over into this Wilderness."[19]

Wheelwright's emphasis on individual assurance, combined with his rejection of works as evidence of grace, accounts for a radical difference in emphasis in the two discourses. While both the speech on the Arabella and the Fast Day sermon are addressed to matters of public concern, Wheelwright subtly transforms the communal ritual of the fast into private terms. Winthrop speaks of the work undertaken by the saints, Wheelwright of the private experience of conversion. For Winthrop these two are identical; for Wheelwright they are wholly unrelated. Their use of the Bible replicates this difference. Winthrop repeatedly alludes to the Bible as a guide for social conduct, while Wheelwright exploits primarily those portions of the New Testament that treat individual union with Christ. Winthrop speaks of the difficulty of the errand and threatens God's displeasure; Wheelwright insists that, once assured of his election, the saint enters a realm of cosmic certainty wherein the things of this world fall by the way.

It is tempting to argue from all this that by denigrating the Law, denying social accountability, and elevating private experience, Wheelwright liberates the individual saint and prefigures nineteenth-century individualism. But this is to discount the language of antinomianism. Whereas for the Puritan the association of secular and spiritual, of public and private, meant that the acts of individual saints were replete with meaning, for the antinomian they were null and void. Wheelwright's language asserts not human dignity or freedom but self-abnegation. The saint, witnessed and sealed, is responsible for neither his failings nor his accomplishments. The denial of self is central to antinomian rhetoric, and with it comes a denial of the meaning of the visible so profound as to make impossible any effort to translate inner conviction into outward form. Only by arguing that the language of the self-in-Christ rationalizes an impulse toward radical self-assertion on the part of the anti-nomian—and this is, of course, what we see in their repeated challenges to the authority of minister and magistrate—can we arrive at the modern view of antinomianism as a liberating doctrine, as enabling and celebrating the individual and his activity.

On such an inversion rests the usual claim that antinomianism served the purposes of those oppressed in one way or another by theocratic rule. Yet other explanations are possible. It may be, for example, that antinomian doctrine relieved for some the acute anxiety that historians tell us plagued the Puritan community. Both of these historical accounts of the rise of conflict in New England assume, however, that we have read the terms of the controversy correctly. When we look at the spokesmen for the two parties to the conflict, a different interpretation suggests itself. The argument over the nature and outcome of conversion takes its importance from the implications these contain for the relationship between saint and community. What Winthrop is at such great pains to demonstrate is that however much Calvinist doctrine might seem to foster passivity, the special circumstances of the New Israel reassert the value of human effort, of works. This implies, in turn, that Puritanism as it was institutionalized in America is itself a new form of Calvinism. The antinomian, viewed in this light, pushes the private, invisible nature of grace to a heretical extreme and, by doing so, places himself in opposition to the "Americanization" of Calvinism. The antinomians insisted that what was hidden could never be made visible; the individual could not be made collective and Calvinism could not be institutionalized. They rejected the revision of the relationship between works and grace on which the New Jerusalem was to be founded.

The Hutchinsonians' rejection of the federal covenant was tantamount to a rejection of the official ideology of the new colony. The idea of a special national covenant had originated among English Puritans before the Great Migration, but nowhere was it more forceful than in Massachusetts, where "messianic themes and biblical texts fused with an official public mission that bound an entire populace to its terms."[20] Recent scholarship suggests that this development was facilitated by the adoption of the 1611 Authorized Version of the Bible. Unlike the earlier Geneva Bible with its extensive marginalia emphasizing the private quest for salvation and insisting on Christ as the "sole object of contemplation," the Authorized Version was entirely without commentary. As Puritans in England and then in New England shifted their attention from the covenant of grace to the federal covenant, the asocial orientation of the Geneva Bible came to be seen as anachronistic. The single-minded focus on free grace of the Genevan commentary only made more difficult the effort to fuse their "original concern with personal salvation to the novel task of model society building."[21] Although the Geneva Bible was not abandoned entirely by ministers of the Bay colony, the Authorized Version became increasingly the Bible of choice. It is telling, then, that Anne Hutchinson and her followers exhibit a decided preference for the Geneva translation. As one scholar has put it: "The Hutchinsonian party spoke from the Geneva Bible, while the leaders accused them from the Authorized."[22] At issue was not only "exegetical anarchy" but the "Americanization" of Puritanism in yet another form. The Geneva Bible, from which Wheelwright drew his Fast Day text and which Hutchinson quoted verbatim and at length during her examination, spoke to an older (in fact, an Old World) Puritanism, free of the special demands of community formation and social cohesion that engrossed the Bay leaders. Resisting the very idea of a national covenant as well as the text on which this idea was taken to depend, the Hutchinsonians pitted themselves against the governing myth of the city on the hill.

As I have already suggested, neither doctrinal nor even exegetical differences alone can fully explain the fervor with which the Hutchinsonians were driven from Massachusetts Bay, for these find their reflection in two wholly disparate visions of community and social order. The Puritans' theory of government provided a perfect counterpoint to their theological position.

Church and state were not inseparable; in fact, the line dividing the two was carefully drawn. But like visible sainthood, good government relied on a shift in the motion of the will toward the good. As "A Modell of Christian Charity" makes clear, ideal community depended on knitting men together into one body with common interests, and this could be realized only by the saints, for the unregenerate were capable only of self-interest. But a community of saints did not mean a community of equals, as the first words of Winthrop's discourse make clear: "God Almightie in his most holy and wise providence hath soe disposed of the Condicion of mankinde, as . . . some must be rich some poore, some highe and eminent in power and dignitie; others meane and in subjeccion."[23] The love men feel one for another will make the "eminent in power" protect the "meane," while keeping those in "subjeccion" from overthrowing the powerful. This form of government, approved by God if not decreed by him in its particulars, offers "mutual safety and welfare" through hierarchy. A man's willingness to submit to authority became yet another test of his standing with God.

But this scheme was too neat. As in the case of the ministers, the origin of the power of the magistrates came into question. Despite the relative homogeneity of the early settlements, they were not free of conflict. The social and economic life of the colony was unsettled, and, as immigration continued, disputes arose over the distribution of chartered lands. A slow increase during the early years in the number of unchurched and therefore disenfranchised settlers, along with an increasingly apparent distance between rich and poor, led to struggles between the magistracy and the freemen who controlled the General Court. In the resolution of these struggles rested the hopes of the magistrates for stable control. The search for a resolution was undertaken by the magistrates in part simply to buttress their own authority, but it expressed, as well, a moral obligation to establish the proper form of civil authority—a Christian authority that would use its power to uphold the covenant. Once the freemen had taken control of the court and had assumed the right to elect the governor, the possibility loomed large that the magistrates would be stripped of their special powers and "mere democracy" would ensue.

The magistrates needed a way to justify their veto over the General Court, their claim to separate legislative power, their right to discretionary sentencing of colonial offenders. But even more immediately, they needed to respond to the antinomian's suggestion that civil, like clerical, authority was superseded by God's immediate word as proclaimed by the chosen. As the antinomians announced their refusal to accept the court's conviction of Wheelwright for "contempt and sedition," as they attempted to gain admission to the magistracy for several of their number, and as they turned their back on the war with the Pequots, this need took on a new urgency. In the 1630s as much as in 1645, when John Winthrop formally addressed the problem, the issue was the relationship between "authority of the magistracy" and the "liberty of the people."

> It is you who have called us unto this office; but being thus called, we have our authority from God; it is the ordinancy of God, and it hath the image of God stamped upon it; and the contempt of it has been vindicated by God with terrible examples of his vengeance. . . . There is a liberty of corrupt nature which is affected both by men and beasts, to do what they list; and this liberty is inconsistent with authority . . . 'tis the grand enemy of truth and peace, and all the ordinances of God are bent against it. But there is a civil, a moral, a federal liberty, which is the proper end and object of authority; it is a liberty for that only which is just and good. . . . This liberty is maintained in a way of subjection to authority; and the authority set over you will in all administrations for your good be quietly submitted unto.[24]

Nowhere in this passage is the authority or accountability of the individual questioned; rather, these stand as the foundation of Winthrop's argument for appropriate control. He assumes that men can and will adopt that liberty which is "just and good" and shun the contemptuous liberty of the self-seeking—a liberty associated with antinomianism. What is more, he assumes that true Christians will be in substantial agreement in their understanding of these. As a result, Winthrop need not define true liberty except to say that it manifests itself as "subjection to authority." He offers a test, not a definition. This reasoning served the magistrates as the distinction between "formal" and "virtual" possession of the keys or between "substantial" and "circumstantial" works served the ministry. It linked piety and good citizenship in such a way as to make palatable continued domination by the magistrates, and it glossed over the inevitable failure of Puritan society to achieve that ideal community of interest which should unite the New Israel.

Conveniently, then, for those seeking power, election was manifest by good behavior, one aspect of which was submission to authority. For the smooth functioning of the community, they depended on that suppression of "self-interest" which would allow the various levels of authority—from the actual to the political fathers—to exercise control. On their ability to succeed in this, they believed, hung God's favor and the world's opinion. In fact, to many Puritan leaders the failure of the New World community would signify God's withdrawal from them. One of the most important ways to insure against this failure was to discover that "instrument of Satan fitted and trained to his service for interrupting the passage, [of God's] Kingdome in this part of the world, and poysoning the Churches here planted as no story records the like of a woman, since that mentioned in the Revelation" (*AC*, 308).

Satan's agent was, of course, Anne Hutchinson, in whose hand invisible witness and immediate revelation combined to form a two-edged sword. Hutchinson wielded her weapon with skill: "You have power over my body but the Lord Jesus hath power over my body and soul, and assure yourselves thus much, you do as much as in you lies to put the Lord Jesus Christ from you, and if you go on in this course you begin you will bring a curse upon you and your posterity, and the mouth of the Lord hath spoken it" (*AC*, 338). Hutchinson's arrogant claim to special knowledge of God's design posed serious problems for the ministry, as we have seen. Winthrop acknowledges this and more during his examination of the heretic. The effect of Hutchinson's revelations was to teach "the country that they shall look for revelations and are not bound to the ministry of the word, but God will teach them." If the ministers could be thus overridden, civil authority too must fall in the face of God's word in the mouths of the saints.

Despite Wheelwright's insistence that "the weapons of our warfare are not carnall but spirituall," the magistrates thought they heard the call to violent rebellion of the kind fomented by the German Anabaptists in 1533. As Thomas Dudley, then deputy governor of the colony, put it, "These disturbances that have come among the Germans have been all grounded upon revelations, and so they that have vented them have stirred up their hearers to take up arms against their prince and to cut the throats of one another, and these have been the fruits of them, and whether the devil may inspire the same into their hearts here I know not, for I am fully persuaded that Mrs. Hutchinson is deluded by the devil" (*AC*, 343). To allow so great an "imposter" as Hutchinson to go unchecked would be to assume the guilt of her heresy and to put themselves and their community in clear and immediate danger. To them, as to the ancient church of Thyatira, the Son of God would say "I have a few things against thee, because thou sufferest that woman Jezebel . . . to teach and seduce my servants" (Revelation 2:20).

Denying the special significance of the city on the hill and defying both ministers and magistrates would have been enough, but this defiance in a woman shook the very foundations of Puritan social organization. The social and economic importance of the family was complemented by the Puritan's belief that marriage most closely mirrored the relation between God and man. The covenant between God and his people was reflected in the one between man and wife, and on that rested all larger covenanted associations. The family provided the prototype for both church and state, and the position of men as fathers in the family justified them as fathers in the state. Hutchinson jumbled the order of things from top to bottom. As one of her judges, Hugh Peters, put it to her, "You have stept out of your place, you have rather bine a Husband than a wife, and a preacher than a Hearer: and a Magistrate than a subject" (*AC*, 382–83).[25]

It has been suggested that Anne Hutchinson was prompted to dissent by her resentment of the lowly status assigned women in New England, that her heresy reflects a "primitive feminism" consisting of "the subjective recognition of her own strength . . . and the apparent belief that other women could come to the same recognition."[26] This argument claims that antinomianism was attractive to women because, by denying the individual any role in his or her own salvation, it made the relation of each Christian to his God analogous to the relation of women to men in Puritan society; its appeal was that it reduced men to the same subordinate status as women in the cosmic if not in the communal scheme of things. This hypothesis seems doubtful on a number of counts, not the least of which is that despite statements like Winthrop's famous one about the insane and bookish Mrs. Hopkins—"if she had attended her household affairs, and such things as belong to women, and not gone out of her way to meddle with such things as are proper for men, whose minds are stronger, etc., she had kept her wits"—recent scholarship suggests a significant disjuncture between expressed attitudes toward women and the latitude actually granted them in their work and lives.

The most important problem with this argument, however, is that it ignores what is most striking in Hugh Peters's accusation and others like it. Peters suggests that Hutchinson, as "husband," preacher, and magistrate, successfully preempted a masculine authority. Hutchinson, unlike the famous Mrs. Hopkins, did not lose her wits, nor did she simply act in ways that ill became a woman. Rather, she declared herself autonomous insofar as the Puritan patriarchy was concerned precisely by representing herself as utterly subordinate to Christ. The abnegation of self urged by antinomianism thus presents itself as an assertion of self, and the antinomian's passivity as power. Instead of an equality of subordination, Hutchinson raised fears of a female autonomy that would disrupt the system of analogies to which the Puritan fathers turned in justifying their authority: as the husband ruled his family, so the minister his church and the magistrate the state. Claiming to be nothing in herself but all in Christ, Hutchinson reduced herself to a medium through which God spoke and, in this way, empowered herself more fully than the men in whom the community vested power.

Nonetheless, in its simplest form, the problem was that Hutchinson stepped out of the role the community defined for her. She ignored the strictures placed upon women, and she exaggerated this transgression by her haughty carriage, by refusing the correction of her "betters," by her impudence. A substantial portion of her civil examination concerns the lawfulness of her role as religious instructress. No one denied that Scripture provided that women might teach, but only under those conditions narrowly defined by the "rule" in Titus. That rule was to be taken "in this sense," Winthrop explained to Hutchinson, "that elder women must instruct the younger about their business, and to love their husbands and not make them clash" (*AC*, 316). Hutchinson not only failed to teach these "good things" but admitted men into her audience as well. By doing so, she both broke the law and disrupted the chain of authority that shaped Puritan civil relations. If a woman could instruct men, then all legitimate authority was in jeopardy.

More important for our present purposes than the question of whether the liberation from earthly authority offered by antinomianism served as a focal point for female revolt is the way in which Hutchinson's assumption of autonomy was used by her judges. This last, more than the alliance between Hutchinson and her female followers, governs the portrait of Hutchinson that was passed from one generation to the next. It seemed obvious to those in power that a woman who would so exceed the limits of female decorum as to expound Scripture to the elders would also be prone to sexual misconduct. Everywhere in the court examination, one finds the insinuation that Hutchinson is, like Jezebel, guilty of fornication. Clearly, antinomianism would lead irresistibly to adultery and worse. At its most extreme, the association of heresy with sexual license is expressed in the charge that Hutchinson held "the foule, groce, filthie and abomonable opinion held by Familists, *of the Communitie of Woemen*" (*AC*, 362). Henry Niclaes's Family of Love believed themselves illuminated and bound together by the indwelling spirit of love. Building from a denial of both original sin and the afterlife, the sixteenth-century perfectionist sect was reputed to practice the communal ownership of property and complex marriage. They rationalized these practices by assuming themselves to live on earth as others thought to live in heaven—in a state of "inter-marriage" with all other beings.[27]

Despite her denial of the concept of the resurrection on which Familism is based, Hutchinson was apparently unable to satisfy her examiners, for the accusation is made again and again.

The question of Hutchinson's sexual conduct is central to John Cotton's denunciation of the antinomians. His reproof is addressed to Hutchinson herself and to the two groups of people most liable to contagion: her grown sons and the women of the congregation. What Cotton considered to be an effective way of addressing these different groups gives an interesting glimpse of the varying attitudes toward them. To Hutchinson's sons his argument is one of filial duty. Their error, according to Cotton, has been to allow natural affection for a parent to come before the love of God: "Though the Credit of your mother be dear to you, and your Regard to her Name, yet the Regard you should have of Christs Name and your Care of his Honour and Credit should outway all the other" (*AC*, 369). Whereas Hutchinson, as a woman, overturns the order of things when she rejects the authority of men in favor of God, her sons, conversely, because they are men, must put God's credit, as interpreted by the fathers, with whom they are naturally identified, ahead of their mother's. Instead, Cotton admonishes them, they have encouraged their mother to "harden her Heart" by their very affection for her: "Instead of lovinge and naturall Children you have proved Vipers to Eate through the very Bowells of your Mother, to her Ruine if god does not gratiously prevent" (*AC*, 370). For Hutchinson's sons to love and respect their mother, despite her errors, would only hasten her damnation; they serve her best, insists Cotton, by allying themselves with male authority.

To the "Sisters of our owne Congregation," Cotton speaks otherwise. He admits that they may have "receaved much good" from their friend, that she may have drawn them away from a covenant of works, but he sees danger in their assuming that since some of what Hutchinson taught was good, all was good. Cotton appeals to the women of the congregation to recognize Hutchinson's errors as a product of her femaleness. "She is but a Woman," he reminds them, and therefore peculiarly prone to error. Cotton assumes that the women will accept his assessment of Hutchinson's theology and her behavior because they, of all people, will be most acutely aware of feminine weakness. He asks that the women of the congregation demonstrate that they are not complicit in Hutchinson's errors by reaffirming the judgment of the patriarchy.

Cotton confronts Hutchinson herself with the disparity between the good she has done and the dishonor she has brought upon the church by her actions. God has endowed her with "good parts and gifts"; he has allotted her a "sharpe apprehension, a ready utterance and abilitie to represe [her]selfe" (*AC*, 370). These abilities, Cotton suggests, are unusual in women and ought to be repaid by proper use. Hutchinson's gifts make her eminently "fitt to instruct [her] Children and Servants and to be helpfull to [her] husband in the Government of the famely" (*AC*, 371). It is to aid her as tutor to her subordinates and helpmeet to her superior that God has made Hutchinson clever, not so that she might meddle in theology. However "good" her gifts, if they are exercised outside the domestic sphere, they yield only "unsound Tenets" and "dangerous principles." But Hutchinson, "puft up" with Eve's pride, has forgotten her place. With her talents, Cotton suggests, she would do better to succeed as a woman than fail as a prophetess.

Cotton regards any good Hutchinson has done in keeping some from "building thear good Estate upon thear own duties and performances" as accidental and believes that that good is more than outweighed by her "poisonous" doctrines. Of her errors, the most virulent in Cotton's view is her opening the way to "Epicurisme," "Libertinisme," and Familism. It is Cotton who says aloud what the other ministers only imply, who questions whether Hutchinson's familism may be more than theoretical:

> Yea consider *if the Resurrection be past then* . . . that filthie Sinne of the Comunitie of Woemen and all promiscuous and filthie cominge togeather of men and Woemen without Distinction or Relation of Marriage, will necessarily follow. And though I have not herd, nayther do I thinke, you have bine unfaythfull to your Husband in his Marriage Covenant, *yet that will follow upon it* . . . and that which the Annabaptists and Familists bringe to

> prove the Lawfullnes of the common use of all Weomen and soe
> more dayngerous Evells and filthie Unclenes and other sines will
> follow than you doe now Imageine or conceave.
>
> (*AC*, 371–72)

By raising so ominously the question of Hutchinson's marital
fidelity, Cotton gave voice to the suspicions of many of the examining ministers and enlarged the grounds for her condemnation. The fact that he had not heard of any unfaithfulness did
not, of course, mean that none had taken place. The language of
Cotton's admonition hints at his feelings—and presumably
those of others of the men involved—toward Hutchinson. His
insistent use of the word "filthie" to describe sexual relations
outside of marriage is especially striking and is echoed by others throughout the examinations. Whether Cotton's scrupu-
lousness is idiosyncratic or representative, there can be little
doubt that Hutchinson was regarded as an object of loathing
and that this loathing arose, in part at least, from the imputa-
tion of sexual crimes. The fear of sexual misconduct may explain the inordinate interest of men like Winthrop in the "monsters" to which Hutchinson and her closest supporter, Mary
Dyer, reputedly gave birth. Despite the lack of evidence of sexual misconduct, the American Jezebel was beginning to look
like her original.

"Men that have sores running upon them must be shut up from
the presence of men sound and whole," wrote Thomas Shepard. "O, thy sins, like plague sores, run on thee; therefore thou
must be shut out like a dog from the presence of God and all his
people."[28] "Non scelus, sed sceleris impuritas (Not wickedness
but the failure to punish wickedness) is the guilt of a society,
whether civil or sacred" (*AC*, 435), John Cotton insisted. The
Massachusetts General Court concurred. To avoid contagion, it
"saw . . . an inevitable necessity to rid [Anne Hutchinson]
away, except wee would bee guilty, not only of our own ruine,
but also of the Gospel" (*AC*, 276). The appearance of Hutchinson and her followers was a test. As Satan himself came to
tempt Jesus in the wilderness, so in this new wilderness he
came in disguise to seduce the saints. And just as surely as this

test demonstrated that the New Canaan was a special place in the eyes of the Lord, so the saints' resounding "Get thee behind me" proved them its faithful stewards.

It is difficult to separate the theological from the social, the psychological from the political in the Puritan response to Anne Hutchinson, and no doubt it was the coincidence of all these that made her excommunication and banishment so urgent a matter. Her unfeminine arrogance compounded her doctrinal errors; her incursions into traditional male territory made more presumptuous her criticism of the clergy; the political turmoil initiated by her followers underscored her unwillingness to recant; the respect accorded her by the Boston congregation made all the more threatening her prophesying; her "greate . . . Wisdome and Understandinge," her intimate knowledge of scripture (albeit Genevan scripture), and her claim to revelation made her a formidable opponent. But finally it was to safeguard the myth of a chosen people laboring for the Lord in the American desert that Hutchinson was banished.

Without repeating the arguments other scholars have so carefully and convincingly made, the nonseparating Congregationalists of Massachusetts laid claim "to the identity of the figural Israel, where to be a believer was *ipso facto* to be a 'true Israelite,' and where, conversely, to be a member in good standing of the society was *ipso facto* to show oneself a saint."[29] The myth of the New Israel embodied in the federal covenant brought together the personal and the historical, the private and the public, the individual and the communal, in such a way as to demonstrate that all of these were bent toward one and the same end: the fulfillment of God's errand in the New World. This did not mean abandoning the Reformation principle of *sola fides*—the translation of authority from the institution of the church to the individual believer—but rather directed individual experience toward community, exemplified by the invisible church and made manifest in the Great Migration. The primary experience of conversion on which all else depended was most centrally a private experience requiring of the saint an abasement of the self before Christ. Paradoxically, the theology of the New Israel at once elevated the individual as the medium of

God's grace and denigrated the self as Satan, while its myth liberated the energies of the self to accomplish the tasks of the elect nation. In America righteousness and redemption, which Puritans elsewhere might take to imply antithetical concepts of selfhood, were understood to mirror each other. Emphasizing the need for each man to cooperate in his election and placing a premium on struggle and self-scrutiny, the theocracy nonetheless took good works to signify election and material success to confirm God's favor.

In the face of this dominant myth, Anne Hutchinson spoke for what she insisted was an older, purer way, the way she believed had occasioned the Great Migration. To the extent that the single-minded focus of the Geneva Bible on justification by faith in Christ shaped her religious thinking, this way did, in fact, reflect an older and immensely popular body of thought. Thus, scholars speak of the proximity of antinomian and orthodox, especially in the New World. One, for example, has suggested that the "Anglo-Christian tradition"

> exists in a tension between legalism and antinomianism, between the belief that religion, taking its impetus from revelation, through reason achieves forms and laws which are essential to the aiding of weak human nature and to the continuity of divine law upon earth; and the belief that since man's relation to God is super-rational consisting as it does of the Lord's gift of grace to the individual believer, laws and rituals are dead except insofar as they are directly informed by the Holy Spirit acting through the individual believer.[30]

There is considerable evidence that a battle not unlike that between orthodox and antinomian raged in most Puritan breasts. Peter Bulkeley, for example, a staunch partisan of the theocracy, in speaking of the gospel covenant points out that "no number of sins exclude from salvation, till they be accompanied with final apostasie, impenitency, and unbelief."[31] Admittedly, he retreats several pages later: "Yet let no man abuse this doctrine unto carnall liberty . . . those that make no conscience of sinning, have nothing to do with this consolation; it is onely to support the weake . . . not to incourage the wicked."[32] Nevertheless, Bulkeley asserts the powerlessness of the saints with a vehemence approaching Hutchinson's. "Do we desire to be in covenant with God?" he asks. "Then trust not to your selves, to your owne righteousnesse, but goe to Jesus Christ . . . give up your selves unto him, put yourselves in his hands, and goe hand in hand with him unto the presence of the Father, that he may mediate for you, and plead your cause."[33] While there is a hint of activity on the part of the saint as he goes "hand in hand" with Christ to the seat of judgment, the similarity between this formulation of the covenant and Wheelwright's in his "seditious" Fast Day sermon is striking.

In one sense, then, we may regard Hutchinson's antinomianism as representing a "residual" aspect of the dominant culture, to use Raymond Williams's term. That is, her understanding of grace can be seen as an element of the culture "formed in the past, but . . . still active in the cultural process, not only and often not at all as an element of the past, but as an effective element of the present."[34] Given her dependence on the Geneva Bible, Hutchinson's insistence on conversion as the sole question of moment for the Christian and her willingness to forfeit all for Christ, while extreme, hardly seems heretical. As Williams points out, however, the "residual" elements of a culture may contain the "oppositional." In Massachusetts the cultural residuum of the Genevan commentary, with its emphasis on individual salvation, was subsumed in the concept of a national covenant. Rejecting the idea of an elect nation in which citizen and saint move in lockstep toward a glorious future—rejecting, that is, the "Americanization" of Puritanism—Hutchinson transformed a quiescent aspect of Puritan doctrine into an actively oppositional one.

In other words, the fact that everyone understood self-abnegation as a condition of salvation and agreed that the "wicked man . . . commiteth the highest degree of idolatry . . . plucks God out of his throne, and makes himself a god, because he makes himself the last end in every action,"[35] did not mean that everyone agreed about the means or the effects of grace. For the orthodox colonists, election entailed a loss of ego that made charity possible; charity, in turn, enabled the saint to act in the larger interests of the chosen community. And these interests, because they were taken to be identical to the interests of God, provided further evidence of grace. Sainthood and citizenship —the one, by common agreement, an invisible condition, the other a series of visible acts—were brought into perfect accord as the sacred errand of the New Israel simultaneously confirmed and exacted the election of those who lent themselves to its fulfillment. The federal covenant provided the context within which personal salvation was to be worked out. In that context, the private quest for assurance and the public mission of the chosen people became one, despite the fact that one seemed to call for an abandonment of self in Christ and the other for energetic, autonomous individuals. The tension between self-abnegation and self-assertion—between being "swallowed up in Christ" and "pressing into the Kingdom"—was resolved by making the visible efforts of the saints signify an invisible state of grace. While the insufficiency of this resolution is perhaps reflected in the pervasive anxiety of Puritan rhetoric, its importance cannot be underestimated. The myth of the New Israel made possible a way of interpreting the world we characterize as "American," a mode of interpretation wherein the private and public correspond.

To the Hutchinsonians' way of thinking, however, conversion signaled not the conflation of public and private but their final separation. The "substantial" self, at once liberated from the things of this world and lost in Christ, was an image of divinity, while the "circumstantial" one was void of significance. The antinomians' dismissal of both ritual and moral law rests on the absolute division of the seen from the unseen, on the assumption that acts denote nothing and that truth is witnessed by the spirit alone.[36] Whether or not one accounts for it by their adherence to the Geneva Bible, the Hutchinsonians effectively challenged the concept of visible sainthood that was the central accommodation of Puritanism to community formation and therefore critical to the fulfillment of the federal covenant. As opponents of the New Israel, Hutchinson and her followers could be characterized as enemies of Christ enacting the "Dragon's old indefatigable Malice with the Serpents subtility."[37]

The fact that Hutchinson's antinomianism contains both residual and oppositional elements is crucial to her story as it is told by the Puritan chroniclers. To the extent that her doctrine contained elements of a still-active past, Hutchinson could legitimately be associated with the sinful Old World, which the orthodox had, in despair, abandoned to its fate. Nonetheless, as the enemy of the chosen people, Hutchinson's existence, like the New Israel itself, had to be authorized in scripture. Her Jezebel, in other words, stands opposed to their Moses. As a heretic, Hutchinson opposed orthodoxy; as a woman, she was pictured as opposing the founding fathers, who, for later generations, stood as heroes in the long foreground of the American Revolution. In the most extreme version of her story, Hutchinson would thus come to be seen as opposing the very idea of America.

3

A Masterpiece of Women's Wit

Anne Hutchinson's death in 1643, in the wake of Willem Kieft's raids on the New Netherland Indians, vindicated the authorities of Massachusetts Bay. Whatever uncertainty they may once have harbored about the righteousness of their judgment against the antinomians, the case was now clear. Hutchinson's arrogant assumption that God would intervene on her behalf and avenge her banishment had proved unfounded. Instead, the heretic herself was the object of God's punishment. In the opinion of Thomas Welde, whose preface opens John Winthrop's 1644 history of the antinomian controversy, the circumstances of Hutchinson's death revealed the extent of God's wrath: "I never heard that the Indians in those parts did ever before this, commit the like outrage upon any one family, or families, and therefore Gods hand is the more apparently seene herein, to pick out this wofull woman, to make her and those belonging to her, an unheard of heavie example of their cruelty above al others" (*AC*, 218). To Welde, in England at the time as an agent of the colony, Hutchinson's death was certain evidence that the Lord had heard New England's "groanes to heaven"; it was a remarkable providence.

A Short Story of the Rise, reign, and ruine of the Antinomians, Familists & Libertines, to which Welde appended his preface, was the first and most authoritative history of the controversy.[1] Compiled by Winthrop, who was not only "an eye and earewitness of the carriage of matters" but the chief adversary of the Hutchinsonians, *A Short Story* gathers together the documents of the controversy, most of them written by Winthrop himself. Containing the catalogue of "erroneous opinions" and "unsavory speeches" assembled by the Cambridge Synod of 1637, the records of Hutchinson's examination before the General

Court, the petition submitted to the Court on Wheelwright's behalf, and the account of Mary Dyer's miscarriage, as well as Winthrop's considerable editorial comment, *A Short Story* is an invaluable record of the attitudes of the ruling elite. But, as Thomas Welde apparently realized, it failed to provide its reader with "the order and sense" of the story of Anne Hutchinson. If we take his preface as an indication of what he meant by this, it appears that Welde found *A Short Story* wanting when it came to interpreting the conflict with the antinomians. Not only was it weak on chronology, the simple "order" of things, but because it was composed of a series of documents, it did not make sufficiently clear the larger pattern revealed by the events of the 1630s, nor did it place these events in the context of New England's special destiny. This was not to say that Winthrop failed to realize or acknowledge the hand of God at work in the controversy, but Welde wanted to make sure that its providential meaning was clear.

His preface begins with the broad lesson to be drawn from the appearance of the antinomians in the New Israel. Having survived "persecuting Prelates," "dangers at sea," and "wilderness troubles," the colonists, Welde tells us, settled down to happy enjoyment of their new home. Their complacency was clearly a mistake. "Lest we should, now, grow secure," Welde explains, "our wise god . . . sent a new storme after us, which proved the sorest tryall that ever befell us since we left our Native soyle" (*AC,* 201). The arrival of the Erronists, with their "packs" full of "unsound and loose opinions," was designed, first and foremost, to save the colonists from themselves, to remind them of their sins and recall them to their labors. But like other misfortunes, the Puritans understood the appearance of heretics in their midst as a blessing in disguise. Insofar as it demonstrated God's reluctance to allow his particular people to fall into a false security, the antinomian controversy offered, at least in retrospect, proof positive that God "watcheth over his vineyard night and day" (*AC,* 202). The antinomians, with their claim that "a man need not be troubled by the Law" but need only "stand still and waite for Christ to doe all for him," offered the colonists "a faire and easie way to Heaven" (*AC,* 203–4).

Their rejection of this way in favor of the more difficult way of truth was a sign of New England's worthiness and God's favor. In other words, God allowed Satan to try his people in order that they might yet again prove themselves, both by their own exertions against the Antichrist and by their unflagging faith in God's righteousness and their own divinely appointed errand.

The historical context of *A Short Story* clarifies Welde's intentions. By the 1640s the same English Puritans who had not hesitated to criticize New England's handling of the antinomians found themselves confronting a similar menace. Antinomianism was on the rise and a second revolution of the seventeenth century threatened—one that, had it happened, "might have established communal property [and] a far wider democracy . . . disestablished the state church and rejected the protestant ethic."[2] What Christopher Hill, writing about England, has called "Calvinism's lower-class alter ego" cannot be so described in America, not because the American version of antinomianism is any less social in nature but because the issues of class to which Hill points are obscured by the language of prophetic history. In fact, it may be that gender figures so largely in the story of American antinomianism because it, unlike class, is comprehended in the language of the New Israel. In any event, insofar as Hill's phrase both raises the specter of class conflict and identifies antinomianism as Calvinism's alter ego—an other, defined always with reference to the one—these same implications are carried by gender in the story of American antinomianism, in which the figure for the disempowered is woman.

Welde's preface, which strenuously defends the banishment of the Hutchinsonians, is designed nonetheless to offer New England's experience of a decade before as a model for the suppression of heresy in England. But in the midst of civil war, antinomianism in England took the form of dissent in the ranks; it was only one of a wide range of radical ideas—theological, economic, and social—that emerged during the English revolution, and it was an idea associated with those disempowered by class. Even had the class bias and the forms of social disorganization in England and America been more similar, Welde's terms would have defeated a shared reading of events. Much as he wants *A Short Story* to serve as an instructive example for the English, his most basic assumptions about the historical roles of England and America undermine his efforts. His interpretation of antinomianism is predicated on his understanding of New England as a New Israel, an understanding that makes his story particular to the colonies and suggests, moreover, that American antinomianism was, in all but its most basic doctrinal assertions, different from its English counterpart. For Welde antinomianism threatened the very structure of significance that defined the new colony, but the antinomian controversy was an episode in sacred history, referring at once to the scriptural past and to the prophetic future. As Welde understands it, the colonists are a choice remnant, saved from the impending universal calamity by their removal to a wilderness refuge. Insofar as their gathering heralds the coming of the millennium, the New Englanders are harbingers of Satan's downfall and thus his special prey.

Welde's story, then, is the story of the serpent in the garden, the story of New England's seduction. The heretics, as he explains, attempted to "insinuate" themselves into the "affections" of the colonists, to "steal into their bosomes." "Seducers" all, they "laboured to worke first upon women, being . . . the weaker to resist . . . and if once they could winde in them, they hoped by them, as by an *Eve,* to catch their husbands also" (*AC,* 205–6). Like the harlot in Proverbs, the antinomians, "with much faire speech . . . caused [the colonists] to yeeld, with the flattering of their lips they forced them" (*AC,* 205). But, as if seduction were not enough, to prove the legitimacy of their deceitful doctrines, the heretics "fathered" them upon the eminent men of the country. The "worst" of these seducers was, of course, Mistress Hutchinson, who, snakelike, "diffused the venome of these opinions into the very veines and vitalls of the People in the country" (*AC,* 207). Led astray by this new Eve, the antinomians set upon the saints to instill in them "a spirit of pride, insolency, contempt of authority, division [and] sedition" (*AC,* 211). But, as Welde goes on to demonstrate, the Lord "hearkened unto" his children and "in a wonderfull manner" freed them from the toils of Satan. The second half of the preface is devoted to God's "Antidotes" to Hutchinson's venom. Welde includes among these the actions taken by the church and the court to restrain the antinomians. The Cambridge Synod, the ministerial conferences, the trials of the heretics, and the sermons of the orthodox all figure as important, though finally ineffective, efforts to subdue Satan. Only when "God himselfe was pleased to step in with his casting voice . . . by testifying his displeasure against their opinions and practises, as clearly as if he had pointed with his finger," (*AC*, 214) were the heretics vanquished.

In keeping with the metaphor of seduction that governs the first half of the preface, the second half is dominated by the "monstrous" issue of that seduction: the stillborn child of Mary Dyer—a committed follower of the Hutchinsonians—and Hutchinson's own multiple "misconceptions."[3] The hand of God was clear both in the extreme malformation of these births and in their striking coincidence with the controversy. "Out of their wombs, as . . . out of their braines," Welde explains, came "such monstrous births as no Chronicle . . . hardly ever recorded the like" (*AC*, 214). Dyer's delivery of a "woman child, a fish, a beast, and a fowle, all woven together," was an event so anomalous that it could only be regarded as a sign of God's displeasure. Moreover, as Winthrop points out later in *A Short Story*, the events surrounding Dyer's confinement were likewise extraordinary: the widow Jane Hawkins, who attended her, was "notorious for familiarity with the devill"; the women who were present at the onset of Dyer's labor were either taken ill themselves or called away to nurse sick children; the fetus was secretly buried, only to be discovered on the "very day Mistris Hutchinson was cast out of the Church," the same day that William Dyer was summoned before the ministers to answer for his opinions. As for Hutchinson, the number of the "births" and their complete absence of human form confirmed their meaning. "See how the wisdome of God fitted this judgement to her sin every way," Welde exclaims, "for looke as she had vented mishapen opinions, so she must bring forth deformed monsters; and as about 30. Opinions in number, so many monsters" (*AC*, 214). This "loud-speaking providence from Heaven" so convincingly demonstrated God's disfavor that, according to Welde, not even Hutchinson's followers dared ignore it.

The interpretation of the "monstrous births" as an instance of special intervention by a God intent on edifying his people is crucial to Welde's affirmation of Puritan authority. Writing about the Salem witch trials, one scholar has argued recently for the striking resemblance between the traditional *maleficia* of the witch and the providences of the Puritan deity. She has suggested that the crime of the women accused at Salem was not simply that they engaged in *maleficia* but that they thus appropriated a power that Puritan culture associated with male sexual identity.[4] Despite the allusions to witchcraft, Welde's account of the monstrous births explicitly denies Hutchinson and her female followers just such supernatural power. Instead, he attributes the creation of the "monsters" to Satan and their revelation to an instructive God. Had he held the women themselves accountable for the births, he would perforce have granted their witchlike power to give tangible form to their heresy. The monsters are neither evidence nor expression of such power. On the contrary, the Puritan fathers insisted that the misconceptions were God's visible demonstration of the monstrousness of the women's ideas. They thus turned the very femaleness of the women against them to prove them wrong.

Insofar as this interpretation of the births demonstrated God's wisdom in fitting the punishment to the crime, it served a dual purpose. It clearly associated the crime with the *female* heretic and, at the same time, elevated the fathers as interpreters of God's will.[5] Hutchinson was an Eve misled by the serpent. Not wholly responsible for her crimes, her offspring were hers and not hers. Revealed by the heavenly Father and interpreted by the earthly ones, the monsters, paradoxically, both signified Hutchinson's errors and denied her power. Because the danger was precisely that just as women's brains might produce misconceptions so might their wombs, Welde's narrative must at once hold Hutchinson punishable for her errors and deny her power to give them tangible form.

John Wheelwright, whose *Mercurius Americanus* was written

in answer to *A Short Story,* thought he saw another significance in Welde and Winthrop's attention to the "monstrous births." Although *Mercurius Americanus* is devoted, for the most part, to a heavily ironic review of the charges leveled against the Hutchinsonians and the behavior of the General Court, Wheelwright considers the use of the births as evidence worthy of rebuke. Winthrop, he suggests, "brings in defects of Nature, amongst defects of Manners. All he can say . . . is, that those are these *reductive,* and as they are effects of sins." To Wheelwright this is a "poore plea," since "by the same reason he may under the same title discover all the weaknesses and naturall imperfections either of man or woman, and fix a kind of morality upon them."[6] Indeed, Welde and Winthrop's attribution of divine significance to the "natural" event of the births appears to Wheelwright to open the way to an anarchy of interpretation, but Wheelwright misses the point of their account. In the eyes of the authors of *A Short Story,* the births were emphatically not "natural." In fact, the very degree of their unnaturalness measured their importance as providential events. In much the same way, the unprecedented violence of the Indian attack on Hutchinson and her family removed their deaths from the realm of the ordinary and suggested to the Puritan mind that the hand of God was revealed in their demise. In both cases the extraordinary quality of the event identified it as an intrusion of the supernatural into everyday life. This "American Jesabel," as Winthrop explains in the final paragraph of *A Short Story,* "kept her strength . . . even among the people of God" till God himself discovered "this subtilty of Satan . . . to her utter shame and confusion, and to the setting at liberty of many godly hearts that had been captivated by her to that day" (*AC,* 310).

Although Welde's preface occupies only twenty of the more than one hundred pages of Winthrop's chronicle, it succeeds in lending *A Short Story* an order and a sense it would not otherwise have. Welde's use of the language of seduction and of childbirth shapes the story to the purposes of the orthodox. The metaphoric structure of the preface insists on Anne Hutchinson—at once serpentine and harlotlike, Eve and Jezebel—as the focus of the story even when the narrative concerns itself with the male Hutchinsonians. Moreover, it conjures up images of irresistible sexual attraction to explain the behavior of the colonists, Eve's unwitting victims. Most important, however, Welde's choice of language serves to demonstrate with some force that sin will, quite literally, out—that is, that the condition of the soul will necessarily be reflected in its visible issue. Welde at once explicates the meaning of the controversy for the benefit of his reader and shows that to the people of God events inevitably unfold their meanings. In this way he accomplished a purpose shared by the historians of New England for the next century. For Welde and Winthrop, as for Edward Johnson, Cotton Mather, Joshua Scottow, and others, the reason for recounting the events of the antinomian crisis was less to confirm the fact or explore the nature of Hutchinson's crimes than to explicate God's intentions in raising up heretics in his vineyard. Seventeenth-century accounts of the controversy are narratives of discovery, in two senses: they reveal God's purpose in trying his people, and, by showing that the same meaning inheres in the visible as in the invisible event, they answer Hutchinson's most dangerous claim—that works evidence nothing, that act and spirit are wholly unrelated.

Both the language and the overall logic of *A Short Story* are typical of seventeenth-century accounts of the antinomian controversy. Recalling the horrors of Familism and the threat of a new Münster rebellion, and intimating witchcraft, *A Short Story* is dominated by imagery that pits Eve/Jezebel against God's chosen—the mother of monsters against the Puritan fathers. It establishes a rhetoric widely employed by later chroniclers and, moreover, it sets the conceptual terms for recounting the crisis. *A Short Story* employs language that simultaneously describes and refutes Hutchinson's errors, it insists on an inevitable process of self-revelation by means of which Hutchinson is brought to expose her own heresies, and, above all, it depends for its interpretation of the conflict on the Puritans' appropriation of Israel's history as their own. This last allowed the Puritans to attribute prophetic meaning to the controversy and, at the same time, addressed the fundamental disagreement between orthodox and antinomian over the meaning of New England. Neither the idea of history as providential nor the ascription of religious meaning to contemporary events is peculiar to American Puritanism—or, for that matter, to the Reformation—but, as one scholar has suggested, American Puritans turned traditional exegesis inside out by transferring "the source of meaning from scripture to secular history."[7] The English might speak metaphorically of a "British Israel," but the colonists regarded themselves not merely as spiritual Israelites, like all Christians, but as inhabitants of a new holy land, "the Antitype of what the Lord's people had of old." In this rendering of New England as a New Israel, they found assurance of the success of their mission. Thus, in the words of Edward Johnson, the soldiers of Christ set forth "to rebuild the most glorious Edifice of Mount *Sion* in a Wildernesse," knowing "this is the place where the Lord will create a new Heaven and a new Earth in new Churches, and a new Common-wealth."[8] To capture the full figural significance of this new Zion, American Puritans evolved what has been called a "rhetoric of inversion," which affirmed "the interchangeability of private, corporate, historical, and prophetic meaning."[9] This rhetoric informs the story of Anne Hutchinson as the historians of New England tell it.

Not surprisingly, it is particularly evident in Johnson's account of the controversy in his 1654 *Wonder-working Providence of Sions Saviour in New England*. There the narrator moves, without explanation, from scriptural analogy to an account of the Antichrist's attempts against the chosen people to a temporal history of the antinomian conflict to the story of a "poor Soule" recently landed in Massachusetts and beset by heretics. In each case the meaning of the controversy is the same: the rise of the hydra-headed monster Error is an "honour" reserved by Christ for those "whose love hee had inlarged to follow him in a dezart wilderness" (*WWP*, 136). Like Welde's, Johnson's purpose is to "bring this disorderly worke . . . into some order" (*WWP*, 121), but this in no way commits him to a single form of narration. Rather, the larger design of his history encourages him to move freely between the corporate and the individual, the universal and the particular. Just as the topography of the country is, at the same time, the anatomy of the Christian soldier in *Wonder-*

working Providence, so the story of the antinomians can be told as personal narrative, community history, or Christian myth.

Johnson begins recounting the events of the crisis by drawing a rather awkward parallel between the defeat of Jabin and Sisera by the armies of Israel and the deliverance of New England from its spiritual enemies. The effect is both to recall the military conceit that governs the history as a whole and to reiterate Johnson's own conviction that a special relationship exists between biblical Israel and the New Jerusalem. But having made the biblical antecedent clear, he moves quickly to enlarge the scene of action. New England's fall into error is not a matter simply of theological dispute or social discord; rather, it is a battle in the war between God and Satan in the latter days. Laboring with "indefatigable paines" to accomplish "not onely the finall ruine of Antichrist . . . but also the advance of Christs Kingdome," the "Souldiers of Christ in New England" attract the wrath of Satan, "who is daily walking to and fro compassing the Earth." So successful is the "worke of Reformation" in the colony that the devil must use all his ingenuity to devise a "new way" to hinder it. This new way takes the form of a simple deception: Satan "stirs up instruments to cry down Antichrist as much as the most . . . but by this project they . . . leade people . . . out of the way . . . and in the Doctrinall part of Antichrists Kingdome, fall to more horrid Blasphemies than the Papist" (*WWP,* 122). Satan's "machevillian" scheme is to divide and conquer the colony, to pit the children of Israel against one another by dividing "those things the Lord hath united in his work of conversion" (*WWP,* 125)—among them the colonists, who should by all rights be united by the Law of Love. In particular, Satan's agents work to divide the Law from the Gospel, Christ from his graces and his ordinances, and the word of God from the spirit of God. In each case the visible is divided from the invisible; acts, rituals, and commandments are alienated from spirit. Out of these "foure dividing Tenents" rise the "forescore grosse errours broached secretly, sliding in the dark like the Plague." As the "fogs of errour" sweep in, muffling the voices of Christ's ministers and turning the "sweete refreshing warmth" of the spirit into "a hot inflama-

tion of . . . conceited Revelations" (*WWP*, 131–32), the true
New England is hidden from view.

As Johnson tells it, antinomianism is the work of the devil
acting through that "Master-piece of Womens wit," Anne
Hutchinson, and her disciples. Like all such trials, this one offered an occasion for the Puritan to fall in with the work of his
God. But whereas Johnson tells the story of the rise of heresy as
an episode in universal history, the story of New England's restoration takes the form of spiritual biography, which we, as
readers, are to understand as another version of the same. The
answer to the "dividing Tenents" is union—here represented
through the union of the individual saint with his Lord, a union
that, in turn, joins him to the children of Israel. The subject of
Johnson's biography is a new immigrant (perhaps the author
himself) who, on arriving in Massachusetts in 1636, is met not
with "the good old way of Christ" but instead with the "new
light" of the Erronists. Beset by heretics at every turn, he wanders into the wilderness where "none but sencelesse Trees and
ecchoing Rocks" answer his confusion: "Oh quoth he where
am I become, is this the place . . . that Christ was pleased
to make use of to rouse up his rich grace in many a drooping
soule; here I have met with some that tell me, I must take a
naked Christ. Oh, woe is mee if Christ be naked to mee, where-
with shall I be cloathed." Like New England itself, the despairing stranger calls upon Christ and is answered. "Oh cunning
Devill," he exclaims, "the Lord Christ rebuke thee, that under a
pretence of a free and ample Gospell shuts out the Soule from
partaking with the Divine Nature of Christ" (*WWP*, 134).

Before crossing "the broade Seas back againe," the newcomer decides to hear the "legall Professors" for himself and arrives
in the nearest town just in time to hear Thomas Shepard preach.
He is "metamorphosed": Shepard's sermon not only clears
"Christs worke of grace in the soule from all those false Doctrines, which the erronious party had afrighted him withall,"
but ends his isolation, both actual and spiritual. Instead of his
own voice echoing off the rocks in the wilderness, his heart now
cries aloud "to the Lords ecchoing answer," and he "resolves
. . . to live and die with the Ministers of New England" (*WWP*,

136). Johnson's use of the echo in this passage nicely schematizes the effects of conversion. Before his metamorphosis, the stranger's voice echoes off the rocks in the wilderness; the self is "echoed" in the world. After his conversion, however, Christ is echoed in the self. His spiritual crisis at an end and his conversion complete, the newcomer becomes one of the company of saints. The trials leading to the pilgrim's metamorphosis and, by implication, to his salvation are the same trials experienced by the community at large. And just as his conversion signals a personal victory, through the agency of the male minister, over the "nimble-tongued Woman" come to tempt him in the wilderness, so too it signifies the corporate victory of orthodox over antinomian and the larger victory of Christ over Satan.

Like Welde, however, Johnson is anxious not only to explore the providential meaning of the controversy but also to defend the actions of the General Court and the Cambridge Synod against English criticism. Johnson's proximity to the American controversy together with the ongoing debate in England over the form of church government make congregationalism a central issue in the temporal history of the conflict that follows the chapter-long biography of the newcomer. He hopes to prove that congregationalism is not "the sluce, through which so many flouds of Error flow in" and, further, to show the means by which "the Lord Christ . . . caused the Heavens to cleer up againe in New-England, after these foggy dayes" (*WWP*, 172–73). But unlike *A Short Story*, Johnson's account of the antinomian controversy is part of a larger chronological history of New England. In this it is more typical of seventeenth-century accounts of the conflict.

Spread out over ten chapters, of which only six treat the controversy exclusively, Johnson's account of the crisis lacks the narrow focus of *A Short Story*; this is reflected in its portrayal of Hutchinson. Although she is held responsible for the crisis in both, the historical Anne Hutchinson is less central to Johnson's story than to Welde's. Identifying her only as the "grand Mistresse" of the antinomians, "who had the chiefe rule of all the roast, being very bold in her strange Revelations and misapplications" (*WWP*, 186), Johnson concurs with Welde in interpreting both the monstrous births and the violence of Hutchinson's death as the "loud speaking hand of God" against her. But although Hutchinson is clearly recognizable as the author of the troubles in New England, Johnson never names her. Claiming to know his own weakness, he is, he says, unwilling to cast aspersions on those who have returned or may yet return to the truth. Given that Hutchinson had died thoroughly unrepentant ten years earlier, this explanation scarcely accounts for Johnson's reticence, but its effect on the story is nonetheless clear. As Norman Grabo has pointed out, Hutchinson "appears not as a particular woman, but as an omnipresent spirit—the 'Erronist' . . . sometimes the lady herself, sometimes her disciples, sometimes the devil, and sometimes all together."[10] Johnson's "Erronist" is a figure sprung loose from temporal history, at once the actual Anne Hutchinson and all those instruments of Satan sent to oppose God's work in New England. On the one hand, the omnipresence of the figure in Johnson's history gives the Erronist increased force as a character. On the other hand, the generalization of the historical Hutchinson into the generic figure of the Erronist prepares the way for Hutchinson's reemergence as a fiction by stripping her story of all but its most essential elements and by explicitly associating antinomianism with dissent from the New England Way.

Not every colonial history of New England retells the story of the antinomian controversy in detail, but most make at least passing reference to it, as do a number of mid-seventeenth-century English tracts against heresy, such as Ephraim Pagitt's *Heresiography* (1647) and Thomas Edwards' *Gangraena* (1646). A few, like the Quaker John Clarke's *Ill Newes from New England* (1652) and Samuel Groome's *A Glass for the People of New England* (1676), express passing sympathy for the plight of the antinomians at the hands of the Puritans; some omit the episode altogether, their focus elsewhere.[11] Wherever the story does appear, however, it tends to rely heavily on the shared language of Welde, Winthrop, and Johnson. Puritan historians have in the past been charged with a lack of originality bordering on plagiarism,[12] but in the case of the antinomian controversy, the rhetorical unanimity of the colonial historians is clearly purposeful. By comparison to Roger Williams, Samuel Gorton, or the Quakers, Hutchinson's errors were difficult to describe. The precise difference between her position on grace and that of the orthodox, for example, seems to have eluded her lay contemporaries, if not the ministers. By their own account, later generations found the difference nearly impossible to recover. Despite Winthrop's explanations, offered in retrospect and with an eye to English opinion, the exact nature of the charges against her remained hazy to the end. When, at the close of her trial, Hutchinson demanded to know "wherefore" she was banished, the best and only answer that Winthrop would give was "The court knows wherefore and is satisfied" (*AC*, 348).

What the Court knew all too well (and what Hutchinson, to her peril, failed to appreciate) was that the force of the female heretic vastly exceeds her heresy. The crime attributed to Hutchinson at her trial is the violation of her role. She is condemned for playing the part of teacher, minister, magistrate, husband. In the later narratives, however, the accusations against her have expanded to embrace her entire nature as a woman. By naming Hutchinson Eve or Jezebel, the historians of the controversy imply an immediate relationship between her heresy and her sexual identity. She brings monsters into the world. Like Eve, she is both seduced and seductress; like Jezebel, her sexual conduct casts aside both scriptural and social law. Johnson seeks out the image of the Hydra, later adopted by Cotton Mather, to express the horror this embodiment of contradiction calls up in him. The Hydra, as an image of the fearful proliferation of error, not only is associated with unnatural fecundity—losing one head, she produces two in its place—but is as well the offspring of Echidna, like Hutchinson half woman, half serpent, and the archetypal mother of monsters. The multiplication of such images inescapably genders Hutchinson's heresy female and reinforces the idea that the essence of that heresy lies in the disjunction of visible and invisible.

The language of the first generation of chroniclers was especially useful, then, insofar as it allowed later historians to confirm the universal and the communal significance of the controversy without engaging the particulars of the theological dispute. To represent Hutchinson as an instrument of Satan and the controversy as a "war of the Lord" was to establish Hutchinson as an agent of evil and disorder and to equate opposition to the New England Way with opposition to God. Ultimately, this language released historians to speak of Hutchinson in a way that, however foreign to those who expelled her, nonetheless came to be hallowed by long repetition. In the long run the nearly complete excision of the doctrinal dispute from accounts of the controversy allowed for a wholesale reversal of its terms. As we shall see, the language of self-abnegation drops out of the record of Hutchinson's errors, and we are left instead with a picture of Hutchinson as advocate of fanatical self-trust. The tendencies of the antinomian toward quietism and perfectionism are subsumed in a new version of the antinomian as radical individualist. Hutchinson comes to be seen not as one who loses her self in Christ and thus ceases to endeavor but as one who falsely claims to be empowered by divinity to pit the demands of the self against those of the community. Whereas the language of heresy positions Hutchinson vis-à-vis the community by defining her role (however marginal) in it, her later identification with radical individualism implies the dropping away of community as a term of definition. The antinomian, that is, presses the limits of community; the individualist bursts its bounds. It required an Emerson to show that society was only one of the myriad expressions of the self. The language once associated with Hutchinson as a religious heretic attaches itself more broadly to those who elevate inner conviction to the detriment of social order.

The beginning of this process is already evident in Cotton Mather's *Magnalia Christi Americana,* written at the close of the seventeenth century. The broad differences between the *Magnalia* and other colonial histories have been much commented on. Most striking among these is the fact that the *Magnalia* is not organized chronologically but rather, in the words of one scholar, "spatially," as "a memorial temple into whose rooms the reader may enter and relive a segment of the New England past."[13] Mather fills this temple with great men whose individ-

ual biographies he regards as an adequate vehicle for his celebratory history of the New Israel. This change in structure is
echoed in the more extravagant style of the *Magnalia*. Replete
with learned allusion and filiopietistic zeal, it is regarded by
some as demonstrating in its most extreme form the tendency
toward prolixity and lack of control characteristic of Puritan
writers.[14] Nonetheless, at first glance Mather's treatment of the
antinomian controversy seems to conform to the treatment of
his predecessors. In describing Hutchinson, he employs the
conventional points of reference—Eve, Jezebel, Satan. The language of seduction that shapes Welde's preface likewise per-
vades Mather's account, and to him, as to Johnson, the Hydra is
the most fitting symbol for the proliferation of heresy. He includes in his account the obligatory report of the proceedings of
court and synod as well as a heartfelt defense of John Cotton,
and he discusses the "monstrous births" in what were by then
the established terms. Despite all this, however, Mather's version of the story signals a subtle shift in emphasis.

From the start, Mather disclaims interest in the particular
errors attributed to the Hutchinsonians. In fact, he insists that
"multitudes of persons, who took in with both parties, did never to their dying hour understand what their *difference* was."[15]
The errors are "needless now to repeat," "dead and gone . . .
and beyond hope of resurrection," and Mather refuses to "trouble the world with the debated questions, much less the de-
bates upon the questions." The fact that Mather does not abide
strictly by his word—he does describe, in brief, both the questions and the debate—is less interesting than his insistence on
their irrelevance. The effect of this is twofold. On the one hand,
it relegates the debate over covenant theology to the past: antinomianism is dead and gone. On the other, it focuses our attention as readers on the "holy temper" of the first settlers evinced
by their handling of the controversy. This emphasis, in turn,
alters the shape of the narrative. Welde spoke of the antinomians as disorderly, Johnson describes the "spirit of giddi-
nesse" that accompanied heresy, and both regarded the heretics as agents of Satan and the controversy as a trial, but Mather
first formulates the crisis as a confrontation between reason

and enthusiasm. He strips away everything but the monstrous woman and the rational power of men.

On one side, as he presents it, stands the party of peace and truth, men of "good understanding" wisely employing the "'sword of the Lord,' the sacred Scripture," to oust the "apostate serpent." Their peaceable temper is apparent in the conduct of the Cambridge Synod, where, instead of indulging in "arbitrary and hereticating *anathemas*," the ministers first "fairly recited" the errors of the sectaries and followed this with "a short reflection . . . after this manner: 'this is contrary to such and such a text of Scripture.'" The effect of this among *"reasonable men"* was to "smite the error under the fifth rib."[16] Opposing these reasonable men were the antinomians, whom Mather characterizes as arrogant enthusiasts; hypocrites and liars, they threaten to use their "virulent and malignant influence" to subvert "all the peaceable order in the colonies."[17] The story of "Hydra Decapitata," like the stories that surround it in "Ecclesiarum Praelia," is the story of the inevitable and prophetic victory of God's people over their enemies, but, as Mather tells it, this story records the victory of human (that is, male) reason and order over unreason, embodied as fecund woman. Mather's subject is not the errors of the antinomians but the triumph of sound doctrine in the hands of rational men; nonetheless, his title suggests the possibility that only a Herculean effort will secure that triumph.

This rendering of the antinomian controversy accounts for Mather's apparent lack of interest in the opinions of the heretics, but it also transforms the story of Anne Hutchinson. The difference between the *Magnalia* and *Wonder-working Providence* is not simply that Mather writes at a greater remove and can, consequently, disown the heresy but that he can dismiss antinomianism without altering his view of the antinomian. He finds Anne Hutchinson's heresy not in her ideas but in her character. Under the subtitle "Dux Femina Facta" (woman made leader), he relates the tale of the "erronious gentlewoman" from Lincolnshire who pretended to be a "Priscilla" but was "rather deserving the name of the prophetess in the church of Thyatira."[18] The allusion to the Jezebel of Revelations is conventional, as is most of the figurative language in Mather's account, but his portrait of Hutchinson differs dramatically from those that preceded it. Whereas Johnson's Hutchinson is an instrument of Satan and of interest only insofar as the devil's agency in the antinomian controversy is revealed through her, Mather's Hutchinson is more nearly a full-blown character whose role in the controversy is an extension of her personality. She is a particular kind of person—a "Virago" (in its archaic meaning, an Amazon), "cunning," proud and impudent—from a particular place, whose "canting harrangues," "vapouring talk," and "gross lying" lead to her banishment.

Mather, in other words, relocates antinomianism. Laying aside the theological errors, he offers in their place a character type. In fact, heresy and heretic are so intermixed that even when Mather lists Hutchinson's errors—her reliance on private revelation, her rejection of works, her censoriousness—we have difficulty knowing whether we are being offered theology or psychology. Edward Johnson left Hutchinson unnamed and produced an account of the Erronist in thrall to Satan. For the sake of her "worthy" descendants, Mather, too, avoids Hutchinson's name, but the effect is quite different. Johnson allegorizes Hutchinson; Mather fictionalizes her. As an allegorical figure, Hutchinson illustrates God's truth; she is a static figure, going nowhere and generating nothing. Mather, by reenlivening her, restores to her the fecundity of fiction. The power to create denied Hutchinson by Welde and Johnson is given back by Mather. Without this power the figure of Hutchinson would remain trapped in the Puritan past; with it she can move forward into the American future as the very type of dissent.

More than any other colonial historian, Mather captures all the disparate elements of the original controversy and reorders them in such a way that they take on a new usefulness. By representing antinomianism as a trait of character rather than as a particular set of religious ideas, he enlarges the figure of the antinomian to include a wide range of "opposers." These opposers are linked less by their doctrinal positions than by their insistence on inner conviction as the source of truth; the impulse which defines their heresy is individualistic, antisocial.

When Mather draws his portrait of Hutchinson, then, he sees her not as abnegating the self but as asserting it; his Hutchinson supplants external authority with fanatical self-trust. Hutchinson was, of course, regarded as haughty and arrogant from the first, and the relationship between this posture and her doctrine of passivity and self-annihilation was problematic for the first generation of settlers. But Mather exposes the paradox at the center of antinomianism more clearly than most early historians. Despite the feminized and feminizing language of dependence and incapacity employed by the heretics, he understands antinomianism to be an empowering doctrine that, by making women leaders, invariably sets the stage for social conflict. Like his predecessors, he rejects the proto-anarchist argument that society will take care of itself if only the saints attend to Christ. Instead, he sees the individual, empowered to act without reference to the community and unhindered by the demands of the errand, as endangering not just the peace of the colony but the very idea of the New Israel. Antinomianism, in other words, emerges from the *Magnalia* as a heretical form of individualism discernible in the bearing of the heretic and peculiarly typified by the Woman.

The shift away from narrow doctrinal concerns and toward the formulation of the antinomian controversy as a battle between masculine reason and female enthusiasm, combined with the emergence of an antinomian "character type,"[19] was a necessary prelude to the exploitation of the story during the Great Awakening. One scholar has proposed that the Great Awakening provided "the means for the 'New Englandization' of American thought."[20] Another has argued that the "genetics of salvation" were such that the Halfway Covenant and Stoddardeanism, those famous departures from the Puritan way, ironically enabled the Puritans to "bequeath their vision to Yankee America."[21] Included in this legacy was the story of Anne Hutchinson. And just as the myth of New England's special destiny grew to include the colonies as a whole, so Hutchinson's story accrued expanded significance. Retold by Mather as a story of reason and enthusiasm, it emerges from the Awakening as a tale of the disastrous effects brought about by those in whom "natural vanity," a "warm imagination," and a "high degree of enthusiasm" are combined. The temperate language of Thomas Hutchinson, who believed that his great-great-grandmother "considered herself divinely commissioned for some great purpose, to obtain which she [thought] . . . windings, subtelties, and insinuations lawful, which will hardly consist with the rules of morality,"[22] is not characteristic of his generation. To those unrestrained by genealogy, Hutchinson was the model of an ever-proliferating dissent.

4

A Flood of Errors

The hundred years that separate the seventeenth-century controversy and the Great Awakening of 1740–45 saw the worst fears of the Hutchinsonians fulfilled. The Halfway Covenant, Stoddardeanism, and the Saybrook Platform conspired to make public and civil all that the antinomians had argued must be private and felt. In view of this, it is perhaps not surprising that new "New Lights" emerged to challenge the new "legalists" and that these were associated with the earlier heretics. Awakening was not, of course, limited to the New World—between 1730 and 1760 England and much of Western Europe experienced similar outbreaks of religious enthusiasm—but the rhetoric of the Great Awakening insists on the special and separate importance of the colonial revival. With the long history of New World exegesis behind them, the American revival could be described by one side as "the New Jerusalem . . . begun to come down from heaven," while to the other it was a chaos peopled by "Antinomians, Familists, and Libertines."

A rash of "surprising conversions" in the Connecticut River valley in 1735 gave the first hint of what was to come, but not until five years later, when the English evangelist George Whitefield made the circuit from Georgia to Maine, did the Awakening reach its peak. In the middle colonies, with their large Scotch-Irish population, the revival was felt most keenly by Presbyterians; the south went largely untouched during the peak years but awoke shortly thereafter; the area most affected was New England. There it was not unusual for ten to twenty percent of a town to experience rebirth and join the church in the course of a year. We can get a sense of the urgency that attended Whitefield's tour from Connecticut farmer Nathan

Cole's account of his "Spiritual Travels." While working in his field, Cole tells us, word reached him that Whitefield was to preach in nearby Middletown. "I dropped my tools," he says, "and ran home to my wife, telling her to make ready quickly to go and hear Mr. Whitefield preach . . . then ran to my pasture for my horse with all my might, fearing I should be too late."[1] Cole and his wife arrived in Middletown in time, only to find a congregation of between three and four thousand of their neighbors assembled to hear the "overheated preacher." If we are to believe contemporary reports, this was an intimate gathering of its kind. In Boston, New York, and Philadelphia a year earlier, Whitefield's audiences ran to some twenty thousand. These audiences, like others of their kind both before and after the Great Awakening, were dominated by women. But, as those writing both for and against the revival acknowledged, a new population swelled the ranks of the awakened as the revival drew to itself a generation of young men displaced by the pressure of their numbers on the land.

Unable, more often than not, to accommodate his hearers in the local church, Whitefield took to the fields. There he exhorted his auditors to attend to the state of their souls and commented on the state of religion in the colonies. His observations were disturbing at best: after his visit to Boston, for example, he noted that the descendants of the original settlers had grown cold in matters of religion, that they indulged the "pride of life," and that Harvard had fallen from light into darkness. The freedom with which Whitefield criticized the "unconverted ministers" for their lack of affection, their inattention to conversion, and their emphasis on learning was imitated by his American counterparts. A flood of criticism was let loose. Attacks on unpopular ministers were venomous, generally taking the form of accusations that the minister in question, not being himself saved, was therefore incapable of facilitating the conversion of his parishioners. Congregations divided and ultimately separated on the issue of ministerial adequacy. In Whitefield's wake, itinerancy and lay exhortation became commonplace, with wayfaring ministers and exhorters—many of them young and some of them black—demanding the use of the local pulpits and, when this was refused, agitating against the settled ministers. Meetings proliferated—many of the awakened attended three or more a week—and "bodily manifestations" of the spirit—fainting spells, frenzies, visions—were admitted by some as evidence of grace. The lines of battle formed, with Old Light antirevivalists standing accused of Arminianism and prorevival New Lights charged variously with enthusiasm, Familism, and antinomianism.

Initially, the majority of the ministers, like the majority of their parishioners, rejoiced in the Awakening. After what they had regarded as a period of religious decline, the sudden and overwhelming interest of the people in spiritual matters came as a welcome sign. But as disorder increased, the opposition camp swelled and the authenticity of the revival was questioned. Measures were taken to limit its effects. Connecticut passed laws forbidding local ministers to open their pulpits to their itinerant colleagues at risk of losing "the benefit of any law of this colony made for support and encouragement of the gospel ministry"—that is, at risk of losing their salary. Clerical councils met and publicly denounced "the errors in doctrine and the disorders in practice that have of late obtained in various parts of the land."[2] Popular support of the revival was such that none of these measures was especially successful. Even the most famous legal case—that launched against James Davenport for achieving such heights of enthusiasm that he called upon his fellows to burn their finery and their books in the streets of New London—ended anticlimactically with Davenport's transportation home to Long Island to recover from what everyone finally agreed was a temporary lunacy.

In its dimensions and its class composition, though obviously not in its politics, the Great Awakening was a revolution tantamount to the one Christopher Hill describes as potential in the rise of antinomianism a hundred years earlier in England. Popular support for the revival threatened to transform the social order. And the Word as it was preached in the fields and pulpits of New England was, in the view of the Old Lights, a new word—one that opposers like Charles Chauncy would castigate as so "loose" and "indefinite" as to allow the people to attach to it whatever meaning they pleased. What was at issue was the authority of both word and speaker, and the two were closely linked. The qualities of language that so dismayed Chauncy were the very ones that made revivalists like Whitefield and, later, Jonathan Edwards so powerful. A consideration of the power of that language returns us to the question of class, this time by way of gender. As we will see, the "feminine" language of religious affection and the more tenuous relation between sign and meaning demanded by a theology of invisible grace brought the disempowered into the revivalists' camp. And this, in turn, set the stage for a collision between a hereditary elite and those newly empowered by Christ himself.

It was as part of the larger effort at containment that the Reverend Charles Chauncy of Boston's First Church published *Seasonable Thoughts on the State of Religion in New England* in 1743. Written in response to Jonathan Edwards's defense of the Awakening entitled *Some Thoughts on the Recent Revival of Religion in New England* and read primarily by the liberal elite of the colonies,[3] *Seasonable Thoughts* is a compendium of letters and eyewitness accounts describing the worst excesses of the times.[4] These accumulated horror stories are useful for what they tell us about the offenses of the reborn, but the essential strategy of the book is revealed in a thirty-page preface, devoted entirely to an account of the antinomian controversy. In Chauncy's view a recounting of the cautionary tale of Anne Hutchinson was "very needful for these days, the like spirit and errors . . . prevailing *now* as they did *then*." In fact, so close a likeness did he see between the two times that he tells his reader, "If I had not spoken in language, part of which was in print fifty, and part eighty years ago, some, I doubt not, would have imagined I had purposely gone into the use of certain words and phrases to make former times look like the present."[5] The particular language to which Chauncy turned in trying to locate the errors of the present times was that of Welde, Winthrop, and Johnson. Quoting at length from these sources, Chauncy attempts to establish the Awakening as an antinomian outbreak like unto the first.

The theological issues that separated Chauncy and Edwards lent themselves to this strategy. In the wake of Whitefield's tour, the question that absorbed both ministers and people was "What shall I do to be saved?" To this Chauncy and Edwards offered radically different answers. A liberal in matters of religion, Chauncy firmly believed that the proper response was to direct men to use their reason. Why else, after all, would God have given men reason if not to help them "know the *Meaning* of a Revelation from God"?[6] If he did not intend men to be within reach of argument, susceptible to a "calm and sober address to their understandings,"[7] why give them the capacity for rational discourse? In the question of conversion, Chauncy, like any good Protestant, admitted that the Spirit works invisibly at first, preparing men "for *faith* and *Repentence*, by humbling them for Sin, and shewing them the *Necessity* of a Saviour; then by effecting *such a change* in them, as shall *turn them from the Power of Sin and Satan,* and make them *new Creatures*" (*STS*, 26). But, "agreeable to our *Make* as *reasonable* Creatures," God enables men to choose to be good and makes that choice one more evidence of grace. Invisible influence issues in "Patterns of good *Works; Examples* to all . . . *in Word, in Conversation, in Faith, in Purity, in Charity*" (*STS*, 11). If the unfailing outcome of grace is good works, then to encourage men to manifest these signs is not in vain. Their capacity for civility makes good their faith. Chauncy, like his Puritan forebears, saw the problem of hypocrisy inherent in this position, but, unlike them, he asserted that although "they may not be the Men inwardly, they appear to be outwardly . . . this is none of our Business."[8]

The fact was, as Chauncy saw it, that "the surest and most substantial Proof" of grace "is *obedience to the Commandments of God*" (*STS*, 26). Like his fellow antirevivalists, Chauncy believed that "we have no way of judging but by what is outward and visible: Nor are we capable of judging any other way."[9] To trust to men's inner knowledge, to give credence to testimonies of grace to the exclusion of good works, was the ultimate in rashness. Asked what men must do to be saved, Chauncy offered an index of behavior against which men could measure themselves and others. What men must do to be saved was to make themselves "patterns." For the revivalists "to leave this way, and go into that of judging from men's hearts," he insisted, "tends to nothing, in the nature of things, but to destroy the peace of the churches, and fill the world with contention and confusion."[10]

There can be no doubt that Edwards abandoned this "way." His way placed greater faith in self-knowledge than in acts, laid a greater stress on God's mystery than on his reasonableness. Edwards's conviction that "all . . . must examine and try themselves, whether they be saints or not,"[11] combined with his willingness to accept the verdict men returned on themselves, put justification squarely in the realm of the invisible. And it laid directly in Edwards's path the tempting arrogance of the antinomian with his claim to knowledge of other men's hearts. Edwards knew that "men are apt to act very treacherously and perversly in the matter of self-examination"; he saw that men "are exceedingly partial to themselves," that they "spare themselves . . . do not search, and look, and pass a judgement according to truth" (*WE*, 4:536). But he firmly believed that the alternative to reliance on self-examination was a dead, legal religion, a religion Christ would not own. Self-examination as a route to conversion was fraught with danger for both the Christian and his church, but it was nonetheless the only route.

The year before Northampton's first revival under its newly appointed minister, Edwards preached his answer to the question of the day: What must I do to be saved? The sermon's title, "Justification by Faith Alone," gives more than a hint of its content. It was, above all else, a vehement and unequivocal reassertion of man's utter dependence on Christ for justification. Man's virtue, his "moral excellency," was for naught in the scheme of salvation. In a perfectly orthodox exposition of his subject, Edwards opened the very doctrine that had plagued his predecessors: "It is none of our own excellency, virtue or righteousness, that is the ground of our being received from a state of condemnation into a state of acceptance in God's sight, but only Jesus Christ, and his righteousness, and worthiness, received by faith" (*WE*, 4:128). Having made clear man's utter dependence, Edwards goes on to contend that God nonetheless sees men as "reasonable creatures, capable of act and choice," and, consequently, requires of them active cooperation in their own redemption—that is, faith. While he does not pretend to describe its mechanics, Edwards knows the function of justifying faith: "[It] is that by which those that were separated, and at a distance from Christ . . . do cease to be any longer at such a distance, and do come into . . . relation and nearness" (*WE*, 4:70–1). This faith, the "foundation of what is legal," is the prelude to justification: "A person is said to be justified, when he is approved of God as free from the guilt of sin and its deserved punishment; and as having that righteousness belonging to him that entitles to the reward of life" (*WE*, 4:66). On faith depends God's willingness to accept men's works.

Edwards's doctrine alone suggests the grounds for Chauncy's identification of him with Anne Hutchinson, but, as if this were not enough, "Justification by Faith Alone" goes on to draw the lines of battle between those who, like Edwards himself, follow a strict Calvinist line on justification and those who oppose this doctrine, between the advocates of an evangelical and those of a legal scheme. Edwards's disdain for "their" scheme, in which "a regard to man's own excellency or virtue is supposed to be first," is undisguised. He sees through the deception of their words: "I am sensible that the divines of that side entirely disclaim the Popish doctrine of merit; and are free to speak of our utter unworthiness . . . but, after all it is our virtue, imperfect as it is . . . by which good men come to have a saving interest in Christ. . . . So that whether they will allow the term *merit* or no, yet they hold that we are accepted by our own merit, in the same sense though not in the same degree as under the first covenant" (*WE*, 4:130). One may suspect that it was small comfort to the "divines of that side" to be thus exonerated of popish tendencies.

"Justification by Faith Alone" was one of a set of five sermons preached with the intention of countering the Arminian tendencies that were beginning to make themselves felt in Northampton. Edwards took sides from the very start. No matter how heretical the revival would become, no matter how thoroughly he would disapprove of its excesses, Edwards's stand on questions of fundamental doctrine would remain unchanged. Grace, he insisted, was freely offered by God to men of faith not in reward for any merit but only by virtue of Christ's intervention on man's behalf. The clash between Edwards and Chauncy has been variously interpreted. Some have seen reflected in their differences the collision between enlightenment and piety, between reason and faith: Edwards is taken to represent the mysterious, emotional, conservative, pietistic strain in American religion, while Chauncy stands for the future, for reason, clarity, humanism, liberalism. Others argue for Edwards's modernity.[12] But neither of these positions addresses the question of what Chauncy and Edwards thought they were fighting about.

The Great Awakening set in conflict two fundamentally different religious attitudes, one tending toward Arminianism, the other toward antinomianism. The first, asserting the efficacy of good works, the ascendancy of reason, the freedom of the will, and, at its furthest extreme, the absurdity of predestination and original sin, seemed to release the Christian from the oppression of a whimsical God and to grant importance to human activity. In fact, the coincidence of Arminian doctrine with the Old Lights' belief in the need for increased clerical authority and relaxed admission argued for domination by the ministers; the opening of the congregation made legitimate the wresting of power from its hands. But the logic of combining increased clerical control with greater individual access to the church did not depend solely on the change in membership requirements. Morality, unlike grace, could be legislated, and the liberal minister took upon himself the task of helping men to find and follow the Law. On the surface, liberal religion freed men to strive, to use their reason, to regard the deity as rational and benevolent, but what looked like freedom manifested itself as restraint. Although he did not fully acquiesce to these principles until well after the Great Awakening, it was on this side that Chauncy stood.

On the other side stood Edwards, as apologist if not advocate. To those who scorned the revival, it seemed not merely an outpouring of ill-regulated religious emotion but a movement dangerously antisocial in character. Enthusiasm, the belief that one is in divine favor or communication, and antinomianism, with its emphasis on immediate witness, pointed toward an end to all authority. Edwards espoused neither of these heresies—in fact, he argued with some energy against them—but his typically New Light insistence on man's dependence on Christ, on the invisibility of grace, and on affectionate religion, combined with the fanaticism these doctrines provoked in the radical wing of the revival, appeared to the antirevivalists to open the way to antinomianism and worse.

When Edwards defended the revival, he spoke out of his conviction that the Awakening was a genuine prelude to the millennium. His reading of the history of New England bolstered his faith:

> If we may suppose that this glorious work of God shall begin in any part of America, I think, if we consider the circumstances of the settlement of New England, it must needs appear the most likely of all the American colonies, to be the place whence this work shall principally take its rise.
>
> And if these things are so, it gives us more abundant reasons to hope that what is now seen in America, and especially New England, may prove the dawn of that glorious day. . . . If these things are so, it greatly manifests how much it behooves us to encourage and promote this work, and how dangerous it will be to forbear to do so.[13]

Certainly Edwards did not forbear to do so. The vehemence of his prorevivalism is bound to his understanding of New England's prophetic history and his association of revival with the latter days. In his view the colonists were faced with a choice. They must either "actively fall in" with God's design for America as conveyed through biblical revelation or be damned as opposers.

But the choice is not really a choice as Edwards presents it. To oppose God's work, as he repeatedly warns, is to commit the "unpardonable sin" of blasphemy against the Holy Spirit. It is to reject the saving knowledge of Christ himself. Thus Edwards emphasizes the danger of defiance. Preaching on "The Nature and End of Excommunication," he recalls the concept of imputed guilt. Religion in all its aspects—God, Christ, gospel, church, and ordinances—is "defiled by the toleration of wicked men in the church." "That the other members themselves may not be defiled," he insisted, "it is necessary that they bear a testimony against sin, by censuring it. . . . If they neglect to so do, they contract guilt by the very neglect" (*WE*, 4:646). If such is the "contagion" of overlooking ordinary wickedness in the church, how much more contaminating to tolerate those among the laity, and sometimes the clergy, who would deny the work of "the author of regeneration." As Edwards saw it, New Light doctrine, with its emphasis on unmerited salvation, self-scrutiny, the rejection of works, the "infusion" of grace at conversion, and the witness of the Spirit, signaled a return to the pure religion of the first churches in the interest of the coming utopia. As stewards of the harvest, it was incumbent upon the ministers to distinguish between true and false awakening, but this could be done only if the nature of saving grace were clearly understood.

Looking at Edwards's writing about and during the Great Awakening, we can see how Chauncy's argument in *Seasonable Thoughts* evolved. To his opponents Edwards's first and germinal mistake was his unbending belief in justification by faith alone, his insistence that no matter how "strict, conscientious, and laborious . . . [men] may be in religion," if they are not savingly converted, they are enemies to Christ. "Not only works of the ceremonial law are excluded in this business of justification," Edwards told his followers, "but works of morality and godliness" (*WE*, 4:64). Edwards spoke from Romans: "To him that worketh not, but believeth on him that justifieth the ungodly, his faith is counted for righteousness" (4:5). But Chauncy replied with Matthew: "Ye shall know them by their fruits" (7:16).

Along with Edwards's position on justification went, in Chauncy's view, the vilifying of good works. Actually, when Edwards describes the effects of revival in Northampton in *A Faithful Narrative of the Surprising Work of God in Northampton* and in *Some Thoughts,* he makes much of the moral reformation that coincided with awakening: the end of vanity and looseness among the young people, the rehabilitation of "one of the greatest company-keepers in the whole town," the decrease in

drunkenness among the Indians. These improvements, however, while good for the town, were of no importance unless
they were accompanied by a change of heart, an inward reformation. In the final analysis sin was no obstacle to salvation,
and, this being so, virtue was of only passing interest. In an
echo of Anne Hutchinson, Edwards assured his flock that they
"need not be . . . more fearful of coming [to Christ] because of
[their] sins, let them be ever so black" (*WE*, 4:426). On Judgement Day good works "will . . . be brought forth as evidences
of . . . sincerity, and of . . . interest in the righteousness of
Christ," but "evil works . . . will not be brought forth against
them on that day; for the guilt of them will not lie upon them,
they being clothed with the righteousness of Jesus Christ" (*WE*,
4:213).

These assertions were not intended to sanction sinfulness,
but it is nevertheless understandable that they caused alarm. If
"the Spirit giveth such full and clear Evidence of my good Estate, that I have no need to be tried by the Fruits of *Sanctification*," then, Chauncy insisted, it might as well be said that "the
darker my *Sanctification* is, the brighter is my *Justification*" (*STS*,
286–87). If all is Christ, as Edwards certainly suggested it was,
then justification cannot be demonstrated and man is reduced
to utter passivity. Furthermore, if works are no evidence, then
assurance must be found within. As Chauncy sarcastically
points out, "the Grace of GOD is so free," in the view of the
revivalists, "that it is enough for us to sit and admire it." And,
he goes on, "some have, upon this principle, arrived to that
Height of Blasphemy as to affirm, that we can never so much
glorify free Grace, as when we make Work for it by stout sinning" (*STS*, 277).

Such a view of sin undercut a carefully devised system of
restraint. If evil works are to be discounted on the day of reck-
oning, if good works are incidental to grace, if the inward
motion of the heart is the only true evidence of election, then
Chauncy saw the way open for men to assume that "there was
no Difference between *moral Good* and *Evil* . . . that *Virtue* was
of no Account in the eye of Heaven, and that the distinction
between *that* and *Vice*, was not worthy to be regarded in Men's

conduct of themselves" (STS, 282). Edwards's retort, although it answers the charge of perfectionism levelled against him, did little to appease the liberals. God offers eternal life only in exchange for perfect obedience to the Law. Were he to accept man's imperfect obedience as sufficient, he would deprive the Law of all meaning. Only through Christ, "accepted to a reward for his obedience, [not] as a private person, but as our Head," can we be redeemed. We "are accepted to a reward in his acceptance" (WE, 4:95). Thus, works, men's feeble attempts at obedience, while they may be a side benefit of conversion and much to be encouraged, signify nothing.

For Chauncy this logic meant a loosening of the restraint that accompanies a sense of sin. Anticipating a later understanding of the problem of antinomianism, he asked whether "instead of being under Restraint from Sin [men] would not be very much at liberty to follow their own Inclinations, and to live and act just as they were moved by carnal Nature" (STS, 282). In Chauncy's vision of things there could be no worse basis for individual action. Given man's nature, without the prod of merit and the restraint of sin, striving would come to an end. And the "quenching of all endeavor" would give rise to a damning spiritual pride: "Who more vain and proud than many of the converts of the present Day? Who more puffed up with a fond conceit of their own Attainments? . . . Why so ready to think themselves fit to be *Teachers*, and to thrust themselves into the Places and Offices of others? . . . How else should that be so often the language of their Practice, if not of their Lips, *Stand off, I am holier than thou?*" (STS, 132–33). Behind all the ills of the Great Awakening, in Chauncy's estimation, stood lack of endeavor. Achieved without visible labor, new birth made men proud of their spiritual achievements, and pride led them to make extravagant claims to revelation of a kind that he was sure had ended with the apostolic age. In their pride the awakened attacked those of the standing clergy who did not share their experience, condemned their learning, and, in some cases, withdrew from their congregations. Lay exhortation, itinerancy, separatism, censoriousness were the natural offspring of a theology that ignored visible signs.

The accusations of the revivalists against the "unconverted ministry" and their insistence on a ministry of "new creatures" would scarcely have convinced Chauncy otherwise. In keeping with his views on conversion, Chauncy insisted that visible holiness was the most that could be expected of a minister, anything more superseding the laws of Christ. The radical revivalists—with Edwards leading the way, though arriving at a different conclusion—insisted on the felt experience of grace and the extemporaneous preaching of a Whitefield. To the most extreme of the New Lights, new birth, not Harvard or Yale, created ministers. At this even Edwards demurred. "If once it should become a custom," he said, ". . . to admit persons to the work of the ministry that have had no education for it, because of their remarkable experiences, how many lay persons would soon appear as candidates for . . . the ministry? . . . And how shall we know where to stop?" (*ST*, 456). Not only would competition for the privilege of preaching become grounds for "uneasiness and strife," but a lay ministry would increase the danger that people would be led into "impulses, vain imaginations, superstition, indiscreet zeal and such like extremes" (*ST*, 457). But this did not mean that "legal" preaching should be tolerated simply because it came from the ordained. A "dead" clergy was no improvement over an enthusiastic laity.

Chauncy suspected George Whitefield of imagining himself "under the immediate, extraordinary Guidance of the Holy Ghost" and saw an anti-intellectualism in Edwards's elevation of spiritual light over human learning that would provoke more of the same. In general, however, Edwards associated the fullness of knowledge through divine light with the millennium. Unlike the traditional Calvinist, Edwards believed that the millennium would precede the Second Coming. This postmillennialism implied the continuity of human and divine history. The premillennialist bides his time, awaiting the miraculous return of his savior, which will mark the beginning of a new historical epoch. Edwards's postmillennialism enlists mankind in the effort of bringing the millennium into being. The flurry of conversions in the 1740s suggested to him that the Awakening was a forerunner of that time when "the visible and invisible church [would be] brought together in the glorious prospect of a downfall . . . of Catholic Rome, the conversion of the Jews, and the enlightenment of the heathen."[14] Learning and wickedness go hand in hand, but eventually, when "God has sufficiently shown men the insufficiency of human wisdom and learning for the purposes of religion, and . . . the appointed time comes for that glorious outpouring of the Spirit of God, when he will himself by his own *immediate influence* enlighten men's minds . . . [then] may we hope that God will make use of the great increase of learning as a handmaiden to religion."[15] In the meantime the millennium would be ushered in by "the preaching of the spiritual, mysterious doctrines of Christ crucified, which to the learned men of the world are foolishness" (*WE*, 4:32). Edwards admitted the possibility of immediate witness in the latter days, he saw the Awakening as presaging the "new world," and these views made him vulnerable to attack. He thought it better to concede the remarkable than commit the unpardonable sin. Edwards walked a cautious line between rejecting all claims to inspiration and lending the weight of his authority to the shenanigans of the Davenports.

The fact that Edwards relegated knowledge by immediate influence to the future did not secure him from attack. By drawing a distinction between the converted and the unconverted clergy, Edwards and his fellow revivalists brought the professional status of the ministry into question just as Chauncy was sure they would. Membership in that special professional class of persons called ministers, the New Lights contended, does not ensure saving knowledge of Christ. Whereas for some, like Edwards, education seemed nonetheless necessary for ministers, many others proclaimed an end to the closed, largely hereditary ministry. If conversion was the test of pulpit worthiness, then not just more people but very different people would invade its sacred precinct. No longer would it be the bastion of a well-educated elite.

It was less a particular body of clerics that the revival attacked than the very basis on which men were deemed ministers. Edwards was one of the first to break through the united front of the clergy and publicly declare that the title might not ensure the reality. Presumably, he did not intend to bring the ministry under the critical gaze of the laity, to wreak schism and separatism, but inadvertently he lent himself to the cause. His support of itinerancy—in violation of the traditional principle of a "settled" clergy—only accentuated the problem. After education, it was a flock that made a shepherd, and just as "experience" called education into question, so itinerancy challenged the stability of the pastoral appointment. Between the two the credibility of the antirevivalist ministers, who tended to be in league with the colonial authorities, was sharply diminished.

But if the end to striving endangered right religion, it also threatened social order. Edwards's attitude toward the duties of the elect looked very much like a challenge to standing authority. He spoke for democracy of a sort in religious affairs. He not only viewed the Bible as "written for the use of all" (*WE*, 4:9) but insisted, further, that the pew take responsibility for "the things of Divinity." The doctrines of Christianity, he told his followers, "concern every one." "The common people cannot say, Let us leave these matters to ministers and divines," he went on, "for they are of infinite importance to every man . . . as it is of infinite importance to common people, as well as to ministers, to know what kind of being God is" (*WE*, 4:8). So important were matters of religion, in fact, that none were to be put off from their Christian duty by ridicule or fear, no matter what their station in life. This did not mean that the elect should so step out of their places as to adopt the boldness of a minister, but neither were the frowns of authority to be taken as conviction of error: authorities, too, could be wrong.

The *"Fruit of the Spirit,"* Chauncy insisted, was a *"peacable Temper and Conduct,"* but the revivalists were "Disturbers of Society . . . Instruments to sow the seeds of Discord and Confusion" (*STS*, 29). How could the conversion that led them to this be legitimate? Order, after all, was the foundation of both church and state, and evidence of piety was to be found in the shoring up of this foundation. "Can there Be Order," Chauncy asked, "where men transgress the Limits of their Station, and intermeddle in the Business of others? So far from it, that the only effectual Method, under GOD, for the Redress of *general Evils*, is, for *every one* to be faithful, in doing what is *proper* for him in his *own Place* (*STS*, 366). Like the orthodox of a hundred years before, Chauncy linked a hierarchical social order to right religion and saw reliance on invisible witness as so far democratizing congregationalism as to bring the downfall of all authority.

But these social expedients did not daunt Edwards. He called for an absolute commitment to the things of religion. In the latter days, there could be no neutrals: a man was either for Baal or for the Lord. Moreover, he could prove which side he was on by accepting as his "high calling" the quest for salvation. To live to God, as Edwards explained, "is the business and, if I may so speak, the *trade* of a Christian, his main work, and indeed . . . his only work. No business should be done by a Christian but as it is some way or other a part of this" (*WE*, 4:10). That the world was "only a thing by the by" Edwards had no doubt, but business was, after all, necessary to men's lives on earth and should, therefore, be shaped by Christian affection. With Winthrop, Edwards claimed charity as the basis for Christian community, and, like his forebear, he linked economic reform with the work of the spirit. One aspect of self-examination was the search for a proper relation to God. The other, equally religious in character, required the saint to scrutinize his day-to-day dealings with other men. The minister could not judge for his people, but he could raise questions for their consideration: "Do you not live in a careless, sinful neglect of paying your debts? . . . Are you not wont to oppress your neighbor? When you see another in necessity, do you not thence take advantage to screw upon him? . . . Will you not deceive in buying and selling . . . when you see that falsehood will be an advantage to you in your bargain?" (*WE*, 4:518). If charity governed, such things would not be, and Edwards had faith that rebirth would bring into being a world in which Christian charity would reign in "temporals" as in "spirituals." And that world would, of course, be America.

Chauncy was skeptical. Anxiety about the future, combined

with the demand that men commit themselves wholly to the quest for salvation, led, in his opinion, to an unwarranted neglect of earthly business.

> Hasn't it been common, among those who have been wrought upon, in these Times, to devote themselves . . . to the Business of attending *Lectures* and Meetings, either to *speak* or *hear,* as though therein lay the Sum of Religion? And hasn't this been done by great Numbers of Persons, to the neglect of their *Callings,* and the real *Damage* of their *Families*? . . . What has been their care about those Laws of GOD, which regard their Conduct, in the *several Relations* and *Capacities of Life*? Have they been, in any Proportion, zealous to be better *Husbands* and *Wives,* better *Masters* and *Servants*?
>
> (*STS,* 304–5)

The fulfillment of social roles was, in Chauncy's "legal" scheme, requisite to the Christian life, and men were accountable to their families, their ministers, their dependents, and their masters for any failure. Neglect of one's calling, like stepping out of one's place, was poor evidence of regeneration. "We were made for business," Chauncy contended, and business was to be conducted in conformity to the "great law of Industry."[16]

Whereas the ministers of the seventeenth century recalled Hutchinson to her role as woman, demanding that she foreswear the activities of preacher, ruler, and husband, Chauncy recalls an unruly populace to its place. The difference and the similarities are equally important. In both cases the issue centers on the failure of those inspired by the Spirit to fulfill their social obligations, but the seventeenth-century version of the problem lacks the class overtones evident in Chauncy's account. As he sees it, those on whose labor the social order depends are being distracted from their labor. By neglecting their callings, they, like Hutchinson, violate their roles, which are, as Chauncy presents it, utterly dependent on their industriousness because generated out of it. To attend meetings when one should be working is once again to put the spirit ahead of the law, but this time the law is explicitly an economic one. Chauncy recognizes economic and social functions as mutually dependent, and, speaking to a class whose steward he takes himself to be but of which he is clearly not himself a member, he elaborates their "place": their industriousness, in itself and as it defines their various roles, is to provide the foundation for the hierarchical social order that denies them power. Sanctified by obedience to the Law, men will stay in the places allotted them; liberated by the immediate witness of the spirit, they will run amuck.[17]

In a post-Awakening sermon entitled "The Idle-Poor secluded from the Bread of Charity by the Christian Law," Chauncy sketches a community in which public and private good coincide not as expressions of grace but as guarantors of prosperity: "For industrious Labour is the Way for *Individuals*, as well as *communities*, to thrive and flourish."[18] But the law of industry that governs such a community—that, in fact, guarantees its prosperity—is an unforgiving one. Chauncy invokes Paul: "If any will not work, neither shall he eat" (2 Thessalonians 3:10). The hand of Christian charity is closed tight to those who do not labor—that is, if they are poor. The rich, Chauncy carefully explains, are exempt from the "Designs of the Apostle", who speaks "not of those who are able, without Labour, to maintain themselves, but of poor People, who, if they won't work, must have their Expectations of Relief from the Charities of others."[19] The class implications are obvious: those who must work to eat *must* work or the order of things will be overturned. The charitable have license to discriminate between those deserving of relief and those not. Since "if a man's circumstances are low, he can rise and prosper in no other Way, but that of Industry,"[20] it is a service to the needy as well as to the community for charity to be given circumspectly. Moreover, since God himself enjoins men from indulging idleness, the ends of religion as well as society are served.[21]

Chauncy thought that all the talk of free grace and the inefficacy of works would encourage men to step out of their places and regarded the theological complement to this as antinomianism. While he did not directly accuse Edwards of the heresy, he apparently believed it implicit in the populist tendencies of New Light theology. Only in *The Late Religious Commotions in New England*, a work of dubious authorship written in answer to Edwards's *Distinguishing Marks*, is Edwards himself charged with Anne Hutchinson's crime. Even if, as seems probable, Chauncy himself did not write either *Religious Commotions* or *The Wonderful Narrative: or, A Faithful Account of the French Prophets*,[22] by his own account most of the works of the opposers crossed his desk to be edited, revised, approved, or published.[23] That he felt no call to delete such accusations is telling. Careful to avoid direct slur, he still felt the insidiousness of Edwards's position. "Mr. Edwards' book . . . upon the *good work* is at last come forth," he wrote to his brother Nathaniel, "and I believe will do much hurt; and I am the rather inclined to think so, because there are some good things in it. Error is much more likely to be propagated, when it is mixed with truth. This hides its deformity and makes it go down the more easily."[24] Like the Erronists of the earlier histories, Edwards's outward holiness, his apparent orthodoxy, allows him to insinuate his errors into the heart of true religion.

But if Edwards was spared the charge of antinomianism, his call for charity was nonetheless regarded by some of the Old Lights as incipient Familism—a horror no less immediate to the liberal clergy of the eighteenth century than it had been to Winthrop and the ministers.[25] But just as the apostle's Law of Industry was not to be taken to apply to the wealthy, so Paul's "All things are yours" called for careful explication. The danger of scriptural literalism, in this case, was both social and economic:

> The *Apostle* . . . says, "ALL THINGS *are yours*." But does this destroy private Property, and make all Things common? . . . 'Tis a Truth as to *particular* Christians, or Churches, in no Sense but what will consist with *every Right* which GOD has given to one Man, in Distinction from another. . . . Notwithstanding these Words of the *Apostle, all* THINGS *are yours; particular* Men have their *own* Wives, and *particular* Women their *own* Husbands; this man has his *own* House or Field, and so has *that:* Nor can they invade one another's Property without sinning against GOD. Christians can be said to have a *Right* in *all* THINGS, only so far, and under such Restrictions, as God has been pleased to give them a Title to them.
>
> (*STS*, 63–64)

Familism, with its double threat of communism and promiscuity, would accompany antinomianism—and who knew to what lengths the revivalists might go to hasten the establishment of the Family of Love?

Arrogance about the meaning of individual and communal regeneration typifies the revivalists, Edwards not excepted. With supreme confidence he claimed that God was calling the awakened congregations though the voice they heard was their minister's: "God is now calling you in an extraordinary manner: and it is agreeable to the will and word of Christ, that I should now, in his name, call you, as one set over you, and sent to you to that end; so it is his will that you should hearken to what I say, *as his voice.* I therefore beseech you in Christ's stead now to press into the kingdom of God." (*WE*, 4:393–94). In yet another echo of the earlier conflict, Chauncy saw that pressing into the kingdom could involve destroying the state. In their audacity the reborn might resort to open rebellion in their effort to hurry the New Jerusalem. The Münster Rebellion of the 1530s had, in the Puritan version of it, been born in just such millennial expectations; who could tell but that the same might ensue from the Great Awakening?

> So it was in GERMANY, in the Beginning of the Reformation. The *extraordinary* and *wonderful* Things in that Day, were look'd upon by the Men then thought to be most under the SPIRIT'S *immediate* Direction, as 'the Dawning of that glorious Work of GOD, which should renew the whole World'; and the Imagination of the Multitude being fired with this Notion, they were soon perswaded, that the Saints were now to reign on Earth, and the Dominion to be given into their Hands: And it was under the Influence of this vain Conceit . . . that they took up *Arms* against the lawful *Authority,* and were destroy'd, at one Time and another, to the Number of an HUNDRED THOUSAND.
>
> (*STS*, 373)

Once again men were claiming that their age was extraordinary, and again the multitudes were following; a new John of Leyden might, it seemed, emerge from the ranks of the revivalists. If so, Chauncy wanted to make sure that the danger of their course was clear.

In fact, what Edwards and others of the New Lights proposed was a society based on invisible grace and legitimized by a strict reading of Calvin. They envisioned a community of saints bound together by love, more concerned about union with Christ than obedience to the Law, and engaged in "pressing into the kingdom of God." This concept of community linked human effort to dependence on Christ and directed it toward fulfilling the promise of New England's history. But, of course, to the degree that it invoked inner light as the route to knowledge, it removed men from ordinary social restraint. In such a community the individual would be rewarded for fulfilling his assigned part in a heavenly rather than an earthly design. No separate interest would detach him from his fellows; interdependence would arise from the coincident private desires of the saints to cooperate in the redemption of the world rather than as a function of economic specialization. Perfect individualism would lend coherence to the community. Each saint would be so "swallowed up" in Christ that when, in solitude, he explored his own heart, he would find his perfect identification with the elect. Thus, what looked like self-assertion would turn out to be self-abnegation, a transformation of the individual self into the Christic nonself. The Edwardsean revivalists thought they had averted any danger of enthusiastic arrogance. They were not antinomians, they insisted, because they did not deny the Law, did not believe themselves incapable of sin. Rather, they claimed that the Law gains significance only in conjunction with the experience of rebirth. Given these terms, the individual quest for grace would issue in perfect social harmony.

But Chauncy saw in the revivalists a combination of arrogance and passivity peculiar to the antinomian. Once justified, the graceful are beyond the Law, but justification cannot be achieved by human endeavor. The effect of the combination was, in his opinion, disastrous; spiritual arrogance would give rise to a denial of all outward authority, a reliance on the inner motion of the heart; utter dependence would make outward reformation—and, by extension, all human effort—futile and unnecessary. In 1740 as in 1636, conflict over the origins of authority summoned up the charge of antinomianism, a charge of neglect of the Law from which would come the end of traditional social relations. And once again the charge would be leveled at those who took Puritan doctrine at its word—those who spoke for self-examination at the risk of error, religious affection at the risk of enthusiasm, dependence on Christ at the risk of antinomianism, and cooperation in the millennium at the risk of disrupting day-to-day society.

Edwards's effort to revivify what he regarded as orthodox religion occurred in response to seeing the churches reduced to agents of morality. The institutional question raised by the Great Awakening was whether the churches would minister to the need of individual Christians for salvation or to the need of the community for a sanctioning body. To the literal Calvinist these functions are mutually exclusive. Edwards's attempt to return to the theology of the past was doomed from the start, but its failure was ensured by the fact that his version of traditional orthodoxy resembled more closely Anne Hutchinson's than her judges'.

"The *old* ANTINOMIANS," Chauncy explains in *Seasonable Thoughts*, "began . . . with much the same Language about the *Law* and *good Works*, that is now in Use: And . . . gradually . . . arriv'd at those Heights of Extravagance, for which they have justly been stigmatised." "Is there no Danger," he asked, "lest this should be the Case, with many, in these Days?" (*STS*, 278). The question is rhetorical. To Chauncy the power of that language was clear, and the danger it posed more apparent with every new manifestation of revival. But as his own careful manipulation of language and his attention to the language of the revivalists suggest, the rhetorical division between New and Old Light was every bit as important as the differences in their doctrine and their deportment. Just as conduct is, for Chauncy, a mirror of grace, so language is an outward show, and the errors of the revivalists were recapitulated in their rhetoric. Mimicking both the name and the five-part structure of *Some Thoughts,* Chauncy, as we have seen, undertook to refute Edwards's argument point by point. But right from the start, Chauncy's book diverges from the pattern established by *Some Thoughts.* While Edwards opens his book with a brief apology for his presumptuousness in attempting such a work and a short exposition on freedom of expression, *Seasonable Thoughts* begins rather ponderously with a thirty-page account of the "ANTINOMIANS, FAMILISTS and LIBERTINES, who infected these churches, above an hundred years ago." This reminder of the events of the 1630s would, Chauncy believed, "prepare" his readers for his treatise on the evils of the present revival and would, moreover, "powerfully tend to undeceive" those beguiled by error.

Aligning himself with Hutchinson's opponents, Chauncy glosses over the dramatic changes in both doctrine and church polity that had occurred in the hundred years since the antinomian controversy and asserts his own orthodoxy. Of course, Edwards, too, by raising the banner of the New Jerusalem, hoped to establish himself as the heir apparent. It has been pointed out that Edwards, in his *Treatise Concerning Religious Affections,* quotes Thomas Shepard more often than any other writer (*AC,* 20). But while Edwards resorts to "right religion" and to the prophetic history of New England for his claims, Chauncy turns to the "methods," both social and ecclesiastical, of the first generation. He finds in the accounts of Anne Hutchinson not only the type of the revivalists but the measures to be taken against them and a mirror of his own fervent need to save the New World from the agents of Satan.

Chauncy's avowed purpose in writing the preface and the effect of the preface on our reading of *Seasonable Thoughts* are, however, two different things. While the story of Anne Hutchinson is meant to caution us against antinomian error, the preface goes beyond this to indicate the terms of argument, both explicit and implicit, on which the whole of *Seasonable Thoughts* depends. The preface defines the appropriate method of judging the Awakening, it asserts the centrality of language as sign in the debate between Old and New Light, and, perhaps most interestingly, it links language and gender in ways that illuminate the social distance between the revivalists and their opponents.

Chauncy's use of the antinomian controversy as the type of enthusiasm in America has not escaped the notice of students of the Great Awakening. Some scholars have dismissed the preface to *Seasonable Thoughts* as "predictable," while others have uncovered in it evidence of a pervasive rhetoric of generational conflict.[26] As minister to Boston's First Church, the site of Hutchinson's rebellion, Chauncy regarded himself as the lineal descendant of the earliest defenders of orthodoxy. By mingling his voice with those of the first generation, the argument goes, Chauncy meant to cast himself as yet another reproving father. Still other students of the Awakening, from Perry Miller on, have exploited the symmetry of Chauncy's analogy: just as the antinomian controversy ushered in the age of Puritanism in America, so, in the view of some historians, the Great Awakening signaled its end. Limited as the comparison might be, these two conflicts, both of them centered on the means of conversion, have provided a suggestive frame for discussions of the rise, reign, and ruin of American Puritanism.

These readings tend to obscure the point of Chauncy's comparison, which is far less oblique than our interpretations of it have tended to be. As we have seen, the theological link between the antinomian conflict and the Great Awakening lay, Chauncy believed, in the problem of visible sainthood, of the proper relation between the private, invisible experience of grace and its outward manifestation. The visibility of God's intentions, on which Chauncy insisted, meant, among other things, that the Awakening itself could be judged by its appearance. The optimistic interpretation of the revival as a prelude to the millennium recorded by apologists like Edwards depended on the assumption, dubious at best, that what looked like disorder was, in fact, the quickening of the spirit. Chauncy was sure that Edwards had misread the signs of the times; his doctrinal errors were recapitulated in his misinterpretation of social phenomena, and that, in turn, was reflected in his misuse of language. As far as Chauncy was concerned, order, peace, tranquillity, and obedience characterized God's work. To identify a period of patent hysteria as the millennium begun to come down from heaven was to misrepresent, to misname, the event.

The story of Anne Hutchinson as story suffers no major revision in Chauncy's hands; on the contrary, his use of direct quotation, not to mention his impeccable sources, ensures against any alteration in the narrative or its interpretation. What is striking, however, in Chauncy's use of the story is his explicit acknowledgment of a rhetorical divide separating Old and New Lights along much the same lines as those that separated Hutchinson and her accusers. In other words, the problem with Edwards is not that he *is* an antinomian but that he *sounds* like one—or rather that he writes out of a set of assumptions about the availability of meaning that are, for Chauncy, inextricably tied to a particular misinterpretation of doctrine, a misinterpretation that achieved its fullest expression in America in the antinomian controversy.[27]

In effect, the preface to *Seasonable Thoughts* proposes the interpretation of signs as the point on which Chauncy and Edwards divide, both as theologians and as writers. Chauncy means to pit the logic of Edwards's defense of the revival against a more persuasive logic of his own. But since Edwards's logic seems to him to deny any necessary coincidence of visible and invisible, Chauncy must refute Edwards's direct claims by addressing the largest assumption that stands behind these. In order to show that Edwards has misinterpreted the revival, in other words, Chauncy must establish the very possibility of interpretation. His intention is to repudiate Edwards's representation of the universe as fraught with a meaning inaccessible to man's limited nature and to demonstrate instead that what we see is sufficient for all our purposes. It is hardly surprising in view of this that Chauncy shows an overwhelming interest in the language of the antinomian crisis and the Awakening *as* language, for language links the two moments and language, likewise, measures the difference between the revivalists and their opponents. As far as Chauncy was concerned, the power of language was perfectly clear and the danger the language of revivalism posed more apparent with each new expression of awakening.

The preface to *Seasonable Thoughts*, then, assumes the existence of two languages, one belonging to the revival and the other to those whom Chauncy considered the spokesmen for truth. Further, it assumes a fixed relationship between language and doctrine. To speak the language of revivalism is, *ipso facto*, to partake of the doctrinal errors of the New Lights. Chauncy himself is perfectly aware of these implications. "Had I wrote [the ensuing treatise] to please my self," he explains, "it would have been without those numerous Quotations, which, I am sensible, have not only taken up a great Deal of Room, but made the Book less agreable to many Readers. My design herein," he goes on, "was to make it evident, that the *Divines*, in most Esteem, in these Churches, for their *Piety* and *Soundness in the Faith*, have spoken in much the same Language, upon the Things now in Agitation, with those who have been called *Opposers of the Work of GOD*, and charg'd with *leading Souls to Hell*" (*STS*, xxviii–xxix). This is partly self-defense. Reviled as an "opposer" himself, Chauncy hopes to submerge his own voice in the multitude of those renowned for their piety; his credibility depends on his words being indistinguishable from those of the estimable divines he quotes.

But this gathering of voices has another significance as well. Chauncy finds in the unanimity of his sources—both contemporary and historical—confirmation of the correspondence between sign and meaning. If, presented with the same evidence, independent witnesses arrive at the same interpretation, the possibility of order in the world is restored. The visible is not only meaningful but stable in its meaning, and authority—the monolithic authority of a particular language and the social authority of the fathers who speak it—is thereby reinstated. By rejecting the idea that signs signify, the revival, Chauncy believed, had forfeited the possibility of an orderly universe. In its place the Awakening offered a world of radical individualists, attentive only to their private experience, arrogant in their self-trust, and incapable of Christian community. The opposers answered the clamor of revival in one voice and, thus, proved the truth of their position; ambiguity, dissension, and idiosyncrasy were banished to the side of revivalism.

Chauncy's attention to language is not, of course, limited to the preface. Rather, it is an obsessive concern of *Seasonable Thoughts*. Again and again Chauncy draws our attention to language as sign and to the revival's apparent repudiation of signs. In describing the dangers of itinerancy, for example, Chauncy asks, "What is the Language of this going into *other Men's Parishes*? Is it not obviously this? The *settled Pastors* are Men, not qualified for their Office. . . . Or, the Language may be, we are Men of *greater Gifts, superiour Holiness, more Acceptableness to God*" (*STS*, 50). The point is oddly stated. The issue, it would seem, is not simply the "going into other men's parishes" but the violation of a traditional language of deference entailed by so extreme a breach of decorum. The real challenge to the authority of the settled ministry—the itinerant's intrusion into the pulpit—is subsumed into the problem of how that act is represented in language, and the language of that representation, for all its apparent ambiguity, is a charged one. To speak uncharitably of the ministers makes "the *Relation*, between *Pastors* and *People*, a *meer Nothing, a Sound without Meaning*" (*STS*, 51). The right relation between pastor and people, in other words, is signified by the language of respect. To dispense with that language, as the itinerants surely did, is to violate the relationship between minister and congregation, and that violation contains in it the potential for a wholesale inversion of the order of things.

If, as Chauncy proposes, the pastoral relationship is made real and apparent by its embodiment in language, then language has the power to undo it. The existence of a language of pastoral authority did not prove the existence of the thing to the itinerants, but this does not, as Chauncy assumes, disempower language. Chauncy suggests that to the itinerants language is only language. But if the dismissive words of the itinerants as much as their intrusion into the parishes reduced the relation between shepherd and flock to "sound without meaning," these words, by the same token, asserted their power.

This brings me to my point (or, rather, to Chauncy's), which is that for Edwards language is, in large measure, sound without meaning. That is, for Edwards, words, like other forms of visible evidence, are accidental and ultimately inadequate signifiers. Despite the fact that Edwards does not address the problem of language directly, the ambiguity of all such signs is apparent in both the logic and the language of part 1 of *Some Thoughts,* the response to which occupies three of Chauncy's four hundred pages. Edwards's argument against *a priori* judging, a "foundation error" of the Old Light position, for example, illustrates the unreliability of visible signs. At the outset Edwards insists that we can judge God's glorious work only from the "effect wrought" and not from "the way it began, the instruments . . . employed, the means that have been made use of, [or] the methods that have been taken . . . in carrying it on" (*ST,* 293). This assertion looks, on the face of it, not unlike Chauncy's claim that we know God's work by its "fruit." But Edwards means something quite different, for the "effect" to which he refers is not a visible but an immediate, sensory one.

Lest we mistake his meaning, Edwards offers an analogy from the natural world. We know that the wind blows, Edwards points out, because "we hear the sound, we perceive the effect." We do not wait, he goes on, "to be satisfied what should be the cause of the wind's blowing from such a part of the heavens, and how it should come to pass that it should blow in such a manner, at such a time" (*ST,* 294). We infer cause from effect, but the only *reliable* effect is wholly private. Our senses tell us that the wind is blowing, and, likewise, the "new sense" lent by conversion reports God's presence.

The wind analogy is intended simply to make the case for *a posteriori* judging, but like many of Edwards's analogies, this one is interesting for both what it says and what it only intimates. In this particular instance, we begin to see the larger problem with which Edwards is grappling if we draw out the implications of his analogy. Certain as I am that the wind is blowing, I cannot prove that I hear or feel it. I can only attest to my felt experience—and I may, of course, lie. If the wind should happen to ruffle my hair, you might infer, if not wind, at

least the movement of air. But this visible evidence is not to
be depended on. After all, the wind may blow without ruffling
my hair, and from this you might wrongly infer an absence of
wind. You can achieve my level of certainty only if you, too,
feel the wind, but in no case need your inference affect my conviction.

The fact, as Edwards caustically remarks, that "God has not
taken that course [in carrying out his work] . . . which men in
their wisdom would have thought most advisable" is nothing
to the point. God's ways are mysterious and his work in America extraordinary. As far as Edwards was concerned, to pry into
the origins of the revival or to question its appearance was to
"expose ourselves to the calamity of those who pried into the
ark of God" (*ST*, 294). Some deny God's work because they lack
the "sense" with which to perceive it; others refuse the evidences of their senses; and still others, like Chauncy, willfully
usurp God's prerogative by demanding that the revival conform, in its outward appearance, to their idea of it. But for Edwards knowledge of God's presence is immediate, internal, invisible. It is not, however, universal. Ironically, to those like
Edwards, for whom the truth of the revival was self-evident, fell
the task of testifying to the "effect wrought" by means of a system of visible signs as unreliable in their way as any other. The
nature of religious experience, as Edwards represents it, renders it wholly private, yet his defense of the revival demands
that he transcribe this experience in language. The language he
devised for this purpose was one that lent enormous power to
its speaker.

One of the places in which Edwards attempts to find a
language commensurate with the experience of grace is in the
spiritual biography of Sarah Pierpont, the nameless, gender-
less "example of evangelical piety" of *Some Thoughts*. The language of Edwards's account of his wife's religious experience is
similar to that of his own *Personal Narrative*. Mistrustful of visible signs as evidence and believing, moreover, that the efficacy
of religious affection cannot be inferred from its conformity to a
conventional sequence of conversion,[28] Edwards is left with a
language stripped of both temporal and concrete referents. In

an early and characteristic passage from the "example," Edwards recounts "the person's" renewed "sense of the holiness of God, as of a flame infinitely pure and bright, so as sometimes to overwhelm soul and body" (*ST*, 336). Here, as elsewhere, Edwards employs a language of intimation and approximation, a language predicated on the inadequacy of language. Repetitious, abstract, and conventional, Edwards's words offer, at best, only a faint glimmer of his wife's "sense" of ineffable holiness. But the very failure of language on one front allows for its success on another. Edwards's self-proclaimed inability to represent the stirrings of grace in human language reminds us of the inexpressible power of God and the limitations of fallen man *and* works to empower his speech. The ambiguous relationship between word and meaning pushes Edwards toward figurative language. Turning him into a poet of sorts, it lends his words the power we take to reside in poetry. All meanings are hidden, but any sign can bear meaning; everything is meaningful. Whereas Chauncy limits the pool of signifiers, Edwards expands it.

Writing about the *Personal Narrative,* Daniel B. Shea, Jr., has suggested that Edwards is faced there with the dilemma of rendering "the perceptions of the 'new sense' with an instrument so imperfect as human language and so indiscriminate in itself as to be the common property of both spiritual and natural man."[29] Not even the sensationalist vocabulary to which Edwards repeatedly turns in his effort to impart religious truth can overcome the limitations of this "instrument." Words cannot bespeak God. Needless to say, for Chauncy, who firmly believed that we should concern ourselves only with visible evidence of God's work—which evidence he defined in the most traditional terms as obedience of all sorts—Edwards's tendency to use "*loose, general* and *indefinite* Words, which People may put a Meaning to, just as they are led by their Imaginations" (*STS,* 397) was deplorable. The "fatal consequence" of a language to which "People," that is, anyone, could put their own meaning was so obvious, in fact, as to demand the restraint of "some men's tongues with Bit and Bridle."

Of course, there is a paradox in all this. Chauncy, for all his attention to language, is highly mistrustful of men's declarations concerning their spiritual condition. The work of God is "secret" and can be judged "only from the *Outward* Discoveries of it." Nonetheless, in a world rife with hypocrisy some outward signs are more reliable than others. Thus, Chauncy insists somewhat platitudinously that *"Action* speaks louder than Words," though clearly the confluence of word and deed speaks loudest of all. Edwards is more generous, or perhaps more resigned. Precisely because he begins from the proposition that language is inadequate to the task of describing the things of God, he is far more willing to accept verbal testimony. At the same time that affectionate religion, by its very nature, devalues the visible signs of grace, it places a premium on the conversion relation, for, imperfect as it is, language is the only instrument men have with which to record their "new sense." Like the old antinomians, then, Edwards seemed to deny outward signs, whether of sin or sanctity, and to elevate the witness of the spirit recorded in a language the unreliability of which Edwards was the first to admit.

Inasmuch as antinomianism builds from a radical mistrust of signs, Chauncy's preface gives us access to the central issue in *Seasonable Thoughts*. His explicit theological argument is reiterated in an implicit one about the efficacy of signs in which words stand as archetypal signifiers and their use stands as evidence of the doctrinal sympathies of the speaker. In this sense the problem of antinomianism informs the whole of *Seasonable Thoughts*. But Chauncy's use of the story of Anne Hutchinson illuminates the subtext of *Seasonable Thoughts* as well as its surface.

Despite the prominence—both social and numerical—of the male Hutchinsonians, the story of the antinomian controversy, particularly as it is told by the writers Chauncy quotes, is about a woman who stepped out of her place. In the terms I have been using, Hutchinson embodies the problem of signification: her usurpation of male roles is the visible emblem of her erroneous theology. But beyond this, the fact that the story of the antinomian controversy is the story of a *woman* heretic alerts us to the possibility that gender, as it stands for a constellation of culturally ascribed characteristics, is an issue in the Great Awakening.

Both Chauncy and Edwards were acutely aware of the disproportionate numbers of women, children, and young men among the newly converted. For Chauncy this preponderance of *"Children, young People,* and *Women,* whose Passions are soft and tender, and more easily thrown into a Commotion," was proof positive of the questionable nature of the revival. After all, he argues, *"Men* may as easily be overcome by the *Power* of the HOLY GHOST, as *Women* . . . what should then be the Reason that they should be, as it were, overlook'd . . . ?" (*STS,* 105). The rise of exhorters not merely young but illiterate— *"Lads,* or rather *Boys:* Nay, *Women* and *Girls;* yea, *Negroes"*— could only "portend *Evil* to these Churches." The case of women exhorters was the simplest to answer: to allow women to preach was, in Chauncy's view, to "give up all Pretence to the *Scripture* as our Rule." As to the young, the illiterate, the black, by exhorting they took "upon them to act the Part that is proper to another" (*STS,* 226–27). Women who acted like men, boys who spoke like ministers, blacks who preached like whites— these were not merely evil tendencies but visible signs of the heretical nature of the revival and the threat it posed to the standing order.

Edwards, of necessity, took a different position. While he associates the errors of the revivalists with their youth and inexperience, he rejects both the notion that only "silly women" and children experience divine joy in the manner of the revivalists and the idea that the revival is discredited either by its youthfulness or its femininity. He wonders, in fact, whether "God has [not] begun at the lower end, and . . . made use of the weak and foolish . . . mere babes in age and standing" so as to "chastise the deadness, negligence, earthlymindedness, and vanity . . . of the ministers" (*ST,* 295). Whereas for Chauncy what links women, children, and boys is their "silliness," their susceptibility to error, for Edwards they are related by their powerlessness. They are a "lower end," lacking "standing" in the world. And while censoriousness does not become them, they are not to be silenced: "'Tis beautiful in private Christians, though they are women and children, to be bold in professing the faith of Christ . . . without any fear of men, though they should be reproached as fools and madmen, and frowned upon by great men, and cast off by parents and all the world" (*ST*, 427). To argue, as Chauncy did, that the converts' lack of standing made their awakening suspect was to argue once again, in a new way, that signs—this time signs of status—were more important than felt experience.

Edwards's account suggests that the new converts were drawn from a relatively disempowered portion of the population. This dovetails neatly with the information modern historians offer about the newly awakened in the 1740s. While women continued to be admitted to the churches in greater numbers than men, historians record a significant increase in the rate of male conversion and in the numbers of youthful converts during the Great Awakening. Richard Bushman has proposed that for these young men, evangelical religion "cleared the air of tensions. Men admitted that they had lusted after wealth, condemned themselves, and afterwards walked with lighter hearts. They ended the long struggle with the social order by denying its power to save and hence to condemn." J. M. Bumstead has pointed to a decline in economic opportunity for young men living in towns suffering the pressure of increased population on the availability of land. Philip Greven has suggested that increased mobility and the consequent anxiety of displacement experienced by young men in this period prepared the way for conversion. In larger schematic terms, James Henretta has located the Great Awakening at a transitional moment in the morphology of New England society when the traditional patriarchal forms founded on an abundance of land and characterized by limited mobility gave way to a new order marked by overcrowding, a relative dearth of land, increased mobility, and the lessening of paternal authority.[30]

These accounts of the young male convert ignore the fact that there is a basis for the association of such young men with women and that that association was confirmed in certain external ways. Like women, young men were apparently relegated to the galleries of the churches. Like women, unmarried men paid neither taxes nor ministerial rates. And like at least some women during the revival, these men were called upon to "step out of their places," both literally and figuratively. By their very conversion, one might say, these young men threatened to displace their "fathers." Given what we know of the young male convert, the appeal of Edwards's theology—and, more especially, the tremendous popular appeal of the language of revivalism—makes sense. Its insistence on experience, its attention to feeling, and its appeal to women have caused Edwards's language and, more broadly, the language of evangelicalism to be characterized as feminine, "feminizing," or even sentimental.[31] But clearly the same characteristics that served to empower women in this language may be seen as similarly empowering the "lower end" of the male social scale as well. Edwards's language, by exalting invisible signs of grace, diminishes the importance of outward marks of status. Election is sealed neither by altered behavior nor by outward signs of God's favor but by the birth of a new self to which the convert can testify only in "loose, general and indefinite words." Edwards's emphasis on the testimony of the hopeful does not imply an antinomian disregard for the Law—in fact, if anything, it restores that tension between works and grace so useful to the first generation of American Puritans—but, by elevating the invisible, his language does empower the individual convert in ways that have nothing to do with his position in a hierarchical social order.

For all the attention paid by historians to the new male convert during the Great Awakening, it may be more useful, finally, to regard these converts as so many more "women," constrained not by their sex but by the conditions attending their lives in the 1740s. In that case, the story of the seventeenth-century antinomians with which Chauncy begins *Seasonable Thoughts* can be seen as a cautionary tale twice over. It urges us to fear the language of antinomianism for both its theological implications and its social ones. Moreover, it brings together gender and class. The "Woman" is once again taken to embody the danger of lawlessness inherent in the repudiation of visible signs, but this time with an expanded significance, for to deny the import of the visible is to empower those *visibly* disempowered. With this conflation of gender and class, it is possible to turn to Emerson, for whom the problem of antinomianism is imbedded, of necessity, in the larger one of the transcendent and autonomous self and in whose writing issues of gender and empowerment need not be broached because the social world in which they exist is itself elided.

5

Emerson and the Age of the First Person Singular

Following the religious strife of the 1740s came a period that Hector St. John de Crevecoeur extolled as one of "religious indifference." In the years after the revival, the spokesmen for the new nation retreated from the problem of private, revelatory experience and directed their attention instead toward the visible and the institutional. Like the liberal clergy whose descendants they are commonly taken to be, the political theorists of the eighteenth century addressed themselves to man in his public aspect. For this reason, perhaps, the period of the American Revolution, a period when one might logically expect the story of Anne Hutchinson's defiance to take on added significance, is not a particularly fruitful one for the purposes of this study. Hutchinson's story remains firmly in the hands of historians like Thomas Hutchinson who alter it very little, while the term *antinomian* is employed primarily by ministers intent on recalling the citizenry to the sacrifices required of them by the war. One might speculate that the relative lack of interest in the story of Hutchinson during the Revolution has to do with the association of antinomianism with problems of dissent within the culture; when the colonists were faced with an external enemy, issues internal to American culture may have diminished in urgency. Whatever one conjectures, Hutchinson's story and the problem it illuminates garnered more attention during the pre- and postwar periods—during the Great Awakening and the first half of the nineteenth century—than they did during the Revolution.

Writing only ten years after the peak of the revival, Benjamin Franklin provides a fitting metaphor for the intellectual temper of his generation. It is not, he points out, "of much importance to us to know the manner in which nature executes her laws; it is enough if we know the laws themselves. It is of real use to know that china left in the air unsupported will fall and break; but how it comes to fall, and why it breaks, are matters of speculation. It is a pleasure indeed to know them, but we can preserve our china without it."[1] Like Chauncy, Franklin insists that we can know with certainty only what we can see and, moreover, that that will suffice, in religion and politics as in physics. Our knowledge of the observed event outweighs in practical value the hidden cause, the invisible motive. The conservative implications of this stance we have seen already in Chauncy's recounting of the antinomian crisis. That the revolutionary Franklin can speak in so much the same terms argues perhaps for an analogous conservatism in the representation, if not the fact, of the American Revolution.

Despite their lack of interest in hidden causes, the enlightened of the eighteenth century knew what they saw. And they were sure, based on their observation of the world, that men, left to their own devices, would act in their own interest. They found nothing to deplore in this. Like Franklin's broken china, it was simply true. For the most part, they were not interested in why it was true or in what could be done about it. Their concern was limited to the practical effect the natural expression of self-interest would have on the operation of the state. Taking the pursuit of the self as a precondition to human happiness, they believed it to be of the utmost importance that a benevolent state guarantee its unhindered expression. As the natural basis for labor, self-interest above all else would insure progress, prosperity, and the continued existence of the state. Whereas the Puritans saw self-love as evidence of man's fallen nature and regarded it as a moral hindrance to the completion of their errand, the utilitarian eighteenth century insisted on self-interest as a stimulus to industry and, thus, as the cornerstone of the new republic. "The happiness of society," as John Adams explained, "is the end of government, as . . . the happiness of the individual is the end of man." "From this principle," he went on, "it will follow that the form of government which communicates . . . happiness, to the greatest number of people, and in the greatest degree, is the best."[2]

The revolutionary new age transformed power itself from an oppressive to a liberating force. "Man has certainly an exalted soul," Adams insisted, "and the same principle in human nature—that aspiring, noble principle founded in benevolence and cherished by knowledge: *I mean the love of power*, which has been so often the cause of slavery—has, wherever freedom has existed, been the cause of freedom."[3] Ambition, the expression of which once (or elsewhere) meant curtailing another's power—that is, meant slavery—is now, in America, the basis of progress, enlightened government, liberty, and freedom. Slavery, which Adams nowhere acknowledges to exist in America, is the concomitant of aspiration only in an old world where a man's capacity to appropriate to himself a greater share of the fixed wealth of the world measured his individuality. In the modern age, the new and newly unique individual generates new things, not the least of them a new world.[4] The relationship between the individual and the state Adams posits is circular, with each eliciting from the other its best.

At the heart of eighteenth century individualism as this was expressed by the Revolutionary generation is the belief that both the happiness of the individual and the welfare of the state are best secured by the free and full expression of self-interest. One scholar, speaking of this idea as it manifests itself in the economic thought of the period, summarizes the argument in another way: "The generalized expression of the commercial republican view was what Tocqueville called 'the doctrine of self-interest properly understood,' the fusing of public interest and private profit to the point where 'a sort of selfishness makes [the individual] care for the state.'"[5] To make oneself the last end in every action was not merely natural and inevitable but also salutary; it was, in fact, identical to making the community the last end. Men serve themselves, government serves the people, and individual exertion prompted by self-love guarantees the success of the state.

As more than one historian has pointed out, Edwardsean postmillennialism is reenacted after the Revolution as a secular march of progress. In both cases, there is a sense in which all the individual need do to usher in the new age of peace and prosperity is attend to himself. For Edwards, of course, this process was cast in spiritual terms: men must examine their souls, bring their very beings into harmony with God's intentions for his chosen few. But contained in the Puritan assertion of the equal moral worth of men—or building on it—was a new conception of the "individual in his own right," the free agent. A new social and economic mobility emphasized the relationship between man as "owner of himself" and society as "a calculated device for the protection of this property and for the maintenance of an orderly relation of exchange."[6] The self-interested activity initiated by this free agent in a fluid marketplace, not his fulfillment of a particular function within a fixed order or his personal control of fixed resources, would advance the nation toward its golden future. In other words, individualism would yield the best of all possible social arrangements. Or, to put it the other way around, the structure of society was taken to be implicit in the self.

With this new conception of the individual came a new sense of the citizen as directly accountable for his condition. "The foundation of our Empire was not laid in the gloomy age of ignorance and superstition," wrote George Washington, "but at an Epoch when the rights of mankind were better understood and more clearly defined, than at any former period. . . . At this auspicious period, the United States came into existence as a nation, and if their citizens should not be completely free and happy, the fault will be entirely their own."[7] The covert threat echoes Puritan sermons on keeping the covenant, but here no hierarchy of ministers and magistrates explicates the contract or exacts obedience to its conditions. In fact, in this rhetoric, there is no longer anything above—or even, in a sense, outside of—the individual. He is arbiter of his own fate, and the success of the nation depends not on his metamorphosis but simply on his fulfillment of a "noble, aspiring" nature.

This representation of the relationship between the individual and his society allowed for tremendous diversity. It assumed an expansive community in which even the man of "irregular ambition" could be accommodated without danger so long as he was sufficiently isolated from his allies. That he would be so isolated was ensured, in the Federalists' view, by the very extent of the republic, taking in so great a "variety of parties and interests" that even where "a common motive exists, it [would] be . . . difficult for all who felt it to discover their own strength and to act in unison."[8] But toleration and pluralism were not sufficient to answer the problem implicit in this new scheme of things, that is, how to adduce and rationalize social limits given the enormous value placed on the individual and his freedom. To distinguish between a lawless antinomianism and the dominant ideology of individualism in a culture where, happily or not, enormous authority accrued to the self must have been difficult. One way to define the new consensus that emerged from the Revolution and to clarify the boundaries within which the newly liberated self was to act was by exclusion.

Against this backdrop, William Emerson, twelfth pastor of the First Church and father of the Concord sage, wrote *An Historical Account of the First Church in Boston*. Ostensibly recounting the major events of 120 years of church history, Emerson gives over a striking amount of space in his book to the linked crises of the seventeenth and eighteenth centuries. About one-fifth of the *Historical Sketch*, published posthumously in 1812, concerns the antinomian controversy, and an equally substantial portion of its 225 pages treats the ministry of Charles Chauncy, with particular emphasis on his role in the Great Awakening. These episodes, which begin and end Emerson's history, lend the book what shape it has.

The figure of Anne Hutchinson looms large in Emerson's *Sketch*. The antinomian controversy was, he thought, "one of the most extraordinary theological controversies that ever was agitated,"[9] so extraordinary, in fact, that "the ecclesiastical annals of no country can furnish a similar instance" (*HS*, 50). Emerson's hyperbole is telling; as he later makes clear, antinomianism is anything but dead and gone, despite Cotton Mather. Yet, although William Emerson identifies the controversy as theological and searches ecclesiastical annals for its equal, the story, as he tells it, concerns the social rather than the doctrinal ramifications of antinomianism. Like the earlier historians, he recounts Hutchinson's errors, makes oblique reference to the "monstrous births," and shows his distress at the fall into heresy of a "married woman," though he does so without hinting at sexual misconduct. But William Emerson's real concern is with the irrational behavior of the Hutchinsonians, behavior he regards as jeopardizing both church and state. Following Mather and Chauncy, Emerson presents the crisis as a confrontation between the forces of reason and those of enthusiasm, but his language, unlike that of his predecessors, is the language of eighteenth-century politics. His attempt to prove that "religion consists not in a heated fancy . . . but in a pure heart and a beneficent life" (*HS*, 188), is couched in terms that are readily transferable from religion to the larger realm of public affairs.

The clash is between two "parties." On one side stand the Hutchinsonians, a party of fanatics who "imbittered, poisoned, and inflamed the popular mind" to such an extent that among the "timid and credulous . . . some became intoxicated with the joys of assurance, some deranged, and others were driven to despair" (*HS*, 42). Opposing these is the "party of order," men of principle, the "rational part of the congregation," led by John Wilson and John Winthrop. For William Emerson the eventual restoration of this party to leadership in church and colony demonstrates the natural and inevitable victory of reason over fanaticism: "Men of prudence have here a fresh stimulus to perseverence in a course of moderation, and a new proof, that principle and truth will eventually triumph over faction and falsehood" (*HS*, 67). For Emerson, as for most of his generation, "prudence" and "moderation" are key virtues, while "faction" and "falsehood" form a natural pair. Firmly committed to the social organicism of the Federalists and deeply fearful of the rise of democracy—"One might almost as well be adrift in the ruthless billows of the ocean as to be overwhelmed by the floods of democracy"—William Emerson .eems to have associated the fanaticism of the Hutchinsonians with the challenge to reasonable government offered by those clamoring for democracy. Like Chauncy, Emerson feared what one Federalist called "a wild furious democracy." As one recent study has shown, for William Emerson, as for his son, the rise of a "Middling Interest" held nothing but terror. The danger such an "interest" represented was the danger of a "marginal and dependent" class "having little interest in the common good . . . [because] they had nothing at stake."[10]

Despite his attempt to write off the Hutchinsonians as fanatics, however, William Emerson's reflections on the antinomian "affair" are full of confusion. He can "hardly help dropping a tear of compassion over the intolerance of the age, and the hardship attending the case of this female fanatick" despite "plenary evidence that she possessed an unquiet, bold, and turbulent spirit, and was full of enthusiasm" (*HS*, 52). Caught between filiopietism and his belief in the reasonableness of toleration, it is hardly surprising that he does not know how to respond to the story he has related. "We are ready to wonder," he muses,

> that the private opinions of a woman, and even the parlour lectures, she was pleased to hold at her house, should excite so strongly the apprehensions of the most learned and powerful men in the state. We are ready to ask, what harm could have arisen from the sentiments, lectures, and even calumnies of this infatuated female, so long as she enjoyed no peculiar political privilege, and could nowise direct the power of the magistrate.
>
> (*HS*, 52)

While the potential for power is at least broached in the Puritans' representation of Hutchinson as Satan's agent, William Emerson is unable even in imagination, much less in language, to empower the "infatuated female." His account of Hutchinson refuses the possibility that the *private* opinions of a *married* woman (and these are the operative terms in his description) could have public consequences. Were he able to credit the specter of woman empowered, he would shed no tear of compassion over Hutchinson's plight. His sentimental response to her story requires her powerlessness.

As he tells it, however, Emerson is clearly of two minds about the Puritans' treatment of Hutchinson. On the one hand, he genuinely abhors the fanatical enthusiasm she represents. On the other hand, his age had taught him well. So thoroughly versed in an organic understanding of the community as greater than the sum of its members was he that he seems to have found it impossible to conceive of the private—out of which the public is generated—as competitive with the public, much less as threatening to it. Hoping to dissociate himself from the intolerance of the Puritans, he is nonetheless unwilling to defend the antinomians. Seeing the direction his questions may take him, Emerson retreats into a conventional encomium on the worth and wisdom of the founding fathers: "We know that those who then held the reins of government in the state and church, were wise and good men. Candour therefore would lead us to conclude, that what they did . . . was best to be done" (*HS*, 59–60). All else failing, he recalls himself and his reader to the merits of those who had, after all, made possible the new republic.

To William Emerson, antinomianism, like all forms of enthusiasm, posed a threat to "reasonable religion"—the very religion his son would denounce as "corpse cold." Following Chauncy, whose *Seasonable Thoughts* he greatly admired, Emerson bemoans the public manifestations of antinomianism—the reckless behavior of the enthusiasts, the disruption of "publick quiet" that accompanies schism, and the delusion of immediate revelation. Chauncy himself, after whom William Emerson named one of his sons, represents the antithesis of this: he embodies the values of the party of order. In the words of his admirer, he is a man "whose indignation against wrong could never be suppressed . . . who loved and cherished the civil and religious liberties of his country . . . who was never carried away by a wild imagination, or weak credulity; who was conversant rather with facts, than fables, with principles, than feelings, and with arguments, than words" (*HS*, 199). Emerson's oppositions—fact versus fable, principle versus feeling, argument versus words—effectively differentiate between male and female modes. Strikingly, they reiterate Chauncy's own argument with Edwards, an argument that, as we have seen, used just such terms to distinguish between the "feminine" revivalists and their masculine opponents.

Himself a model of male rationality, Chauncy's account of the analogy between the antinomian controversy and the Great Awakening contained an essential lesson. William Emerson was sure that "the story of the early spread of antinomianism in this country," as told by Chauncy, would be "interesting to every lover of american history as well, as to divines," not only because it cast light on the ancient past but as it applied to the present. Chauncy, Emerson tells us, "could hardly have better described . . . the temper and conduct of modern enthusiasts, than he has described them, in the practice of the antinomians of his own days" (*HS*, 191). Chauncy, of course, had insisted a hundred years earlier that his gleanings from Johnson and Winthrop were likewise "needful for *these days* . . . the like . . . Errors prevailing *now* as they did *then*."

The sense one has in reading William Emerson's *Historical Sketch* is, as Joel Porte has pointed out, that "two hundred years of history have collapsed in on themselves."[11] And in a sense the times had collapsed in on each other, at least insofar as the new "commercial" times, like the old colonial times, increasingly required a public rhetoric that would offer assurance that the self-reliant man, now primarily an economic rather than a religious construct, "was on the side of society and not against society"[12]—that is, that self-reliance did not imply a secular antinomianism. Ironically, the emerging capitalist economy of the first half of the nineteenth century presented Americans with a problem analogous to the one the Puritans faced: how to foster individualism, especially economic self-reliance, while, at the same time, averting the lawlessness that might be its result. The concept of "self-interest properly understood"—producing, as it surely would, an "orderly, temperate, moderate, careful and self-controlled citizenry," if not a populace committed to disinterested virtue—answered the problem in the limited sphere of economic behavior. But the larger answer came from William Emerson's son, in whom his father's fear of antinomianism and the new commitment to individual self-creation came together. What Tocqueville acknowledged as an expedient ideology for an expanding nation professing ideas of equality and individual freedom, Ralph Waldo Emerson universalized and offered back to his culture not as social strategy but as ideal philosophy.

Professor Cornelius Felton of Harvard University, reviewing Ralph Waldo Emerson's *Essays, First Series* in 1841, predicted that self-reliance, "if acted upon, would overturn society, and resolve the world into chaos."[13] Felton's alarm may seem excessive, but his estimate of the subversive possibilities inherent in Emerson's thought has nonetheless been shared by a long line of Emerson scholars. According to these scholars, Emerson "brought to full consciousness . . . the antinomianism latent in the thought of his Puritan forbears."[14] He was, in other words, the spiritual descendant of Anne Hutchinson. Remote from the constraints of seventeenth-century dogma and liberated by Romantic thought, he is represented as giving free play to the antinomianism Hutchinson had, of necessity, to disavow.

Emerson himself admitted that the Transcendentalists "easily incurred the charge of antinomianism" by virtue of their claim that "he, who has the Law-giver, may with safety not only neglect, but even contravene every written commandment."[15] But to link antinomianism and Transcendentalism is to imply that the social implications of the two "heresies" are the same. Whereas Emerson uncovered and described the perfect correspondence of the universe, Anne Hutchinson insisted that the visible and the invisible, the public and the private, bore no necessary relation to one another. And whether she intended it or not, the reinterpretation of doctrine that grew from this "error" undermined the elaborate myth the Puritans used to justify settlement and to enforce social norms just as its implied reinterpretation of selfhood undermined community. Antinomianism, in this sense, represents a rejected alternative to Puritanism as it was practiced and understood in colonial Massachusetts. By casting Emerson as a latter-day antinomian, we come to think of him as likewise offering an alternative to a dominant ideology that we locate elsewhere. In fact, he discovered a disturbing tendency toward antinomianism in his own philosophical stance. However, rather than celebrating the dissenting view implied by this antinomian tendency or glorying, as Anne Hutchinson in some sense did, in his liberation from the Law, Emerson applied himself to the task of demonstrating how it was that the perfect self-reliance of the American was precisely not antinomianism.

It should come as no surprise that Emerson concerned himself with the "ancient heresy." We know that he owned—and presumably had read—his father's account of the seventeenth-century controversy. And in the course of preparing his "Historical Discourse" on the town of Concord in 1835, he read as well John Winthrop's *Journal* with its entries on the disruptions of the 1630s. Moreover, he could hardly have been unaware of revivalists of dubious orthodoxy like Charles Grandison Finney, who, citing Jonathan Edwards at every turn and insisting on the primacy of feeling and the universality of grace, rose to prominence in the 1830s.[16] Fearing a fall into heresy, then, Emerson transformed the antinomianism potential in his thinking into a conservative idealism, the language and structure of which were widely shared by his contemporaries.

In other words, Emerson excised antinomianism from his philosophy to create Transcendentalism. Even as he unquestionably "removed the task of self-validation within,"[17] he saw by this very act that he must "beware of antinomianism." And, treading a fine line between "heresy" and "orthodoxy," he tempered his idealism and transformed it into a doctrine that served the realities of his time. To accomplish this he had to play the Puritan to his own Anne Hutchinson. His problem was to refine his theory of individualism to allow self-reliance, to encourage faith in human intuition and in the divinity of man, without thereby justifying lawlessness. The solution began with his disavowal of Unitarianism. To a nation espousing democratic principles, Unitarianism, with its stress on human capability and activity, on the demystification and universality of religion, on the historical nature of Christianity, was comforting. To Emerson it was "corpse cold." What Americans needed, in his view, was not history but "an original relation to the universe." As Emerson set about describing this new relation, he became increasingly uncomfortable with its resemblance to the antinomianism of an earlier generation.

Assuming the whole world to be infused with the same truth, Emerson looked to nature for a demonstration of how all its myriad parts cohere. What he discovered was a "radical correspondence" between all things. Finding "no fact in nature which does not carry the whole sense of nature" (*CW*, 1:20), he went on to assert that "mind is the only reality, of which men and all other natures are better or worse reflectors." Emerson's doctrine of correspondence asserts a unity that the material philosophy of the Unitarians denies, but it does not solve the problem of how man, bound to a "biographical Ego," confronted continually with distinctions of time, space, and circumstance, trained to think in terms of a sequence of events, arrives at a perception of this unity. It does not explain how it is that at certain moments "all mean egotism vanishes. I become a transparent eyeball; I am nothing; I see all; the currents of the Universal Being circulate through me; I am part or particle of God" (*CW*, 1:10).

Emerson's rejection of historical Christianity and his understanding of reason as imagination and intuition combine to suggest self-reliance as the key to truth and the source of cosmic unity. The "error of the religionists"—their willful ignorance of "the extent or the harmony or the depth of their moral nature," their dependence on "little, positive, verbal, formal versions of the moral laws"[18]—led them to so complete a reliance on authority that its absurdity was self-evident: "You must be humble because Christ says, 'Be humble.' 'But why must I obey Christ?' 'Because God sent him.' But how do I know God sent him? 'Because your own heart teaches the same thing he taught.' Why then shall I not go to my own heart at first?" (*JMN*, 4:45). Emerson's writings are replete with statements of this kind. Self-trust, the "infinitude of the private man," the rejection of all but the heart's authority—these constitute a major theme in both journals and essays and are repeatedly invoked by scholars as evidence of Emerson's radical individualism. When we hear Emerson proclaim of the American scholar, "The world is nothing, the man is all . . . it is for you to know all, it is for you to dare all" (*CW*, 1:69), it is indeed tempting to understand him as proclaiming the emancipation of the individual. Trust yourself, he seems to insist, and you will not err.

But Emerson's appeal for self-trust was not a call to egotism or to an arrogant disregard of social forms, nor was it intended to give men license to do as they pleased. Potentially, it was far more subversive than any of these; actually, it could be seen as far less so, for the same interplay between self-abnegation and self-assertion that we saw in Hutchinson's doctrinal position informs Emerson's philosophy. Ultimately, the transcendent self, like the antinomian one, is no self at all, but God: "To reflect is to receive truth immediately from God without any medium. . . . A trust in yourself is the height, not of pride, but of piety, an unwillingness to learn of any but God himself. It will come only to he who feels that he is nothing" (*JMN*, 3:279). Self-assertion is defined as the obliteration of self. Man at the moment when he sees himself and the universe most clearly—at the moment of "grace"—sees himself no more. In fact, "the object of the man, the aim of these moments, is to make daylight shine through him" (*CW*, 2:93); the individual who looks to himself for the truth loses all opacity, all form, and becomes thereby a perfect medium for the transmission of that light which is God. At moments of heightened awareness, "from within or from behind, a light shines through us upon things and makes us aware that we are nothing, but the light is all" (*CW*, 2:161). Like Hutchinson and Edwards, Emerson saw that at the very instant a man discovers the true harmony of the universe, he is "swallowed up in God."

Attractive as this vision of the self absorbed into the Oversoul was, however, it prompted Emerson to caution. In his effort to counter the rational theology of the Unitarians, he found himself, despite himself, seeming to speak for immediate access to divinity, for an arrogant denial of the authority of teachers, for the equation of self and selflessness, for the invisibility of "grace," for reliance on intuition or "revelation"—all of which pointed toward a rejection of the Law. This configuration, as he knew, typified the antinomian:

> Beware of antinomianism. All men have a slight distrust of your novelties and think you do not esteem the old laws of true wit-

ness, just dealing, chaste conversing, as much as they. They have some reason. For as they make a bad use of their old truths, so we make a bad use of our new ones. They know that we have brought with us the clinging temptations that whisper so softly by night and by day in lonely places, in seductive company, and they query whether the loss of the old checks will not sometimes be a temptation which the unripeness of the new will not countervail.

(*JMN*, 5:496)

The new truths of the Transcendentalists did, in fact, open the way for disdain of the old laws, and the unripeness of the new checks did encourage some to wander. Emerson, however, insisted that the tendency toward antinomianism that grew out of his critique of Unitarianism could be turned to another purpose. The same revelation that led the seventeenth-century antinomian to challenge the dominant social order could, in the nineteenth century, be shown to yield inner peace and outward harmony.

Were he less careful to qualify his meaning, it would be tempting to find in Emerson's doctrine of compensation a more profound antinomianism than any yet espoused by an American. Instead, his assertion that the world is formed of opposites—ebb and flow, male and female, darkness and light—each of which contains and completes the other and none of which exists independently begins a process of redirection. To Emerson "all things are moral. . . . The world looks like a multiplication table, or a mathematical equation, which, turn it how you will, balances itself" (*CW*, 2:60). This understanding of the world might be seen as resulting in an ethical nihilism so complete as to make all actions a matter of indifference, but, with his usual acumen, Emerson preempts this charge: "The doctrine of compensation is not a doctrine of indifferency. The thoughtless say, on hearing these representations,—What boots it to do well? there is one event to good and evil; if I gain any good, I must pay for it; if I lose any good, I gain some other; all actions are indifferent" (*CW*, 2:70). The charge finds its answer in the meaning Emerson attributes to self-reliance. Actions are not indifferent; they are without force. The standard against which they are to be tested is not external but in the soul, which "is" and which contains its own compensation. All things bespeak the Law—"every globe in remotest heaven, every chemical change . . . every change of vegetation . . . every animal function from the sponge up to Hercules, shall hint or thunder to man the laws of right and wrong, and echo the Ten Commandments" (*CW*, 1:25–26). But access to the Law, as well as its fulfillment, depends on bringing the soul into harmony with eloquent nature. And harmony with nature depends, in turn, on the discovery that "there is God in you," by virtue of which you shall "be informed of all and . . . pervaded with a great peace" (*JMN*, 5:230). Thus, self-trust means neither impulsiveness nor egotism, nor does it imply that ethical categories are to be dismissed. Instead, to "trust thyself" means to trust God, and this, in turn, means accepting "the place divine providence has found for you, the society of your contemporaries, the connection of events" (*CW*, 2:28).

The doctrine of compensation makes nature "optimistic." It demonstrates that "there is no need of struggles, convulsions, and despairs" (*CW*, 2:79). A "higher law than that of our will regulates events," and if man is to be in harmony with the universe, he must see that "painful labors are unnecessary and fruitless." He "need only obey" to "become divine" (*CW*, 2:81). To find God in you and to manifest his presence by a passive acceptance of the world and its conditions is, in Emerson's terms, the height of self-reliance. All circumstances, "famine, typhus, frost, war, suicide, and effete races," are merely "calculable parts of the system of the world";[19] they are balanced elsewhere in the cosmic multiplication table. Human intervention is not what is needed, for in the perfect identification of the self with the universe lies the promise of the reformation of the social world. To focus on the intermediate term—that is, the community—rather than the immanent one—that is, God—will only lead man astray. Man must see his fortune as "the fruit of his character"; to do otherwise would as surely loose chaos as if "a particle of lead were to prefer to mask its properties, and exert the energies of cork" (*JMN*, 8:75).

Individualism, then, need not threaten the social order but

can instead be its mainstay. The proper mixture of passivity and optimism, self-reliance and humility, these qualities in their natural proportions will produce not rebels but the perfect Franklinesque American, a citizen whose every act, however self-interested, redounds to the benefit of society, albeit without his ever acknowledging its importance. For the rejection of popular standards is not a rejection of all standards and "mere antinomianism." Compensation calls not for indifference but for a change in man's thinking about morality. What matters is the "law of consciousness":

> There are two confessionals, in one or the other of which we must be shriven. You may fulfill your round of duties by clearing yourself in the *direct*, or, in the *reflex* way. . . . But I may also neglect this reflex standard, and absolve me to myself. I have my own stern claims and perfect circle. It denies the name of duty to many offices that are called duties. But if I can discharge its debts it enables me to dispense with the popular code. If any one imagines this law is lax, let him keep its commandment one day.
>
> (*CW*, 2:42)

Morality has reference only to each man's perfect circle, but the perfection of that circle depends on the divinity within. Each circle repeats the configuration of that larger one whose center is nowhere and circumference everywhere. Every time a man follows the commandment of his own heart, he takes a step closer to all mankind, for in every heart the same law is imprinted. Were all men to "dispense with the popular code," the result would not be anarchy. Rather, in the course of absolving themselves to themselves, men would learn the doctrine of correspondence. Public morality would flow from private judgment; society would mimic nature; all laws would be one Law.

This optimistic vision depends on the intermixing of the ethical and the natural meanings of the law. The theoretical principles according to which nature functions and the system of ethics to which men adhere echo one another. Moral qualities, like natural facts, are paired: one good implies the absence of another. Both generate their opposites, but both also attract their kind. The same laws that govern nature govern man as part of the natural world: "All things are moral. That soul which within us is a sentiment, outside us is a law" (*CW*, 2:60). Emerson posits one law that incorporates both rules of behavior and principles of nature. If a man looks honestly at himself and speaks what he finds, he speaks the truth. He knows it is the truth because he can find its analogue in every particle of nature. Law is just another way to describe truth, perfect because it is natural, natural because it follows the constitution of things: "But speak the truth, all spirits help you with unexpected furtherance. Speak the truth and all things alive and brute are vouchers, and the very roots of the grass underground there, do seem to stir and move to bear you witness. See again the perfection of the Law as it applies itself to the affections, and becomes the law of society" (*CW*, 1:78). Prescriptive law is absorbed into the larger concept of the law as a perfect description of nature. This thinking moves inexorably toward the subversion of all moral authority, but the extravagance of the conclusion does not deter Emerson from articulating it: "Good and bad are but names very readily transferable to that or this; the only right is what is after my constitution; the only wrong is what is against it" (*CW*, 2:30). The constitution of the individual soul, its natural affinities, lead to heaven or hell "of their own volition."

Emerson's equation of moral, social, and natural law further complicates his theory of self-reliance and also sharply limits the social implications of "natural" justice. Trusting oneself, granting priority to one's natural constitution, is not an act of self-assertion in the sense that we ordinarily understand. Rather, the perfectly balanced endowments of man, given full expression, reveal the God within and the perfect law that governs God's creation. This same law is "sovereign over all natures." If men were genuinely self-reliant and followed their intuition, the law of society would complement the law of nature. No distinction would exist between descriptive and prescriptive law; only their forms would differ. In the world as it is, Emerson conceded, self-reliance seems to foster isolation. Each man must look to himself; he may be "provoked" but he cannot be taught. His primary concern must be with discovering his own ideal law, his perfect circle, and not (as Emerson pointed out to Carlyle) with the discrepancies between this and any other purported law: "But what you say now and heretofore respecting the remoteness of my writing and thinking from real life, though I hear substantially the same criticism made by my countrymen, I do not know what it means. If I can at any time express the law and the ideal right, that should satisfy me without measuring the divergence from it of the last act of Congress."[20]

Emerson's answer to Carlyle epitomizes the contradiction that runs through his writing. Claiming personal access to ideal law while renouncing formal earthly law is the height of antinomian arrogance. The last act of Congress, like visible sainthood, is a mechanical accommodation of the Law to the conditions of society; what is binding is that invisible, ideal law written on the heart. With all the antinomian's certainty that it is not so, Emerson thus proclaims, "If I am the Devil's child, I will live then from the Devil" (*CW*, 2:30). Were this the final outcome of his reasoning, we would be forced to see Emerson as an undaunted antinomian, Melville's Ahab brought to life. In fact, however, he undermines this position as quickly as he adopts it by insisting that the universe is composed of interchangeable parts: "This is the ultimate fact which we so quickly reach . . . the resolution of all into the ever-blessed One. Self-existence is the attribute of the Supreme Cause" (*CW*, 2:40). However genuine, Emerson's rebellious disregard for Congress, like his proud acknowledgment of diabolical patrimony, is short-lived. Cautious as ever, he retreats quickly into a vision of unity in which resistance to social forms is no longer necessary. Antinomianism identifies a point of maximum distance between the individual and his society; the two are engaged in perpetual conflict, neither willing to grant the other meaningful authority. Emerson pauses at this point, then passes on, arriving, as we shall see, at the identification of individual and collective interests.

The doctrine of correspondence sets the stage for such a conflation. It posits an analogy between individual men identical to the one between man and nature. Variety does not mean disharmony: "Every man comes at the common results with the most conviction in his own way. But he only uses a different vocabulary from yours; it comes to the same thing" (*JMN*, 4:50). Vocabularies simply provide diversity in the utterance of truth. Emerson sees even so distant a figure as Luther as merely another version of himself: "I have only to translate a few of the leading phrases into their equivalent verities, to adjust his almanack to my meridian, and all the conclusions, all the predictions shall be strictly true. Such is the everlasting advantage of truth. Let a man work after a pattern he really sees, and every man shall be able to find a correspondence between these works and his own" (*JMN*, 4:352–53). The tacit assumption behind statements like these is that since there is only one truth and since the human heart leads unerringly toward that truth, all men move always in the same direction, albeit along different paths. Individualism cannot lead to discord, for eccentricity and idiosyncrasy are nothing more or less than expressions of the endless variety of nature. In a distant echo of Thomas Shepard, Emerson insists that conformity lies not in the suppression of idiosyncrasy but in its full and honest expression. Thus the man who lives truly according to the dictates of his heart is completely idiosyncratic and utterly representative; he manifests the substantial work of the Spirit in the circumstantial one. All vocabularies, truly spoken, generate the same sentence.

Conveniently, then, indulging the idiosyncratic brings men into alignment with the universal: "Culture . . . consists in the identification of the Ego with the universe, so that when a man says I think, I hope, I find,—he might properly say, the human race thinks, hopes, finds . . . he shall be able continually to keep sight of his biographical *ego* . . . as rhetoric, fun, or footman, to his grand and public *ego*, without impertinence or ever confounding them" (*JMN*, 11:203). Neither conflict nor contradiction nor confusion is inherent in the movement from the individual to the universal, from the private to the public. A man need only "speak [his] latent conviction, and it shall be the most universal sense" (*CW*, 2:27); what is more, "the more exclusively idiosyncratic a man is, the more general and infinite he is. . . . In listening more intently to our own reason, we are not becoming . . . more selfish, but are . . . falling back on truth itself, and God" (*JMN*, 3:199). The abnegation of self, which, in another context, we have seen as the antinomian's defense against accusations of self-love, in Emerson provides a philosophical bulwark against the dangers of individualism.

The irresistible and unalterable fact underlying the correspondence between the particular and the universal is the fact of God in man. Hutchinson, who regarded felt knowledge of the indwelling of the spirit as a prelude to grace, saw God in some men, the saints. Metaphorically speaking, she maintained that justification meant an automatic adjustment of her "almanack" to God's "meridian." If her bearings coincided with those of the Puritan community, so much the better, but if not, her alignment was nonetheless perfect. Since the antinomian cannot invariably reconcile the dictates of the graceful heart with the demands of society, the individualism implicit in such a stance prefigures competition between these. This competition Emerson disallows by defining the social order out of his paradigm.

In a grand democratic gesture Emerson ascribed divinity to all men. Some, the "secondary men," by refusing to listen to God within, act as though they are evil. These are, at worst, misled: the potential for virtue resides undiminished in their hearts. "Representative men," on the other hand, are the true exemplars of individualism. Paradoxically, they are those whom Emerson calls "no individual, but a universal man." Neatly inverting the usual paradigm, he argues that out of conformity—imitation, in Emerson's parlance—come secondary men, mere parrots of social convention and current opinion. Individualism, self-reliance, gives birth to the representative, universal man, and that man perfectly embodies the ideals of his society, if not its forms. Emerson's representative man, insofar as he is one expression of the Universal Mind, arrives by way of idiosyncrasy at a set of values universally acknowledged.

Emerson assumed that "what was right for Emerson was happily right for the nation. And this because the world was made so, with individualism generating public morality as surely as free enterprise in the marketplace did the general welfare."[21] Recent histories have cast a shadow across our rosy picture of America in the "era of the common man" as an expanding, fluid, idealistic, and increasingly democratic nation. We no longer believe with Tocqueville that Jackson's America was marked by unusual equality and social mobility. Rather, the early nineteenth century appears to have been a period of rapid industrialization and urbanization, punctuated by economic depression, suffering from an unprecedented concentration of wealth, fraught with unemployment and labor strife. Despite their "pronouncements in favor of laissez faire," the Jacksonians, one scholar has claimed, were "beset by fears of a world out of control."[22] Massachusetts, in spite of its relative insulation from economic hardship, was no less fearful than the rest of the nation. As Anne C. Rose has pointed out, by the 1830s "Bostonians had moved away from the Christian beliefs and institutions which had structured social life in the preindustrial city." Old cultural boundaries had grown increasingly indistinct, and the need to mark out new ones by identifying "heretics" of all kinds had become pressing.[23]

Increasingly, the prevailing ideology assuaged these fears by representing a world in which unfettered self-interest would exploit the limitless resources of the nation and produce, at once, individual affluence and national prosperity. Inequality was, indeed, to be seen everywhere, but this only reflected the difficulty some men had in identifying or acting in their best interest; certainly it was no necessary product of the social structure. By the 1830s the myth of the land of opportunity had come into being. Given elbow room and a little ambition, not *any* ordinary man but *every* man with the capacity to do so could rise. This vision of boundless opportunity not only promised the success of individual endeavor but allowed as well for the equation of personal and public well-being. As each American busily pursued his fortune, he contributed, however unwittingly, to the affluence of the nation. Self-interest would insure the welfare of all.

Emerson's individualism bears this same relation to public morality. As each man looked to himself and found the perfect law written in his heart, he would be brought into harmony with all other men. Self-reliance would provide the set of individual judgments from which the social ethic would be gleaned. Despite Emerson's distaste for the Jacksonians, it is no accident that his philosophy should mimic in this odd way the Smithian economics that increasingly dominated Jacksonian thinking. Just as Adam Smith posited that if the market mechanism—the laws of accumulation and population—were permitted to function undisturbed they would prompt a movement toward national prosperity, so Emerson was sure that the laws of correspondence and compensation would bring into being a society of representative men. Self-reliance would not pit men against one another but would, instead, usher in a public morality to which all would assent because the boundaries between one and all, self and other, the unique and the ordinary would have disappeared.

The analogy between Emersonian individualism and free enterprise is apt. The logic that funnels the private into the public is, in both cases, the same. More important, however, this analogy highlights the fact that Emerson's mode of presentation confounds economic and moral terms. In fact, Emerson's writing is so full of commercial rhetoric that one can scarcely open an essay or journal without discovering examples of its use: "Put God in your debt. Every stroke shall be repaid. The longer the payment is witholden, the better for you: for compound interest on compound interest is the rate and usage of this exchequer" (CW, 2:69). Whether or not we call this the language of "moral ledgerism"[24] and see in it an expression of Weber's Protestant ethic, the ease with which Emerson uses the language of the marketplace to describe the moral universe is telling. Free enterprise offers one more vocabulary through which to enunciate universal principles: it is a metaphor for the system of law that prevails in nature. That is to say, free enterprise is not, for Emerson, merely one of a number of equally artificial economic arrangements: unlike socialism, for example, it is natural, it corresponds. The evidence of this is that it teaches the necessary lessons.

In a striking resemblance to Chauncy, Emerson insists that "you shall not so arrange property as to remove the motive to industry. If you refuse rent and interest, you make all men idle and immoral. As to the poor, a vast proportion have made themselves so" (*JMN*, 10:312). Property, debt, and industry, in other words, like the roses outside Emerson's window, teach all that men need to know. Here, as in Chauncy's sermon on the idle poor, industry and morality are linked in such a way that the failure to fulfill one's calling itself signifies moral failure. Like Chauncy, Emerson speaks from outside the problem, and, like Chauncy, he is horrified at the specter of an idle and thus poor and thus immoral—and thus, of course, dangerous—populace. In defending against the threat of the disempowered, however, Emerson turns not to the prerogatives of class—having written community out of his transcendent scheme of things, he can hardly invoke its terms—but instead to a monolithic assertion of the ratification of free enterprise in nature itself. Morality, then, is not only analogous to but dependent on the incentives of a free enterprise system. Or, to put it the other way around, Emerson can use free enterprise as a metaphor for the perfect system of law that prevails in nature because he sees in it the paradigm for a natural morality.

The fact that the economic system does not work flawlessly in no way invalidates its principles. In every realm of human action, man's gifts are adequate, but that does not ensure their proper use:

> There is imparted to every man the Divine light of reason sufficient not only to plant corn and grind wheat by but also to illuminate all his life his social, political, religious actions. . . . with this inseparable condition; Every man's Reason is sufficient for his guidance, *if used* . . . Democracy/Freedom, has its roots in the Sacred truth that every man hath in him the divine Reason or that though few men . . . live according to the dictates of Reason, yet all men are created capable of doing so. This is the equality and the only equality of all men. To this truth we look when we say, 'Reverence thyself. Be true to thyself.'
>
> (*JMN*, 4:356–57)

That this passage echoes the rhetoric of the Declaration of Independence and of other Revolutionary documents suggests how thoroughly Emerson had incorporated the lessons of the nation. If free enterprise fails to produce prosperity, if individualism does not lead to an ideal public morality, it is only because the world has not yet achieved that state of "American" perfection toward which it tends by the laws of nature and of providence.

Having observed the facility with which Emerson slips from the economic to the moral, and having seen how readily he puts the vocabulary of commerce to use in describing divine law, it is not surprising to find that the individual subsumes the social in his writings. This is not to say that Emerson had no quarrel with America as he found it. His father's son, he detested the violent activism of the Jacksonians—the grasping materialism, the leveling influence, the violent activism of his countrymen—and he greatly feared the rise to power of what he called "the Middling Interest." "Eager, solicitous, hungry, rabid, busybodied America," he called it. While acknowledging the evils of slavery and imperial adventure, however, he held himself aloof from the reform movements of his day.²⁵ Ultimately, he would argue that the remedy for all these accidental social ills, from the false relations of the marketplace to the removal of the Indians, would come, in the fullness of time, when the true principles of America were embodied in a self-reliant citizenry.

Emerson shared the national faith in equal opportunity, individual responsibility, and inevitable progress. The Jacksonian dream of material success and his vision of a nation of representative men mirror one another. In both cases nature outweighs circumstances; given that man is endowed with the capacity for self-improvement, on the one hand, or reason, on the other, individual failure, like poverty, is simply the result of not putting natural gifts to good use. Nonetheless, the "infinite potential of man" is infinite only in some men. The myth of social equality did not prevent Americans from accepting class distinctions, poverty, the misery of some as inevitable any more than its philosophical counterpart prevented Emerson from asserting that "you may as well ask a loom which weaves huckabuck why it does not make cashmere, as expect poetry from this engineer, or a chemical discovery from that jobber. In certain men," Emerson goes on, "digestion and sex absorb the vital force. . . . The more of these drones perish the better for the hive."[26]

The trouble with America, as Emerson saw it, was that its citizens did not take the lessons of the republic to heart. Unfortunately, the ordinary man thought that his intervention was required to bring about a better world. As a result, he neglected the true route of progress: he failed to attend to himself and thus failed to discover the universal movement toward perfection. He did not see that "every man finds a sanction for his simplest claims and deeds, in decisions of his own mind, which he calls Truth and Holiness" and that "in these decisions all the citizens find a perfect agreement. . . . All forms of government symbolize one immortal government" (*CW*, 3:124–5). If once the average man saw this, he, like Emerson, could say, "I will let the Republic alone until the Republic comes to me" (*JMN*, 5:479) and be sure that it would. He would see that reformers and great men of action, admirable characters that they are, are to be admired not for their deeds as deeds but as these signify an unflagging faith in the self. Truly self-reliant, grand examples of the representative man, these heroes provide the pattern for all men to follow. What Emerson offers, finally, is the optimism of passive cooperation with a world changing always for the better. His is a perfectionism stripped of all danger. Self-trust "will lead . . . to perfection which has no type yet in the universe, save only in the Divine Mind" (*JMN*, 3:199), but which is not beyond "the bounds of reasonable expectation from a man" (*JMN*, 5:97). This typeless perfection manifests itself in the equation of the "exclusively idiosyncratic" and the "general and infinite." Individual and social good fuse in the quest for perfection as in all else:

> Build, therefore, your own world. As fast as you conform your life to the pure idea in your mind, that will unfold its great proportions. A correspondent revolution in things will attend the influx of the spirit. So fast will disagreeable appearances, swine, spiders, snakes, pests, mad-houses, prisons, enemies, vanish . . . the advancing spirit . . . shall draw beautiful faces, and

warm hearts, and wise discourse, and heroic acts, around its
way, until evil is no more seen.

(CW, 1:45)

In Emerson everything depends at last on point of view.
Look at the world in the ordinary way and idiosyncrasy divides
men, society seems inequitable, government evil, and man selfish. But look again, from the vantage point of "that Unity, that
Over-Soul, within which every man's particular being is contained and made one with all other" (CW, 2:160), and the world
is transformed. All that once seemed unjust, all that once caused
despair, now seems "wisdom and virtue and power and beauty." The change in point of view alters the face of reality. Things
as they are become, conveniently, things as they should be:
"The radical tragedy of nature seems to be the distinction of
More and Less. . . . It seems a great injustice. But see the facts
nearly, and these mountainous inequalities vanish. Love reduces them. . . . The heart and soul of all men being one, this
bitterness of *His* and *Mine* ceases. His is mine. I am my brother,
and my brother is me" (CW, 2:71–72). Whether "Less" would
assent to this as readily as "More" is at least debatable. What is
striking in this passage is the degree to which Emerson relies
on altered perception to make intervention in the world's arrangements unnecessary. Inequality, the evils of government,
injustice, egotism are all swept away by the simple act of re-
adjusting one's vision. While Emerson carefully refuses to lend
his support to the status quo, he describes the relationship between the self and society in ways that nonetheless make it
more easily acceptable. By insisting that, rightly regarded, all
men are one, for example, Emerson invalidates indignation; he
writes class conflict out of his universe. If all men are brothers,
if his really is mine, then there are no longer grounds for such
conflict. If the world Emerson inhabited was not yet the one he
"thought," it nonetheless promised to become so.

Despite his reliance on invisible sources of knowledge and
morality, Emerson ruled out the possibility that his philosophy
would give rise to the antisocial, the irreligious, or the merely
egotistical. The Puritan distinction between "substantial" and

"circumstantial" works served to contain idiosyncrasy by discounting its significance. It allowed the ministers to assert the validity of visible signs of conversion while leaving room for individual variation. Emerson made a similar, though far more encompassing, distinction. Men differ from one another as a crystal differs from a drop of water; their "circumstances" are so totally unlike that men tend to assume that they are intrinsically different. But at base all men—all nature, for that matter—are part of the same "substance." They are unified because they all reflect the same moral laws; the same Over-soul infuses all things. Thus is evil transitory in Emerson's world, and justice permanent and *a priori*. Compensation is reflex: "He who does a good deed, is instantly enobled himself. He who does a mean deed, is by the action itself contracted" (*CW*, 1:78). Society is, finally, only a conglomeration of individual men, all of them sharing the same divinity, all moving ever closer to a state of perfection. In this sense, it is not the larger organic sum his father took it to be but a mere accident. If, at a given moment in history, society metes out rewards and punishments wrongly, this neither detracts from the lessons of the inner self nor makes any less inevitable universal progress.

But Emerson believed as well that men are prone to concentrate on means rather than ends. They see danger in diversity, anarchy in self-reliance, safety in conformity. The world moves in its appointed course regardless, but this fundamental misunderstanding impedes its progress. Like the enthusiast, "enraptured with the grandeur of his discovery," who "imagines that whosoever would make the same must think as he has thought," man fails to see the essential unity of all things: "In his wanderings he has come out upon the shore of the Ocean and astonished he believes you must walk thro' the same woods, climb the same mountains, and be led by the same guide." The "wise Christian," on the contrary, "sees and rejoices in the evidence brought by so many and independent witnesses that the Ocean has been discovered" (*JMN*, 3:207). Governments, churches, reformers—societies of all sorts— share the attributes of the enthusiast. Lacking faith that any but themselves can find the Ocean, they dare not turn men out on their own. Convinced that many will be lost in the forest or perish on the mountain, they pass out maps, make rules, appoint guides. They fail to understand that all routes, however circuitous, lead to the same Ocean.

Writing about the social experiments of the New England reformers in 1844, Emerson makes clear the "magic" by which "actual individualism" will yield social union. Praiseworthy as he thought the work of the reformers, Emerson believed it founded on an erroneous faith in "covenants." The joining together of men in contractual relationship only "cramp[s] and diminish[es] the individual of his proportion." The reformers fail to realize that "the union is only perfect when all the uniters are isolated." Their methods work against them. All they need do is leave the individual alone "to recognize in every hour and place the secret soul," and he will "go up and down doing the works of a true member, and, to the astonishment of all, the work will be done with concert, though no man spoke" (*CW*, 3:157). Just as Emerson was sure that the abstract principles of democracy and capitalism were as natural as the laws governing the physical universe, so he believed that our discontent with the world only measures the distance we have strayed from that perfect self-reliance which ensures its right ordering. To a society worried about the decline of old values and the impact of a newly empowered class of self-made men, Emerson offered a failsafe method for distinguishing true individualism from false: the genuinely self-reliant man would inevitably prove to be the perfect member; true individualism would yield "union," not anarchy. The proof of the man was in his works. If antinomianism has a place in our consideration of Emerson, it is in its capacity as boundary marker, as Emerson's way to differentiate between that self-reliance which guarantees social harmony and a misguided and potentially subversive assertion of self.

My use of the masculine pronoun throughout this discussion of Emerson's philosophy is not accidental. In every respect, from his advocacy of a "spermatic" language to be ejaculated by newly empowered men to his assumptions about individual autonomy, Emerson's essays assume the subordination—social, natural, and grammatical—of women. As Emerson's oversized Man-God incorporates dissent into himself, so Emerson enlarges the masculine to include the feminine, which comes then to exist only as an ideal version of what men might be. Ironically, the greater restraints imposed on women in the seventeenth century seems to have allowed them greater leeway to create themselves as others. The infinitely expansive social universe pictured by the nineteenth century, on the contrary, simply absorbed Woman as its ideal form.

In the seventeenth-century accounts of the antinomian crisis, we traced the empowerment of the figure of Anne Hutchinson and the emergence, through that empowered figure, of the antinomian as the type of dissent. The fulfillment of the figure of Hutchinson depended on the rendering of woman as fecund seductress. The mother of monsters, she was liable at any moment (and in a multitude of forms) to bring the downfall of Truth and established order. The danger that social roles would be abandoned was located in the very nature of Woman. As we have seen, the association of gender and dissent made possible the further association of women and the disempowered during the Great Awakening. And this called up the specter of overwhelming democracy, a democracy Chauncy saw as implicit in the fluid relationship between sign and meaning in the language of the revival.

The subordination of Woman both in Emerson's language and, as we shall see, in his direct representation of her alters the gender implications of the early narratives. By doing so, it changes as well the relationship between women and power those narratives asserted. Located exclusively in a role that defines her out of society and thereby makes her the ultimate guarantor of social harmony, Woman is, in Emerson, wholly without danger. The power to create, the power to bring monsters into the world, which was conferred on her, however reluctantly, by the colonial narratives, is absent in Emerson. This form of power had allowed Woman to stand as an emblem for the empowerment of others, men among them. And insofar as the disempowered were defined as other the Woman could

stand as the figure for dissent. As less—and therefore better—
she is a cipher. Even as he asserts the special power of Woman,
Emerson ensures that that power not be understood as generating disorder. Shifting the balance of the gender argument we
have located in the story of Anne Hutchinson, he enables the
sentimentalization of the figure of the female dissenter in Hawthorne and Stowe.

6

The Lady or the President

Emerson's views on the nature of female power are set out in a little-known lecture delivered to the Woman's Rights Convention in Boston in 1855. Entitled, "Woman," this lecture indicates how the danger of the empowered female we have seen typified by Anne Hutchinson might be contained. Or rather, it shows why, properly empowered, she need not be contained. For "Woman" makes the case that true womanhood, with its natural and peculiar powers of affection and divination, is not antithetical to representative manhood but, rather, its ideal. By much the same means that he used to demonstrate that perfect self-reliance yields perfect membership, Emerson transforms the empowered woman from a figure of defiance to one of deference. That disempowering transformation stands at the heart of my argument.

The subject of Emerson's lecture is the literal empowerment of women, the extension of the franchise. Gathered to consider the position of women in America seven years after Seneca Falls, the Boston convention apparently concerned itself with both the equality of the sexes broadly construed and the specific question of women's suffrage. In any event, these two considerations—the essential nature of Woman and the matter of the vote—structure Emerson's lecture. The argument Emerson offers in support of female suffrage depends, in fact, on his prior assertion of the inevitable and natural disempowerment of women. As historians of feminism have pointed out, the eventual extension of the franchise to women did not result in their larger social enfranchisement, as many had hoped it would. The rendering of Woman on which Emerson's argument rests may suggest some of the reasons for this disappointment. But beyond this, "Woman" establishes the relevance of definitions and redefinitions of gender to the concept of individualism in America. Whether as quintessential other or as the ideal form of generic Man, from the periphery or from the center, what Woman defines is the problem of individual autonomy.

In the story of Anne Hutchinson the woman who claims total dependence on Christ is by that very dependence empowered to act without reference to temporal community and thus, potentially, against it. The private and unassailable authority to which she gives her allegiance competes with the authority of the community. As a woman—that is, as one whose identity is taken to be conferred by that community—the claim to autonomy (even masked as dependence) itself makes her monstrous. And it implies, further, the monstrousness of all those others whose autonomy is not assumed. In this sense Woman marks the limits of individualism, the boundary at which self-assertion becomes heretical and, therefore, subject to restraint. In Emerson's address this sequence is inverted. Dependence remains a source of empowerment, but it empowers a feminine virtue that, by definition, precludes the possibility of autonomy. In this version Woman stands as the fixed center that counterbalances the centrifugal force of a male individualism.

Emerson opens his lecture with an account of women's strength, a strength he represents as equal to the strength of men but different from it. Women are, he begins, oracular and intuitive beings. Their wisdom, which is "all wisdoms," reveals itself not in the reasoned statement or the logical discourse of men but in the "inconsiderate word." Knowing everything by virtue of her extreme sensitivity, Woman, it seems, does not know that she knows—and this is her greatest virtue. Whereas Man is strong by "will," Woman is "strong by sentiment," or, in Emerson's metaphor, he is the "rudder," she the "sail."[1] But will is not what God—or Transcendentalism—requires of us. In fact, as Emerson quickly points out, true religiosity demands humility just as transcendence requires the "transparent" self. And humility is, for Emerson, the "omnipotence" of Eve. Clearly this Eve is not the powerful seductress of the Anne Hutchinson story, yet the humility of Emerson's Eve is unquestionably a kind of power. Woman's power, he explains, consists of affection and sentiment. Hers is the "power of divination," by virtue of which all women are, potentially at least, as threatening as Anne Hutchinson.

But only potentially. The very impressionability that makes "what [women] say and think . . . the shadow of coming events," that allows women to achieve a "religious height" unattainable by men, is a direct function of their position in society. Naturally in command of special powers of divination, Woman would be dangerous were it not for her "sequestration from affairs." Domesticity—or, one is tempted to say, disenfranchisement—both keeps and makes her safe, not because she has no place in the world she might defy but because her "place" confers what power she has. Protected from "the injury to the moral sense which affairs often inflict," Woman has a moral force unmatched by men, but she maintains this force only insofar as she keeps her place. Power, Emerson explains, resides not in the "masculine woman," who "is not strong," but in the "lady," sequestered and pure.

Emerson himself acknowledges the class issue involved in this representation of Woman. "We commonly say," he points out, "that easy circumstances seem somehow necessary to the finish of the female character" (W, 341). And indeed the "civilized" and sequestered lives of the humble Eves and patient Griseldas he pictures would appear to require the leisure of a middle-class existence. But as is the case for "universal" men, true women create by their nature the circumstances that best suit them: "They are always making that civilization which they require; that state of art, of decoration, that ornamental life in which they best appear" (W, 341). The "lady" in whom power reposes is, then, the lady who properly exercises that power by overseeing the "department of taste and comeliness" (W, 342). Emerson's lady lives in a world of "society, conversation, decorum, dances, colors, forms . . . fair approaches . . . [and] agreeable architecture." She emits from her very pores "a colored atmosphere . . . wave upon wave of rosy light" through which she regards "all objects" (W, 343). She need not *be* a lady of leisure, for, in her proper place, she shares the sensibility, if not the circumstances, of the middle-class lady.

Sensibility, in "Woman," is the female complement to vision elsewhere in Emerson's writing. Whereas for Man, to see the world anew is to rebuild it, for Woman there is no analogous transformative act. Receiving impressions and emitting light, she is medium, not seer, oracle, not prophet, or, to shift the terms, poem but never poet. Emerson's friend Margaret Fuller, whose *Woman in the Nineteenth Century* shares the language of "Woman," had tried to have it otherwise. In fact, one measure of the inevitability of Emerson's logic given the terms he uses to represent Woman is their intransigence in the hands of Fuller whose agenda in *Woman in the Nineteenth Century* is explicitly feminist. Speaking at once for the right of women to be sea captains if they wish and for their "especial genius," Fuller argues for women's equality on the grounds of both sameness and difference. But neither argument, as it turns out, yields a vision of Woman as autonomous.

Fuller's allusion to the story of Orpheus and Eurydice illustrates the problem:

> Not a few believe . . . that the time is come when Eurydice is to call for an Orpheus, rather than Orpheus for Eurydice; that the idea of Man, however imperfectly brought out, has been far more so than that of Woman; that she, the other half of the same thought, the other chamber of the heart of life, needs now to take her turn in the full pulsation.[2]

Woman here can either reproduce Man or stand as his alternative; what she cannot do is stand alone. As muse become poet, Eurydice singing Orpheus's song, she is simply absorbed into Man. As the "other half" of a completed being, she is defined vis-à-vis the first half. Moreover, as Fuller explains, the qualities of her different, female genius—"electrical in movement, intuitive in function, spiritual in tendency"—make it "more native . . . to her to be the living model of the artist . . . to inspire and receive the poem, than to create it."[3] If she chooses to be the poet, Woman becomes Man. If she acts out of her feminine nature, she can only be poem.

Feminine qualities are not Woman's exclusively, of course, but only in greater proportion. Nonetheless, Fuller's vision of Woman as the complement that completes Man suggests the origins of her inequality and the impossibility of her autonomy. Harmony, Beauty, and Love—the feminine side of "Man considered as a whole"—are virtues that can be expressed and appreciated only in relation to others; in the absence of observer or recipient they cease to exist. The masculine virtues of Energy, Power, and Intellect, on the contrary, are virtues of agency and autonomy. They require a world in and on which to act but they require an other only to embody the spiritual ideal that they themselves enact.

The vision of Man made "whole" by Woman—of a transcendent being, twofold in his development but finally and inevitably one—that obstructs Fuller's argument for female "self-subsistence" shapes Emerson's exposition on Woman. Fuller's argument against the idea of Woman "absorbed by . . . relation" and for "Woman as Woman" is undermined by an ideal of a human wholeness achieved by the joining of feminine and masculine complements; Emerson's far less radical effort to defend female suffrage depends on that ideal.

In fact, Emerson's sequestered lady, enveloped in a "warm-tinted mist," whose "starry crown" is her affection, the "victim" of a "finer temperament" than that of men and, consequently, subject to "tears, and gaieties, and faintings, and glooms, and devotion to trifles" (W, 349), resembles no one so much as the sentimental heroine of mid-nineteenth-century fiction, a figure whose usual function is to marry and, in that way, "complete" man. It is to this woman that Emerson would give the vote. If at first this seems a paradox, it is a paradox that Emerson fully exploits. Emerson's support of female suffrage is founded on his understanding of women as empowered only insofar as they fulfill their traditional subordinate role. Women are, "in their nature, more relative" than men: "Out of place they lose half their weight, out of place they are disenfranchised" (W, 341). The play on words here is crucial. Since Nature, of its own accord, will disenfranchise the woman who steps out of her place, there is nothing to fear in the extension of the franchise to women. In fact, the woman thus enfranchised—the lady—is the ideal occupant of the ordered universe that defines her place: "Let us have the true woman, the adorner, the hospitable, the religious heart, and no lawyer need be called in to write stipulations, the cunning clauses of provision, the strong investitures,—for woman moulds the lawgiver and writes the law" (W, 355). In the early Hutchinson narratives, Woman as other is the personification of dissent; in Emerson, Woman as other becomes the ideal aspect of the one and, in this sense, the lawgiver. As Emerson puts it, the "organic office" of women as "mediators between those who have knowledge and those who want it," that is, their maternal and educational office, is fulfilled in a law enacted by the well-tutored sons of the perfect mothers who themselves embody it.

In Emerson's lecture Woman is the representative in Man and thus entirely safe. Isolated by the very contract that calls community into being and thus invulnerable to its corruption, she is immediately capable of that perfect identification with the universe to which men aspire. Still, vis-à-vis Man, Woman is a "relative" self. Emerson quotes one Mrs. Lucy Hutchinson writing about her late husband to the effect that "all that she was, was *him*, while he was hers, and all that she is now, at best, but his pale shade" (W, 339). Woman may be the ideal in Man, but she is not all of Man. And, incomplete except in him, she is herself a nonself, a "shade"—or a pure medium for God's beams. "Delicate as iodine to light, and thus more impressionable" (W, 337) than Man, she is the light, he the transparent eyeball. Herself incomplete, she is the God in Man but never the Man-God.

In the interest of showing that women's suffrage poses no threat to the status quo, Emerson demonstrates that it is the status quo that lends women their greatest power. In fact, so entwined are the interests of women and those of the prevailing social order, as Emerson represents these, that the enfranchisement of women can be offered as a way to guarantee the hegemony of the standing order. Answering what he sees as the most urgent objections to female suffrage, Emerson makes clear the interests with which he imagines the woman voter will identify. The claim that women are unfit to vote because they are ignorant of the world and therefore prone to aim at "abstract right without allowing for circumstances" is, for Emerson, "not a disqualification, but a qualification" (W, 352). It is a qualification not only, as might be expected, because right is right but even more compellingly because "an educated and religious vote, representing the . . . desires of honest and refined persons," as women invariably are, would, Emerson hoped, offset the vote of the "half-brutal intemperate population" (W, 353) of poor immigrants whom he so deeply feared. The virtuous votes of women might, Emerson thought, outnumber the votes based on "imperative class-interests" (W, 353). Being virtuous—that is, having nothing to do with either action or the public sphere —women, unlike men, transcend class; conveniently, they prove their disinterestedness by aligning themselves with the refined and the educated. In Emerson's lecture enfranchised Woman is associated not with the disempowered, as she was for Chauncy, but with those in power. As to the objection that women will be "unsexed" and "contaminated" by their participation in political affairs, this Emerson regards merely as demonstrating the barbarity of "our existing politics," a barbarity he associates with the corruption of politicians who, beset by class interests, fail to enact into law the true principles of the republic, embodied, of course, in Woman.

In every respect, then, "Woman" reverses the meaning of female empowerment as it was imagined in the narrative accounts of Anne Hutchinson. The by now familiar oracular and generative powers of the American Jezebel are attributed to generic Woman in Emerson's lecture, but rather than raising the specter of autonomous (and therefore dangerous) selfhood, they are tied to a vision of Woman as nonself, a vision akin to the antinomian's self-in-Christ. The relationship between Woman and society in Emerson's lecture is perfectly circular: she is simultaneously the product of her circumscribed setting and its creator. Without that setting, Emerson insists, she is not Woman but a thoroughly anomalous being, the "masculine" woman, who, like other anomalies, is too monstrous to contemplate. In fact, although he defines Woman in social terms,

Emerson dismisses the problem of the "masculine" woman by asserting that she is so *unnatural* as to be without force. In her proper place, however, Woman is perfect medium, both as she focuses God's beams and as she focuses social intercourse. She is at once less and better than her male counterpart but she is other only insofar as she is ideal.

As Emerson imagines her, Woman empowered is by that very fact disabled, and the particular form of her disablement guarantees her perfection. The same assumptions about the private nature of Woman that elicited William Emerson's more conventional incredulity at the Puritans' fear of Anne Hutchinson inform his son's thinking, but the implications of the younger Emerson's representation of Woman extend much further. The disinterested virtue of women is virtue indeed, but its disinterestedness contains its potential force. Thus, Emerson can argue that "the new movement" for female suffrage will not result in an equal competition for power between men and women. Quite the contrary, since every woman is "the wife or the daughter of a man" (W, 355), since Woman is by nature a "relative" rather than an autonomous being, competition is unthinkable. The movement for women's rights is necessarily, then, "a tide shared by the spirits of man and woman" (W, 356). "You may proceed" Emerson assures his suffragist audience, "in the faith that whatever the woman's heart is prompted to desire, the man's mind is simultaneously prompted to accomplish" (W, 356). The reciprocal relationship between women's desires and men's acts not only gives evidence of universal truth but also precludes conflict. Ratifying female suffrage by way of the powers of divination and affection, powers simultaneously enabled and contained by Woman's sequestration from affairs, Emerson demonstrates that suffrage cannot, paradoxically, confer power. Thus, Woman as prophetess invariably predicts a rosy and harmonious future, not a coming catastrophe.

In Emerson's lecture enfranchised Woman is denied the power to oppose; at the same time, Woman empowered—that is, autonomous—is by nature disenfranchised. Of course, by insisting on the complicity of Nature in the maintenance of the social design, by demonstrating with such care the naturalness of existing social arrangements, "Woman" silently acknowledges the frightening possibility of an Anne Hutchinson. It is precisely the specter of female autonomy and the allied possibility of equal competition, albeit between incomplete beings, that is banished by Emerson's assertion of a perfectly complementary relationship between Man and Woman. Yet insofar as the paradox on which Emerson's case for women's suffrage rests renders female dissent unnatural, "Woman" also refines Emerson's solution to the larger dilemma of individualism: the possibility that, encouraged to pursue the self, autonomous Man will move ever further from that "feminine" center which is ideal community. By first defining the feminine *as* the interior, the intuitive, and the relational and then enfranchising it, Emerson not only contains any threat Woman might represent but makes possible (perhaps even necessary) the location of the feminine in the masculine. A potentially lawless and exclusively male individualism is thus checked, externally, by the civilizing influence of women and, internally, by the "feminine" heart. Conflating the requirements of society and the imperatives of Nature, "Woman" resolves what Fuller called the "great radical dualism" of the sexes into yet another image of universal harmony, another completed circle, and suggests that Man completed by Woman answers the problem of individual autonomy.

Just as the story of Anne Hutchinson is implicit in Emerson's rendition of Woman, so the potential for the shift in meaning we have traced in Emerson is implicit in the story of Anne Hutchinson. Once gender itself (and its alter ego, class) could be taken to image the danger of antinomianism—that is, the danger of the nonself asserting selfhood—then gender could be used to contain that danger. The arrogant Jezebel and the humble Eve imply one another, not just in Emerson's lecture but in the larger cultural discussion of dissent and individualism in nineteenth-century America. If we turn from Emerson to his contemporary George Bancroft, who addressed the problem of heresy and individual autonomy as a historian rather than a philosopher, the dramatic implications of Emerson's transformation of the antinomian into the lady becomes clearer. For if the antinomian is an autonomous dissenter, dangerous because she refers only to herself, the lady is a lady by virtue of her dependence on and completion of Man. Once duality is replaced by perfect unity, the feminine can be understood as an ideal aspect of Man, and Woman need not be invoked at all. In this form, gender informs history as thoroughly as philosophy.

As Russel Nye has pointed out, George Bancroft discovered in "the study of the American past" proof of the same march toward perfection that Emerson would later find revealed in "the voiceless intimations of his soul."[4] Despite their friendship and the similarities in their backgrounds—both were sons of Unitarian ministers, Massachusetts-bred and Harvard-educated—we do not expect the Democratic historian to share so thoroughly the language of the Transcendentalist philosopher. Bancroft, after all, not only was a committed Jacksonian but also aspired to be a modern historian. His *History of the United States* was to be a new and "authentic" history, founded on the "principles of historical skepticism" and derived "entirely from the writings and sources which were the contemporaries of the events that are described." It is surprising, then, to find Bancroft in 1834 struggling with the same distinction between true and false individualism that would exercise Emerson a few years later and to find him arriving at a similar conclusion.

Recounting the story of Anne Hutchinson in his effort to find the "germ of our institutions," Bancroft, like William Emerson and others, is divided in his loyalties.[5] Believing that "the spirit of the colonies demanded freedom from the beginning," he is at once distressed at the intolerance and exaggerated fears of the first settlers and certain that the enthusiasm of the Hutchinsonians could not be countenanced. Rather than see the controversy as a conflict between reason and enthusiasm like those who came before him, however, Bancroft attempts a more sophisticated reading of the episode. "Amidst the arrogance of spiritual pride, the vagaries of undisciplined imaginations, and the extravagances to which the intellectual power may be led in its pursuit of ultimate principles"—all of which Bancroft took to

characterize the antinomian controversy—he, like his predecessors, locates "two distinct parties." But he differentiates
these not by their doctrine but, first, by their composition and,
second, by their goals for the settlement.

As Bancroft represents it, one party consists of the "original settlers, the framers of the civil government . . . intent on
the foundation and preservation of a commonwealth." These
"dreaded unlimited freedom of opinion as the parent of ruin-
ous divisions" and, longing instead for "patriotism, union, and
a common heart,"[6] were reproached as being under a covenant
of works. Bancroft's description of this party is couched in terms
both collective and consensual—these are "settlers," "framers," unanimous in their desire for union. The Hutchinsonians,
on the contrary, are not really a "party" at all but *"individuals,"*
notably Anne Hutchinson, "who had arrived after . . . the
colonies had been established" (my italics). Following Calvin
with "logical precision," they came "to the wilderness for freedom of religious opinion; and they resisted every form of despotism over the mind" (*US*, 306). While their adversaries dreaded unlimited freedom, the antinomians, led by Hutchinson,
"sustained with intense fanaticism the paramount authority of
private judgement" (*US*, 1:306).

The antinomians' resistance to despotism may be commendable, but it quickly becomes clear that *fanatical* self-trust is no
better than intolerance. Taking immediate revelation as the
"guide of their conduct" and insisting on the Holy Spirit as the
"inward companion of man," the antinomians "avowed their
determination to follow the free thought of their own minds,"
little realizing that "individual conscience is often the dupe of
interest and often but a more honorable name for self-will" (*US*,
1:308). Bancroft appears here to deny the very infallibility of
private judgment on which Emerson's optimism will rest, but
in fact the case is more ambiguous. The key term for Bancroft is
"fanatical"; this, unlike "conscience" or "self-trust," defines
antinomianism as a socially destructive expression of the individual will.

Bancroft's distinction between those who emigrated to the
colonies in 1630 and those who arrived in 1634 does little to

solve the problem built into the antinomian controversy for the post-Revolutionary generation. Unwilling to remain simply neutral, Bancroft is faced with the impossible choice of aligning himself either with intolerance or with fanaticism. The antinomians have in their favor an admirable intellectual curiosity. They tried, Bancroft believes, to address "the most profound questions relating to human existence and the laws of the moral world" (*US*, 1:305). Unfortunately, they did this with little thought of the "shipwreck" that might be its result. The founding fathers, by contrast, are quite simply the founding fathers, men whom Bancroft, as their heir, wants to find reasonable and orderly. But they, he admits, may have acted out of blind intolerance: they feared, or maybe only "pretended to fear" (*US*, 1:308), a disturbance of the public peace. In the end, Bancroft sides with the party of order, orthodoxy, and intolerance almost despite himself, but he does this having established, in advance of telling the story of Anne Hutchinson, that repressive intolerance and wild fanaticism are false alternatives.

The story of Roger Williams, which immediately precedes the account of the antinomian controversy in Bancroft's *History*, offers us an alternative to the representation of colonial dissent as a conflict between male repression and female fanaticism. Here, as in the later story, Bancroft extends his sympathy to those who banished Williams, but in this case his generosity is, as it were, purely historical. Living when they did and knowing what they knew, the colonists cannot be blamed for failing to recognize in Williams the spokesman for that perfect individualism which would leave its impression "in characters so deep" that they remain "to the present day, and can never be erased without the total destruction" of the republic. As a spokesman for the modern age, however, Bancroft is unequivocal in his admiration of Williams. Like Penn, like Descartes, like Copernicus, Kepler, and Newton, Williams advocated "the great doctrine of intellectual liberty." He "advanced moral science" and made himself a benefactor of mankind.

Juxtaposing the accounts of Williams and Hutchinson renders the difference in Bancroft's judgments of the two both striking and resonant. Bancroft's varying attitudes toward Williams and Hutchinson rest on a distinction very like the one Emerson draws between the enthusiast and the inquiring Christian—or the antinomian and the lady. Despite the Puritans' mistrust of Williams, it is clear to Bancroft that Williams was anything but subversive in his thinking. Unlike Hutchinson, he was a pure tolerationist. He "would permit persecution of no opinion, of no religion, leaving heresy unharmed by law." Whereas Hutchinson is cast as an opposer, Williams embodies a perfect charity. In her heretical reliance on private judgment, she defies the world; he, insofar as he combines feminine humility and masculine freedom, implies an ideal world even as he renounces the real one. As Bancroft tells it, Williams "was willing to leave Truth alone, in her panoply of light, believing that if, in the ancient feud between Truth and Error, the employment of force could be entirely abrogated, Truth would have much the best of the bargain" (*US*, 1:298). According to Bancroft, Williams stands for nothing less than that perfect liberty out of which both men are convinced Truth will emerge. In contrast to the unfeminine arrogance of Anne Hutchinson, Williams's "most touching trait" was his affection for his persecutors, an affection both Christlike and, in Emerson's terms, womanly in its self-effacement. About these persecutors, Bancroft reports Williams as saying, "'I did ever from my soul, honor and love them, even when their judgement led them to afflict me'" (*US*, 1:301).

In other words, Hutchinson's antinomianism is represented as an enabling, an empowering, doctrine that, insofar as it challenged received truth and insisted on the priority of the self, led inevitably to schism and controversy. Williams's doctrine of intellectual liberty, on the contrary, is "magic," in the Emersonian sense. Leave man to his own devices, meet idiosyncrasy with equanimity, Bancroft's Williams seems to say, and self-reliance will reveal one truth and individualism will yield membership. The genuine alternative to both fanatical self-will and ancient prejudice, then, is a self-reliance so complete that it fails even to engage the world. For Bancroft, this self-reliance is most perfectly exemplified by the Williams who withdrew into soli-

tude—who, literally, sequestered himself—and waited passively, humbly, and forgivingly for those around him to discover the common truth.

Williams is Bancroft's most rarefied example of the individualism to which all Americans should be committed, but perfect
self-trust is not limited to those in retreat from society. His representation of the self-effacing Williams as the model of self-
reliance echoes Emerson's paradoxical solution to the paradox
at the heart of antinomianism: "A trust in yourself . . . will
come only to he who feels that he is nothing." But Bancroft does
not stop with Williams; rather, he goes on to use language that,
in the past, was identified with dissent and disempowerment
to describe a powerful man in charge of the state.

Andrew Jackson died in 1845; among the notables who delivered eulogies in his memory was his ardent admirer George
Bancroft. Bancroft's eulogy, like others of the twenty-five gathered together to form a memorial volume a year later, ascribes
to the late president the very traits formerly attributed to wom-
en and the disenfranchised. That the language of antinomianism could be used to characterize Jackson, whom these eulogists regarded as the best of public leaders, suggests how
complete a transformation of terms had been accomplished by
the 1840s. A male public figure whose greatness is directly associated with his reliance on an intuitive, oracular, and feminine
private self, Jackson is at once the president and the lady.

"Behold . . . the unlettered man of the West," Bancroft begins,

> the nursling of the wilds, the Farmer of the Hermitage, little
> versed in books, unconnected by science with the tradition of
> the past, raised by the will of the people . . . to the central post
> in the civilization of republican freedom. . . . What policy will
> he pursue? What wisdom will he bring from the forest? What
> rules of duty will he evolve from the oracles of his own mind?[7]

Anne Hutchinson's conscience may have been the "dupe of
interest," but not so Andrew Jackson's. In the case of the seventeenth-century antinomian, Bancroft challenges the very possibility of disinterested conscience and associates private judg-

ment with fanaticism. When it comes to Jackson, however, the same law is within and without the man. The forest and the farm that, according to legend, gave birth to Jackson bear good fruit—men in whom the "rules of duty" and "the oracles of the mind" are one and the same. Like Emerson's Man-God, the legendary Jackson comprehends in himself all of America—farmer and frontiersman, high and low, west and east—and, crucially, male and female. Thus enlarged, he incorporates—and negates—all possible dissent.

Bancroft is not alone in portraying Jackson as Emersonian man. The eulogies delivered at Jackson's death, like the popular representations of him during his lifetime, insist again and again on Jackson as the embodiment of that perfect law known only to the "fearless, intuitive, and bold." Jackson is no "slave of routine and detail," no lackey of the written law. In fact, what distinguishes him from his rival, John Quincy Adams, is that he "was the very man to d——n Grotius, Puffendorf, and Vattel; and Adams was the very man to condemn him for that. . . . Jackson cared only for his justification; but Adams was horrified at its mode. Jackson made law, Adams quoted it."[8] Jackson's "love of justice" was so great, says one eulogist, that "he disobeyed the positive orders of his government." Lest we misunderstand the import of that disobedience, however, another echoes Emerson's claim that "there is no crime but has sometimes been a virtue" and observes that "nothing can be more obvious than the distinction between nominal and real obedience."[9]

Clearly, Adams confused the two forms of self-reliance that Emerson and Bancroft alike were at pains to differentiate. He failed to appreciate that in Jackson "the heart inspires the intellect. Its warm and instinctive impulses are more to be trusted than the cold inductions of the understanding . . . the heart sees further than the head. In its deep and silent revelations, flashes, as it were, from another world—Jackson was made conscious that he was an instrument in the hands of Providence."[10] Jackson is imputed the power of immediate revelation; his mind is "clogged by no forms, but goes with the lightning's flash," and the pathway it illuminates is the one best adapted to the glory of America. But beyond this, as the eulogist's language makes clear, Jackson's manly deeds are informed by a feminine self, a self of the heart, impulsive and intuitive. Astonishingly—though, of course, logically too—the inversion Emerson accomplishes in "Woman" reaches its apotheosis in the eulogists' vision of the activist president imbued with feminine virtue. In Jackson, what Woman desires is precisely what Man accomplishes; moreover, wish and act coexist in one body.

The "femininity" of the legendary Jackson has long suggested him as a version of the sentimental hero,[11] but my point goes beyond this. By attributing to Jackson the virtues of the sequestered lady—her powers of divination and affection—the eulogists "complete" him in precisely the sense that Emerson and Fuller alike understood ideal Man to be complete. And, locating feminine virtue not just in a man but in the president, the eulogists propel these virtues out into the world as principles of action as well as ideals. As a way to celebrate Jackson's perfection in retrospect, this vision of masculine action informed by feminine virtue works perfectly well. As we will see, however, the representation of this completed being in action, in a novel, becomes highly problematic.

The celebratory portraits of Andrew Jackson as the "great pioneer" leading the unlettered masses, "educated only by the spirit of freedom," into the American wilderness "whose woods in spring put to shame . . . the cultivated gardens" of the Old World, only partially masks the tension between individual freedom and public law that emerged from the Revolution and was exacerbated by the rapid expansion of the nation. The movement west, as Bancroft knew, might bode ill for America. The same "doctrines of freedom" that made Americans "lovers of adventure" might lead the western settlers "to live in unorganized society, destitute of laws and fixed institutions." From this dire fate Jackson saved them. His function, in Bancroft's account of it, was to lead America away from a dangerous lawlessness by the very liberty he embodied. Paradoxically, Jackson—"bold, determined . . . shrinking from nothing that his heart approved"[12]—assured by his presence that the new territory would not remain an untamed wilderness for long. Bancroft's eulogy for the late president reiterates the lesson that Emerson gleaned from his philosophical musings: the perfect self-reliance of the genuine man will mirror the public world around him; the "isolato" is only the perfect member by another name.

At once actor and medium, male and female, Jackson embodied, in Bancroft's view, the perfect union of inner and outer worlds. "No man with truer instinct received American ideas," he says of Jackson, and "no man expressed them so completely, so boldly, or so sincerely."[13] In the man, Bancroft insists, is the best of the nation, and in the nation, the man. Though Jackson would not have been his example, Emerson too had no doubt that such a conflation would characterize the union ideal in "actual individualism."

Invoking self-creation as the basis of the commonweal, the reigning ideology of the early nineteenth century empowered the interior self. But once empowered, that self could be seen as containing all the subversive possibilities of the unrestrained heart. The interior space marked out by Anne Hutchinson in the seventeenth century had somehow to be filled with a self whose power would guarantee rather than disrupt the larger social arrangement of which it was taken to be the most basic unit. Antinomianism, now understood as a fanatical self-trust generating both social and exegetical anarchy, had to be distinguished from the self-reliance of the true American, with its promise of an ideal social cohesion. The alternative stories of Winthrop's Jezebel and Emerson's Eve worked to clarify this distinction.

Behind their celebrations of liberty and self-sufficiency, Transcendentalist philosopher, Romantic historian, and historical romancer alike worried about how inner and outer selves were to be brought into proper relation. They worried about whether liberty might not slip into lawlessness and about whether the "oracles of the mind," so eminently trustworthy in a Jackson, might not yet lead to a secular antinomianism. The story of Anne Hutchinson became a way to reenact the drama of that interior self which at once authorized and endangered the structure of society. But whereas the historian recounted this drama in male, public terms, the historical novelist spoke a language both feminine and private.

The shade of Anne Hutchinson lingers over any number of historical romances of this period. Throughout Harriet Cheney's *A Peep at the Pilgrims in 1636* (1850), the romantic history of the heretical courtship of the Anglican Edward Atherton and the Puritan Miriam Grey, runs an animated discussion of the charges against Hutchinson. A range of opinions are represented, from Miles Standish, who, at the distance of Plymouth, insists that "if the magistrates would only let her alone, she would soon come to her senses"[14] to an "austere looking man" who sees in her "the spirit of a devil!"[15] The more temperate view that we come to associate with both author and hero is that Hutchinson, though well-intentioned, is carried away by her fanatical beliefs. Daily "advancing some new and absurd doctrine," she, "with a subtlety of argument, and a versatility of talent," gives "error the appearance of consistency and truth."[16] A "golden apple of discord," Hutchinson is legitimately alarming to the "friends of peace and good order" at the same time that she is unquestionably the victim of an "unchristian" persecution. Her fanaticism is such, however, that it leads even Winthrop, that model of Christian charity, to play the role of bigot, although Cheney redeems this foremost of the founders by having him privately defend Hutchinson's motives to Major Atherton. The central issue in *A Peep at the Pilgrims*, however, is intolerance, not antinomianism, and Anne Hutchinson serves as one example among many of the effects of religious bigotry. Yet the problem of intolerance, which Hutchinson, like the young protagonists of the novel, dramatizes, is never adequately resolved in the novel. Miriam and Edward marry, Mr. Grey, who has opposed their union, arrives mysteriously at a new position of universal tolerance, and the story ends. In *A Peep at the Pilgrims*, as in many novels of its kind, fiction solves the problem of history.

Earlier, in John Neal's *Rachel Dyer* (1828), intolerance and, as one scholar points out, filiopietism had emerged victorious in spite of the author's best intentions.[17] Here, Anne Hutchinson, misnamed (or renamed) Elizabeth and cast as a Quaker, returns to Boston in 1660 quite literally as a specter. As the Puritans prepare to execute Mary Dyer, grandmother of our heroine Rachel, Hutchinson's voice commands them from beyond the grave to "set their houses in order" and "get ready the accounts of their stewardship." Later, revealed to a traveler "on the very spot where she and her large family . . . were put to death by the savages," Hutchinson appears with a "look of wrath" and "a speech of power" to denounce the witch hunts and to prophesy disaster to the colony.[18] Neal's Hutchinson speaks across the years not to defend her errors but only to urge against further persecution. She is part of a strategy that pits an enlightened present against a superstitious past.

Hutchinson appears more prominently in Eliza Buckminster Lee's *Naomi, or Boston, Two Hundred Years Ago* (1848). In this case she serves, along with the Quakers, as a foil to our heroine's perfect faith. The trouble with Mrs. Hutchinson, as Lee presents it, is that, succeeding as a prophetess, she perforce failed as a woman. Her "masculine and independent spirit," although it foretold the age of "intellectual insight," obliges the author to see her "martyrdom" as "the fruit of her inordinate self-esteem." "Her blameless life," Lee tells us, "perhaps, left her conscience free from reproach; but when . . . she looked back upon her career, she must have feared that the slimy trail of spiritual pride had sullied the white robes of her martyrdom."[19] Not so the author's creation, who is "too truly a woman" ever to broach "the struggles of her soul" as matter for "public discussion." Naomi is humble, "the soul of benevolence and loving-kindness." Quaker though she is, Naomi partakes of none of the spiritual pride that Lee regards as the Quakers' legacy from Anne Hutchinson. She is "among them . . . but not of them," and lest we wonder what Lee means by this, she explains that her heroine *"thee-d* and *thou-ed* no one" and that her "dress differed from the reigning fashion" only by its "more tasteful simplicity" (*N*, 336).

The difference between Naomi and the fanatical sectarians with whom the Puritans mistakenly associate her lies not in the nature of her essential faith but in its outward tokens—or, as the case may be, in the absence of these. The Quakers are arrogant, and their arrogance is expressed in their singularity of speech and costume. This singularity constitutes, for Lee, a form of contempt for the community, a dramatic, unacceptable, and ultimately "un-Quaker" assertion of self. Naomi, however, is as private and as self-effacing as a woman can be. Her dress and comportment, unlike that of the Quakers, does not merely conform to the "reigning fashion" but perfects it by its simplicity. The Quakerism represented by Anne Hutchinson is an alternative to Puritanism, but Quaker Naomi is its ideal.

Nonetheless, Lee's distinction is problematic at best. On the one hand, she insists that the very "principles" of Quakerism "flattered self-esteem and fostered spiritual pride, and gave to [the Quakers'] deportment an offensive degree of arrogance and contempt for other" (*N*, 336). On the other hand, it is exactly "the essential *principle* of their faith, the belief of the inward voice of truth in the soul" that Naomi holds "above all other inspiration" (*N*, 336). Yet sharing this belief in an inner voice "to be obeyed and honored as the voice of God . . . obeyed rather than the authority of any church" (*N*, 336), she mysteriously remains free from all manifestations of spiritual pride. It has been observed that Lee distinguishes between "two kinds of Quakerism . . . two kinds of religion of the heart,"[20] but nowhere has it been noticed that the "slimy trail" of Anne Hutchinson's arrogance metaphorically separates these two. Like Bancroft and Emerson, Lee understands a difference between those intimations of the truth that lead to humility and compliance and those that point toward antinomianism, between those that confirm membership and those that signal dissent. And, like them, she genders this distinction: the "masculine" Anne Hutchinson is the forebear of the arrogant Quakers, but Naomi is all woman and thus all ideal. Quakerism appears quite literally in two different guises in *Naomi;* Naomi is not Anne Hutchinson, though she is perhaps what Anne Hutchinson might have been, stripped of her self-esteem and thereby feminized. How it is that Naomi can share Hutchinson's faith in the invisible witness of the spirit yet remain perfectly humble Lee never explains.

The closest we come to the terms of the distinction—and to Lee's purpose in invoking Anne Hutchinson—is when, in an explicit reenactment of Hutchinson's trial, Naomi is taken up and examined about her beliefs. From the outset, we are asked to recall Hutchinson's examination, as Naomi contemplates confiding in the sympathetic Reverend John Wilson. Remembering that Hutchinson "gained nothing by her reliance upon the Puritan saint,—the Rev. John Cotton" (*N*, 401), she forgoes all assistance. Naomi, "the orphan girl, ignorant of all but the wisdom of truth and honesty, unlearned in all but the love of the heart," goes to meet the "iron-willed" Puritan fathers unsupported. Clearly, Naomi will not repeat the mistakes of the earlier martyr. In fact, we realize before she even enters the court that Naomi will, in every respect, redeem Hutchinson's errors and thus avert martyrdom altogether. A girl, not a woman, much less a middle-aged mother of fourteen (monsters excepted), Naomi is unversed in theology. No Biblical exegete, she is incapable of challenging the ministers on their own ground as Hutchinson did. Moreover, she is wholly disinclined to challenge them at all, fervently believing as she does in the private nature of religious faith. Whereas Hutchinson's inordinate self-esteem provoked her conflict with the Puritan authorities—in Lee's rendition of the story—and sullied the white robes of her martyrdom, Naomi's confrontation with the Puritan ministers measures not the dimensions of Naomi's pride but the extent to which the fathers have fallen away from their own ideals and, therefore, confirms her sanctity.

Still, the fears articulated by Naomi's interrogator, John Norton, are much the same fears as those Anne Hutchinson tried so unsuccessfully to put to rest, although they are couched in different language. Naomi is accused of relying too heavily on private means of devotion, of refusing public forms of worship. She is queried as to her state of grace, a matter Lee unequivocally asserts should be broached only "in the intimacy of nearest friendship." She is asked whether she denies the Trinity, whether she believes "in the Scriptures as the only rule of faith and practice," and whether she will submit to the rule of the church.

As readers, our understanding of Naomi's response to these questions is at odds with the conclusions of her examiners, although they too come, ultimately, to appreciate Naomi's perfection. We are clearly meant to find Naomi humble, submissive, and more than willing to admit the limits of her "powers of comprehension." Her answers to the court are curiously like a faint, feminine echo of Emerson as she explains, "modestly," of course, that the Bible "appears to me, not religion in itself, but the records of a formal and ceremonial religion" (*N*, 412) or insists that "I must live by the light which God has given me . . . I must live by my own faith. . . . The laws of men are but the injunctions of mortals; but what the spirit dictates is the voice from heaven within us" (*N*, 413) or tremulously points out that "there is a . . . secret and acceptable prayer . . . breathed in the silent heart" (*N*, 409). Naomi's insistence on the authority of the spirit within could, of course, be dangerous, but in case we are not sufficiently reassured by her manner before the ministers, Lee states outright that Naomi "had no sympathy with the Quakers *as disturbers of the church or of the civil order*" (*N*, 411). Oddly enough, it is not Naomi's dissent but her perfect compliance that is at issue.

Thus, when Norton finds in Naomi "the spirit of pride, of an unconverted soul" and claims that this dictates her "arrogant difference from [her] spiritual teachers," (*N*, 414) we know that he is mistaken. Naomi speaks for "those natural feelings" that to her "uninformed spirit . . . took the form of revelations from God." Only in her essential faith in "the sensible and constant direction of the spirit of God in man" does she resemble Hutchinson and the Quakers. In Naomi this faith represents no danger to the standing order, as the conclusion of the novel makes clear. Naomi does not grow into a fanatic, an antinomian, or an egotist, but into the very epitome of true womanhood; she embodies all the missing virtues of the martyred, "masculine" Anne Hutchinson: "Humility continued to form the foundation of her character, upon which had been built the beautiful proportions of Christian grace, forming an harmonious whole, lovely to look upon, comforting and elevating to those who lived within the shadow of her blessed influence" (*N*, 447–48).

Naomi's "naturalness" redeems her from vulgar Quakerism and saves her as well from antinomianism or worse. What defines that naturalness is Naomi's innocent faith in the lessons of the feminine heart. Her repudiation of public authority is safe because the private revelation that supplants that authority prompts her to a "natural," that is, a feminine, virtue indistinguishable from the virtue urged upon her from without. In other words, Naomi's intimations of the truth are true; guided by God, she cannot go astray. Like Emerson, Lee assumes that the "religious heart" of Woman "moulds the lawgiver and writes the law."

But even as Lee insists on Naomi's virtue, she complicates matters by offering the counterexample of Hutchinson's heirs, the Quakers, whose hearts apparently impel them to civil rebellion and spiritual pride. False revelations, Lee insists, lead to lawlessness and heresy and, by their outcome, prove themselves false. That the Puritans in the novel fail to grasp the distinction between Naomi and the other Quakers is hardly surprising, however, since that distinction rests entirely on the authority of the author. The reader is asked to take it on faith that some revelations are truer than others and that this difference is made visible in the deportment, not to mention the clothing, of those who claim special access to the truth. While Lee argues, on the one hand, that Calvinism—a religion "revolting" to "natural feeling"—only exposes its own weakness by finding in Naomi an Anne Hutchinson, she speaks, on the other, for a notion of visible sainthood that closely resembles the Puritan one.

Lee cannot do otherwise than contradict herself, for she fails to engage the larger contradiction implicit in her novel. By refusing to address the question of how Naomi's feminine interior self can be authorized other than by granting her masculine agency, Lee opens the possibility of Naomi as subversive. This possibility she then disallows by asserting what the visible difference between Naomi and the actually subversive Quakers symbolizes: Naomi, who idealizes the civil order, looks different from the Quakers, who jeopardize it. Lee claims, in effect, that we will know a Naomi when we see one by the "tasteful simplicity" of her otherwise ordinary dress. Having established femininity and dissent as mutually exclusive possibilities, Lee is able to write the problem of Anne Hutchinson out of her book simply by dressing Naomi differently from the Quakers. Hawthorne, however, setting the dual nature of Anne Hutchinson as woman and dissenter as his problem in *The Scarlet Letter*, allows his heroine two dresses.

7

An American Jezebel:
Hawthorne and *The Scarlet Letter*

If Naomi is all simplicity, by the same token Hester Prynne is all embroidery. Claiming for Woman a natural and naturally superior feminine morality, Eliza Buckminster Lee skirts the danger of radical individualism implicit in her story of private revelation. In fact, Lee manages her novel in such a way that the power of the individual is the very power on which the status quo rests. The term that brings the two together is Woman—Woman, that is, as Naomi, in whom the "voice of heaven" is embodied as Harmony, Beauty, and Love. The tastefulness of Naomi's dress pays homage to the "reigning fashion," while its simplicity distills and perfects that fashion. Likewise, her feminine humility perfects a masculine world. In Lee's novel, for a woman to choose *tasteful* simplicity over singularity of dress is to choose humility over assertion, sanctity over selfhood, and this, in turn, is to choose to fulfill her feminine nature. For a woman to choose to be "masculine," as Lee's Hutchinson demonstrates, renders her neither male nor female but only singular and, in that sense, monstrous.

To return to the terms of Emerson's "Woman," Naomi is better but not other, and this poses a novelistic problem. Singularity—or, as one critic has put it, "individual experience which is always unique and therefore new"[1]—stands at the center of the novel as a genre. Its subject is the autonomous individual, and the elements of its plot emerge as this individual, in possession of himself, moves out into a social world. Naomi is, of course, anything but the autonomous character required by the novel. In fact, possessed of the spirit and a model of feminine humility, she might be said to be dispossessed of herself twice over:

once as Christian and again, as Woman. To say that Lee's novel is, as a result, full of incident but without the tension that characterizes the introduction of the autonomous individual into society might only be to say that *Naomi* is not a novel at all but, in good American fashion, a romance, invoking rather than rejecting universals.[2] The difficulty with this view is that the universal truth Naomi embodies is precisely individuality; being female, however, her individuality is representative rather than singular—better but not other than the social universe she inhabits. On the deepest level, then, *Naomi* recalls the stories of Anne Hutchinson because its heroine, too, paradoxically combines self-assertion and self-abnegation. But whereas in Hutchinson's story self-assertion and self-abnegation are opposite extremes and equally problematic, in *Naomi* they are identical and, together, prove her perfectly feminine nature. Tastefully but simply dressed, Naomi moves through the social world of the novel as an embodiment of its highest ideals.

The elaborately embroidered dress in which Hester Prynne first appears is in every respect the opposite of Naomi's simple garb. Not only is it singular but it explicitly violates both the "reigning fashion" and the sumptuary laws governing that fashion. As we first see her, Hester, a figure of dissonance, not harmony, at the mercy of her society but apparently fully in possession of herself, would seem inevitably to call a novel into being. We quite reasonably expect incident, action in the social sphere of the novel, but we also anticipate conflict as this haughty and self-dramatizing Hester meets the world. But *The Scarlet Letter* belies these expectations. From the outset, we are presented not with action but with what might best be called tableau vivant. We are introduced into not a historical social world but an art world. In fact, history, and with it plot, is suspended. We are in an interlude like the one in "The Custom-House," in which the narrator discovers ghostly Surveyor Pue's parchment, or like the "neutral territory" between objective reality and attributed meaning in which the romancer imagines his tales. The story of Anne Hutchinson, the long foreground of the novel, is complete, and, likewise, the more proximate story of

Hester's adultery ends before the novel begins. In lieu of a story we are offered a "view."

But this refusal of *The Scarlet Letter* to be a novel despite the initial force of its central character does not therefore make it a romance, at least in the traditional sense that romance, by engaging the abstract and the ideal, tends to flatten character and exaggerate plot. In fact, in *The Scarlet Letter* novelistic action of the usual sort is supplanted by endlessly elaborated characterization. The crucial "action" of Hawthorne's tale occurs inside Hester, who is in every sense immobilized by her crime. Rather than set his character in motion as the novelist would or reduce her to a type as a romancer might, Hawthorne instead slowly revolves the stage on which she stands, revealing her anew with each turn. The staginess of *The Scarlet Letter* is not that of drama but that of tableau, as we see Hester on the scaffold (with and without Dimmesdale), Hester at her needle, Hester in "another view," and so on. The difficulty in discussing Hester—and I mean here to focus on Hester, not to offer a reading of *The Scarlet Letter*—is a product of Hawthorne's method, for as the stage turns, what is revealed is not another Hester but another interpretation of Hester. Because change occurs on the level of interpretation and not that of action, its effect is to turn the endless multiplication of meaning into the plot of the novel. Thus, the scarlet letter is Hester, who is adulteress, antinomian, artist, and angel, and it is Pearl, who is sin and redemption, and it is Dimmesdale, who, as feminized male, is himself a version of the masculinized Hester.

My point is that in attempting to tell the "real" story of Naomi by bringing the dangers of the interior self to the fore, Hawthorne cannot simply reverse *Naomi*. For what, in a neat paradox, makes Hester singular is her multiplicity, a multiplicity that mirrors her fecundity, both physical and imaginative, and suggests her danger. Acknowledging the dangerous fertility of Hester, Hawthorne, then, repudiates the naive optimism of Lee—or, in another sense, of Emerson—both of whom claim that the truth of the female heart is the Law. But, having rejected the sterility of Naomi—a sterility that makes her action in the novel perfectly safe—Hawthorne is faced with the danger inherent in permitting the fertile Hester to act. He solves this problem, ultimately, by endorsing the view of Woman's nature that rendered Naomi safe in the first place and that, as we will see, transforms Hester into her twin. Like Lee and Emerson, Hawthorne finds in gender the solution to the problem of individualism. His singular heroine, who might live out the subversive potential of all the Naomis who preceded her, is instead barred from action, and her story is subsumed by the exegetical exercise needed to set the terms of action.

Logically, then, *The Scarlet Letter* begins with ambiguity, the occasion for exegesis, in the form of a bouquet composed of the "black flower of civilized society," the wild rose of Nature, and the narrator's "sweet moral blossom." The first of these, of course, describes the "beetle-browed" prison linked by its iron-work door to the iron men who govern Puritan Boston. The high contrast between its blackened facade, which "seemed never to have known a youthful era,"[3] and the red roses that adorn its threshold suggests classic dichotomies; the new wilderness world set against the old; the works of Nature versus the works of civilization; the "deep heart of Nature," which can "pity and be kind" (*SL*, 158) to the worst sinners, as against the harshness of Calvinist justice. But dichotomy quickly gives way to multiplicity. The prison, while wholly "unnatural" in one aspect, is, in another, as inevitable as Nature itself. And the signs of age which make it, like crime, "more antique than anything else in the New World" (*SL*, 158) propose it as a fixed necessity. Utopian aspirations aside, the narrator tells us, where men live in community, prisons exist; America is a New World, but it is no Eden.

The wild rose bush, likewise, is no simple sign of a benevolent Nature. Associated with the "stern old wilderness" of pre-Columbian America, we nonetheless find it not in the forest but at the portal of the town prison. It is linked to the "sainted Anne Hutchinson," (*SL*, 159) who we suspect from the author's tone (and know from history) was less saintly than she hoped. The rose bush is, on the one hand, an expression of Nature's sympathy with "natural" man and, on the other, a token of Hutchinson's martyrdom, having, as some believe, "sprung up under [her] footsteps . . . as she entered the prison-door" (*SL*, 159). Nature may be "unadulterated," but it is also lawless and ungovernable. Ambiguous as Hawthorne's language is, however, his introduction defines quite clearly the appropriate stance for the reader of his "tale of human frailty and sorrow." The unexpected antiquity of the prison informs us of an undeniable human need for ordered society, even as the natural beauty of the rose bush urges sympathy with the victims of that order. If we would pluck, with Hawthorne, the sweet moral blossom of this tale, we must understand the black flower and the red rose not as alternatives but as doubles.

From the outset, our attention is directed to the multiplication of meaning, a figure for the problem of individualism that Hester embodies. And, not surprisingly, Hester herself is multiplied before she is even introduced. Anne Hutchinson enters the prison, but Hester Prynne comes out of it; the historical figure yields the fictional one. And just as the rosebush springs into being as Hutchinson enters the prison, so its double, the scarlet letter, comes to life as Hester leaves it. The letter itself likewise appears from the first in two forms: as the fantastically embroidered token on Hester's breast and as Pearl, herself the sign of both Hester's sin and her redemption. Fiction elaborates history and art Nature. And as art—*The Scarlet Letter* and the scarlet letter both—unfolds its proliferative nature its relevance to the story of Hester, as artist and as object of art, is established.

Hester Prynne is not the antithesis but the fictional embodiment of a "fictional" Anne Hutchinson. The figure to whom she refers is not the historical Anne Hutchinson but rather a figure bearing her name, created by the Puritan chroniclers and kept alive by their heirs. Hester, as one critic has put it, is "literally what orthodox Puritan metaphor said Anne Hutchinson was 'really' or spiritually."[4] The heretic who metaphorically "seduced" the Puritan community, according to Welde, Winthrop, Johnson, and Mather, is reborn in Hester, who actually seduces the highest representative of that community, the minister. And just as the "misconceptions" of Hutchinson's brain come to fruition in the misconceptions of her womb, so Hester's crime of passion quite literally begets her ungovernable offspring, Pearl, symbol of a broken law both by virtue of her illegitimacy and insofar as she is the creation of Hester the artist.[5]

To say that Hester is Anne Hutchinson twice removed is to suggest the complexity of Hawthorne's character, a complexity likewise suggested by our initial view of her on the scaffold. An oversized figure, beautiful and arrogant, Hester faces the townspeople with a "burning blush" and a "haughty smile." Everything about her is excessive, luxuriant, abundant, and, as our narrator tells us, "lady-like, in the antique interpretation of the term" (*SL*, 163). Not, however, in the contemporary one. Hester, in some ways typical of those lusty, overripe English-women of whom the paler and more genteel women of nine-teenth-century New England are the "fair descendants," is nonetheless free of the moral and material coarseness that characterizes the "matrons" of the crowd. Not yet the reduced, refined, and desexualized lady of Hawthorne's own age—the "lady" Emerson invokes—Hester stands rather as a transitional figure between two types of womanhood. What moves her away from one and toward the other is not so much her sin as the heightened consciousness of sin imparted by the atmosphere of Puritan New England, a heightened consciousness which is, "The Custom-House" suggests, a prerequisite to art.

Guilty, then, of the adultery that Anne Hutchinson seems not to have committed but that, nonetheless, provided the language of her tale, Hester is ambiguous from the start. For all intents and purposes abandoned by her husband in a wilderness, she is tempted and she falls. And we are asked, first, to believe that her adultery is the result of an unfortunate but understandable excess of passion. Hester's loveless marriage, the betrayal of her "budding youth into a false and unnatural relation" with an aging scholar's "decay" (*SL*, 182), while it does not justify her fall, at least explains it. Given Woman's nature and Hester's particular circumstances, we must consider the possibility that Hester's sin was "natural." Unprotected—not sequestered but abandoned—Hester's fall was, as Chillingworth himself reminds us, only to be expected.

Removed from normal social relations by the "taint of deepest sin," she is further isolated by the severity of Puritan justice, which, by forbidding "the culprit to hide his face for shame" (*SL*, 186), forces Hester to a "desperate recklessness." Whatever she might have been, by the time we meet her on the scaffold she is barred "from ordinary relations with humanity . . . enclos[ed] in a sphere by herself" (*SL*, 164). She can approach others only by bringing them into her "magic circle" of sinfulness—a "magic circle" that is at once the image and the opposite of the domestic, fireside circle, just as the "sphere" in which Hester is isolated, like Woman's sphere more generally, both impedes and defines her social intercourse.

In one sense, then, the "fantastically embroidered" scarlet letter epitomizes the spiritual pride that is Hester's contribution to her own isolation. Signifying her antinomian propensities as well as her adulterous act, it is both a symbol and an object of art. In this way, it ties the liberation of the creative, the generative, impulse to lawlessness. And insofar as the creative impulse that produces art depends on or implies lawlessness, it endangers the social order. Loosed in fecund Woman, this danger is multiplied. But the scarlet letter is also that "letter" of the law which accomplishes Hester's transformation into a "living sermon against sin" in the eyes of her neighbors. Hester's letter, that is, simultaneously liberates and fixes her.

As a history of Hester's spiritual journey, *The Scarlet Letter* records a seven-year progress[6] from her first impulsive violation of the law to her systematic rejection of all institutional authority, from a haughty and painful defiance of her judges to a self-sufficiency so complete as finally to deny history, religion, and community alike—or, one might say, from adultery to antinomianism, its intellectual counterpart. With each "view" of Hester, we become more acutely aware of the deleterious effects of the isolation that inevitably follows crime. And with each step in the downward slide that ends in the forest scene, we become more conscious that what we are being given is an inversion of the Puritan scheme of conversion. Hester, "transfigured" on the scaffold, begins a process of conversion that will lead to her rebirth as surely as her "conversion" from wife to adulteress led to the birth of Pearl.

Lest we miss the point, Hawthorne formulates this change in the conventional language of Puritan regeneration. Hester's sin is a "new birth" that cuts her off from her past selves—most particularly from the natural self that the Puritan community deems most in need of redemption. "Happy infancy" and "stainless maidenhood" alike are as "garments put off long ago"; her own past is "foreign" to her (*SL*, 186). And just as in the classic Puritan experience of conversion the natural self is discarded in favor of union with Christ, so Hester relinquishes her "individuality" and becomes instead a "general symbol" not of God's grace but of "woman's frailty and sinful passion" (*SL*, 185).

In her altered condition Hester is endowed with that "new sense" which orthodox Calvinists like John Cotton associated with the chosen but which was more conspicuously claimed by Anne Hutchinson and her followers. The antinomians' "new sense" purportedly enabled them to identify other members of the invisible church; thus, the witness of the spirit would be confirmed by mutual recognition among the saints. In Hester's case, of course, that recognition is not of other saints but of other sinners. The scarlet letter reveals to her a "mystic sisterhood" of fallen women, and this "sympathetic knowledge of the hidden sin in other hearts" (*SL*, 192), by utterly depriving her of faith in the essential goodness of humanity, deepens her isolation. Having relinquished her past and become, in the eyes of the world, a general symbol, Hester becomes more radically singular than ever.

Left with nothing to "revere" outside herself, she turns increasingly inward, and the more she turns to herself, the more prominent the scarlet letter becomes, until at last she looks at herself in the mirrored breastplate of Governor Bellingham's armor and finds herself "absolutely hidden behind it" (*SL*, 208). In one sense her natural self is as completely subsumed by the letter of infamy as that of any saint in Christ, but, in another, she has, in her spiritual pride, come to regard herself as the only object worthy of contemplation. As in the earlier story of Anne Hutchinson, self-assertion and self-abnegation go hand in hand. The more self-sufficient Hester grows, the more exclusively a symbol she becomes until, no longer a self at all, she is, even to herself, an object. Just as she lives only for Pearl—"the scarlet letter, only capable of being loved, and so endowed with a million-fold the power of retribution for my sin" (*SL*, 214)—so she lives only in the scarlet letter. For Hawthorne, however, everything is proximate: antinomianism is contained in Puritanism just as sin lurks in the most saintly saint. The difference is in the outward show.

This attention to outward show returns us to the matter of Hester's clothes. Her sexual crime may be natural, in both the positive nineteenth-century sense and the negative seventeenth-century one, but her "transfiguration" on the scaffold is accomplished not by Nature but by art. Hester's attire, "wrought for the occasion" and "modelled . . . after her own fancy" (*SL*, 164), is, like all art, an expression of the "spirit" of the artist. But Hester's art is also specifically feminine, in its materials and its form. As we learn when we view Hester at her needle, she plies the only art "within a woman's grasp" (*SL*, 188), the art of needlework. Her splendid apparel, appropriate perhaps to the seventeenth century but hardly to New England or to a criminal, is an example of the art that will at once provide her meager income and allow for the expression of her sensual nature. Intimately associated with her illicit sexuality, Hester's artistry, while greatly in demand, is never "called in aid to embroider the white veil which was to cover the pure blushes of a bride" (*SL*, 189). In this sense, her art, like her adultery, profoundly, if only figuratively, distances Hester from action by distancing her from marriage, the central action of Woman's life. Moreover, Hester's obsessive, labor-intensive embroidery confirms her identity as an artist by associating her with the obsessive teller of the tale, himself engaged in the endless embroidering of his character.

Feminine, then, insofar as needlework is always feminine, Hester's is an art of embodiment and is in this respect, too, feminine. She is presented to us in tableau, but it is a tableau for which she herself is the costumier, and her choice of costume exacerbates her condition. Her lush beauty is so heightened by her garb that it makes a "halo of the misfortune and ignominy in which she was enveloped" (*SL*, 163). This halo, although it hints at another transfiguration, is here ironic, at least insofar as Hester's dress is another expression of her lawlessness, greatly exceeding "what was allowed by the sumptuary regulations of the colony" (*SL*, 163). This irony, moreover, generates another, since it calls into question the transfiguring power of art: Hester's halo does not make her into a saint but rather exaggerates her sinfulness.

Hester on the scaffold is engaged in a species of self-dramatization. Dressed in a way that both draws attention to her sinful nature and violates the law, Hester's clothing simultaneously acknowledges her crime and flouts the law that demands her repentance. The art that accomplishes this is feminine not only as its materials are feminine but also as it is an art of embodiment rather than of interpretation or enactment. Creating herself as an object of art, Hester is, to use Margaret Fuller's terms, poet and poem at the same time. To be poet and poem simultaneously is not, however, simply to be double but to embody a contradiction, for while art requires the feminine, female art involves a transgression into masculine territory as criminal as adultery. The female as object of art, on the contrary, is sanctified. Hawthorne's apparently casual allusion to portraits of the Madonna and child is contrived to illuminate this contradiction.

A papist, he tells us, might see in Hester and Pearl "an object to remind him of the image of Divine Maternity, which so many illustrious painters have vied with one another to represent" (*SL*, 166). The shift from a Puritan to a Catholic point of view, it would seem, transforms Jezebel into Mary, turns Hester into ideal Woman, and suggests Pearl as the product of a virgin birth. The suggestion is ironic, on the face of it, alluding in part to the mystery of Pearl's paternity and in another way to Hester's flamboyant sexuality. But just when we have grasped this suggestion and its irony, Hawthorne goes on: Hester and Pearl would, he says, "remind [the Papist], indeed, but only by contrast, of that sacred image of sinless motherhood, whose infant was to redeem the world" (*SL*, 166). This second statement makes the requisite moral point and exposes the irony of the first, but it is structured to encourage misreading. The "by contrast" is so submerged that the sentence leaves undisturbed the possibility of Hester as Mary and Pearl as child Redeemer. And well it might, for as we read on we discover that in her maternal aspect—"viewed," that is, as mother—Hester is, like all mothers, Madonna-like. Moreover, we learn that Pearl, regarded by almost everyone as of supernatural paternity, although usually as the issue of Satan, will, as children do, redeem her parents from further sin. Mary may be divine mother and Jesus the son of God, but all mothers and all children share in their perfection.

Whether she is understood as a "living sermon against sin" or an image of divine maternity, Hester on the scaffold demands interpretation. But off the scaffold she is no less a puzzle, for, in a sense, all that changes is her dress. With the loss of her individual—her "natural"—history comes as well the loss of her sexuality, which, Hawthorne reminds us, was the problem in the first place. Hester is sadly altered, her "rich and luxuriant hair" hidden completely, her dress austere, her manners subdued. There is "no longer anything in Hester's face for Love to dwell upon" and nothing in her form that "Passion would ever dream of clasping in its embrace" (*SL*, 258–59). No longer an object of passion, she would seem no longer to risk a fall. Without the attractions of a woman, she can hardly be a seductress. For one brief moment, we think that Hester has been contained, albeit at an enormous cost. But the turn from passion to thought that accompanies this change, while it desexualizes and, in that sense, tames Hester, also ungenders her and thus leads her to a different kind of lawlessness.

Assuming "a freedom of speculation" that the Puritans, we are told, "would have held to be a deadlier crime than that stigmatized by the scarlet letter" (*SL*, 259), she casts away the fragments of the "broken chain" that once bound her to the rest of the human race and commits a "deadlier crime." Concluding that "the world's law" is "no law for her mind" (*SL*, 259), she contemplates an entire rearrangement of society of a kind "common enough on the other side of the Atlantic" (*SL,* 259) but wholly inappropriate to a world already new. As her heart loses its "healthy throb," she wanders in a "dark labyrinth of mind" from which there is no escape and in which there is only danger—"deep chasms" and "insurmountable precipices" (*SL,* 261).

Though newly clothed in "the coarsest materials" of the somberest hue, stripped of her individuality and become the general symbol of feminine frailty and sinful passion, Hester is as singular as ever, as criminal in her thoughts as she once was in her deeds. To put it another way, insofar as her new costume *is* a costume, Hester remains as much the artist and, thus, as lawless as ever; *only* a costume, a new dress does not signify a change of character. Not surprisingly, Hester's costumes exactly parallel Hawthorne's settings: just as Hester's dresses provide the changing ground against which we regard the scarlet letter, so the backdrop against which we view Hester herself also changes. The scarlet letter is to Hester's dress as Hester is to her setting, a focal point pricked out in scarlet and gold.

If Hester is always both artist and object of art, however, so too she is always both adulteress and mother. Only in one sense has she cast away the chains of relation; in another she has tightened them. The fact of Pearl, like the intimations of feminine perfection contained in Hester as object of art, works to contain Hester's lawlessness. In fact, redemptive motherhood explicitly prevents her from coming "down to us in history, hand in hand with Anne Hutchinson, as the foundress of a religious sect" (*SL,* 260). Without Pearl—the scarlet letter come to life—Hester might never have questioned the morality of her deed; the "something wrong" in Pearl's nature suggests, more powerfully than anything else, the possibility of her wrongdoing. Without Pearl—the human child—Hester would have no regard for her own life: "in the education of her child," in her domestic rounds, we are told, "the mother's enthusiasm of thought had something to wreak itself upon" (*SL,* 260). And not, of course, just something but the right thing.

Hester's maternity constitutes both a reassertion and a revision of gender, and this in two senses. On the one hand, the seductress is supplanted by the mother; Mary replaces Jezebel. Passionate sexual love gives way to maternal love, and just as one weakens, so the other proportionally strengthens the moral character of woman. In fact, maternity alone has the power to save Hester. On the other hand, maternity and not the prospect of damnation—or rather, maternity as it both teaches and expresses virtue—checks her career as an Anne Hutchinson. It continually recalls Hester from masculine thought to feminine feeling. Pearl is the agent of her mother's redemption. Unlike her precursor, Quaker Catherine of "The Gentle Boy," whose religious enthusiasm is such that not even her son's welfare can check it, Hester is unwilling to part with her child. Her commitment to Pearl proves the depth of Hester's maternal love, but it also requires that she submit to Pearl's tormenting questions about the reason for the scarlet letter.7 Thus is mother love paired, albeit obliquely, with suffering and self-sacrifice. Catherine, abandoning motherhood, abandons all; Hester's maternity prefigures her redemption, which, in turn, implies her ultimate containment as a figure of danger and dissent.

Even so, the scarlet letter, as emblem or as child, does not entirely fulfill "its office." It brings neither genuine repentance for the sexual crime nor conviction of error. Rather, it seems to push Hester toward a complete lawlessness of mind. Freed from the outward constraints of community by her extreme isolation, Hester is freed by her letter from the inward ones of faith as well. Sexual passion, requiring as it does an object, had linked Hester to the world outside herself, if only in sin, but thought, wholly self-sufficient as it is, not only advances her isolation but divides her external behavior from her inner life. She becomes "false."

The further Hester wanders "without rule or guidance" in that "moral wilderness" of speculative thought to which the scarlet letter is her "passport," the more outwardly compliant she becomes. Self-sacrificing and submissive, Hester conforms "with the most perfect quietude to the external regulations of society" (*SL*, 260). Outwardly, Hester is a saint—or, as the narrator somewhat ambiguously puts it, "a martyr, indeed." Living a public life of "blameless purity," inwardly she wanders in "regions where other women dared not tread" (*SL*, 290). A "Sister of Mercy," tending the sick and consoling the unfortunate, Hester rises so far in the regard of her fellow townspeople that they come to think of her *A* as standing not for Adulteress but Able, while all the while "her intellect and heart . . . roamed as freely as the wild Indian in his woods" (*SL*, 290).

The speculation that may, our narrator informs us, "keep woman quiet" (*SL*, 260) as certainly it does Hester leads to a dangerous duplicitousness. Furthermore, the problems Woman hopes to overcome by the masculine "exercise of thought" can be solved, we are told, only "if her heart chance to come uppermost" (*SL*, 261), that is, only if she lives as Woman. We wonder, at this juncture, what has become of the human Pearl, but, of course, she does not really come into being until the final scaffold scene. And without her Hester poses what seems to be an insoluble problem: with her "heart uppermost" and her hair down, so to speak, she embodies an awakened female sexuality, the consequences of which we see, on the one hand, in Pearl's demonic qualities and the suffering of Dimmesdale, for which Hester is held accountable, and, on the other hand, in her passionate art. With her hair bound and her intellect ascendant—in her "masculine" guise, that is—she is lost in an "unredeemed, unchristianized lawless region" where "the clerical band, the judicial robe, the pillory, the gallows, the fireside [and] the church" (*SL*, 290) count for nothing, a region in which she foolishly imagines herself the prophetess of a new revelation. To press the limits of the metaphor, one might say that *The Scarlet Letter* proposes an ideal feminine state in which the hair is bound and the heart ascendant—in which sexual and artistic passion are overwhelmed by maternal love—and an ideal masculine one of impassioned intellect. What makes Hester powerful and dangerous, artist and antinomian, is that she contains all these permutations: she is not simply adulterous Jezebel or humble Mary but both and, therefore, neither.

There is no "middle way" for Hester because she is constantly rewriting herself—or perhaps I should say reembroidering herself. Her fertility, however masked, is such that it continually generates new possibilities for meaning. An image of unchecked individualism, this fertility impedes not only Hester's progress in the novel but the progress of the novel itself. The ceaseless interpretation and reinterpretation of Hester, the endless embroidering of character, defers plot, calls history to a standstill. Hawthorne dare not set Hester in motion until the terms that govern her as a character are established, for to set in motion so unstable a character would be to destabilize the world of the novel. Hester, as she is represented, could only be launched into rebellion, and, as rebel in a novelistic world, she would revert to Anne Hutchinson and history.

But if there is no middle way for Hester, so there is none for Dimmesdale, Hester's silent partner in crime. The distance between Hester's inner and outer lives, increasing with each year of her isolation, typifies their shared tragedy. In fact, Dimmesdale's first words to Hester, spoken from the elevated (and exclusively masculine) viewpoint of the gallery of the meetinghouse overlooking the scaffold, are symptomatic of his infidelity. Reluctantly urging her to speak the name of her "fellowsinner," Dimmesdale blames Hester for his misery—"Heaven hath granted thee an open ignominy, that thereby thou mayest work out an open triumph over the evil within thee. . . . Take heed how thou deniest to him . . . the bitter, but wholesome, cup"—and, in the same breath, implies that to name Pearl's father would be an act of selfishness on Hester's part—"If thou feelest it to be for thy soul's peace . . . I charge thee to speak" (*SL*, 175). Arguing that Hester's silence can only "tempt him—yea, compel him, as it were—to add hypocrisy to sin" (*SL*, 175), Dimmesdale insists that Hester take responsibility for his soul and represents her as an Eve tempting him, an unwitting Adam, to disobedience by her silence.

A silent partner in the adultery, Dimmesdale is nonetheless a speaker in the novel. In fact, while Hester's difficulties are associated with her refusal to speak—to name Pearl's father, to tell

Pearl the meaning of the scarlet letter, to reveal Chillingworth's identity—Dimmesdale's arise from speaking. This difference, in the terms of the novel, figures the difference between Hester and Dimmesdale as artists. One, silently plying her needle, transforms herself, her letter, her daughter—all the versions of the scarlet letter—into embodiments of sin, symbols ripe for interpretation. The other speaks, interprets, preaches, enacts his sinfulness on the pulpit, on the scaffold, and in the closet.

In fact, if Hester refuses to repent, that is, to unspeak her sin by speaking, Dimmesdale does almost nothing else. But the more he tells his congregation that he is the "worst of sinners, an abomination, a thing of unimaginable iniquity" (*SL*, 242), the greater a "miracle of holiness" (*SL*, 241) they quite reasonably believe him to be. Taken by the community to be a veritable "saint on earth," he regards himself as a "pollution and a lie." Engaged in "constant introspection," Dimmesdale tortures himself but achieves no purity. In fact, his suffering leads him, if not quite to heresy, at least to unorthodox practices. Scourging himself like a repentant Catholic, fasting and keeping midnight vigils, he achieves, as he later tells Hester, "penance" but not "penitence" (*SL*, 283). True neither to himself nor to those who depend on him, whether as pastor, partner in crime, or parent, Dimmesdale finds the "whole universe . . . false" and becomes himself "a shadow." Dimmesdale's "introspection" is the other side of Hester's "speculation," just as his self-inflicted torture mirrors the "torture" Pearl inflicts on Hester.

Dimmesdale's suffering works a change in him that parallels the change wrought in Hester by the scarlet letter. Part of the circle of sinners himself, he has, like Hester, an uncanny knowledge of the secret sins of others. His guilt gives him "sympathies so intimate with the sinful brotherhood of mankind . . . that his heart vibrate[s] in unison with theirs" (*SL*, 240). He too acquires a "new sense." In fact, his brilliant popularity as a preacher is associated with his fall into sin. Had he not fallen, the narrator tells us, Dimmesdale would in all likelihood have been another of those "true saintly fathers, whose faculties had been elaborated by weary toil among their books, and by patient thought," but fallen, he is gifted with the "Tongue of Flame" (*SL*, 240). A sinner among sinners, he addresses "the whole human brotherhood in the heart's native tongue" (*SL*, 240).

But Dimmesdale is trapped in the central fallacy of the very creed he represents. A "true priest" who needs to "feel the pressure of a faith about him, supporting, while it confine[s] him within its iron framework" (*SL*, 223), he represents the very best that Puritanism has to offer. Yet it is precisely Puritan doctrine, with its emphasis on visible sainthood, that fails him. The orthodoxy to which Dimmesdale is committed, by encouraging his colleagues and his congregation alike to accept his outer self as an expression of the inner one, prolongs his torture. Dimmesdale, knowing himself a hypocrite, resists the all too logical conclusion that the world is as false as himself. He is forced unwillingly toward that denial of works as evidence which Hester embraces as a kind of freedom. His chronic inability to breathe the "fresh air" of speculative thought figures his resistance to the heretical implications of his own circumstances.

The contrast Hawthorne draws between Dimmesdale and his fellow minister, John Wilson, is interesting in this regard. In reality, Wilson shared the Boston pulpit with John Cotton, Hutchinson's mentor, both during and after the antinomian controversy. An object of derision among the Hutchinsonians, they did not just accuse him of preaching a covenant of works but also attempted to oust him from his position. As Hawthorne portrays him, Wilson is so perfectly the Puritan that he looks like "the darkly engraved portraits which we see prefixed to old volumes of sermons" (*SL*, 173). He is, however, a particular kind of Puritan, one who speaks for the Law, the Old Testament, the world of the fathers. When he addresses Hester as she stands on the scaffold, his carefully prepared discourse treats sin "in all its branches . . . with continual reference to the ignominious letter" (*SL*, 176), its symbol. A "kind and genial spirit" in his private life, as minister Wilson is a religious taxonomer, classifying and systematizing sin "in all its branches." Disallowing ambiguity and complication, he has "no right

. . . to . . . meddle with a question of human guilt, passion and anguish" (*SL,* 173). Wilson is the epitome of "legal" Puritanism.

Dimmesdale, younger and softer, speaks not from the head but from the heart, not from the Old Testament but from the New, not from the law but from the spirit, not with the wisdom of age but with that of feeling. Full of "religious fervor," he has "a white, lofty, and impending brow, large, brown, melancholy eyes, and a mouth which . . . was apt to be tremulous" (*SL,* 174). Effeminate in aspect, his manner and speech are effeminate as well. His look is "startled, half frightened," and his thought has a "freshness, and fragrance, and dewy purity . . . which, as many people said, affected them like the speech of an angel" (*SL,* 174). In part the affectionate preacher of the great revivals, he even more closely resembles the "sentimental" ministers of the mid-nineteenth century, those "meek," "sensitive," "delicate" men beloved of their female parishioners.[8] Gaining both physical and intellectual strength from her ostracism, Hester turns from passion to thought and becomes "masculine." Plunged into a world of feeling, timid Dimmesdale is, on the contrary, weakened and "feminized," constantly in need of a strong arm, human or doctrinal, to support him. This confusion of gender is a correlative of lawlessness, as Hawthorne presents it, but it is also—or therefore—intimately associated with art.

Like everything else in Hawthorne's novel, his characters are invested with meaning at every turn. Their guilt or innocence is in the eye of the beholder, and the discrepancy between outward appearance and innermost self that defines them as false is replicated so often in the book that it comes to seem unavoidable. Nothing is what it seems—or rather everything is only what it seems at a given instant from a particular vantage point. Meaning originates in the "colored, magnifying and distorting medium" of the individual imagination. Thus, each character in *The Scarlet Letter,* including the narrator, is presented with the red letter and required to interpret it, and we quickly learn that each will ascribe to it the meaning lent by his or her own point of view. The famous ambiguity of the letter, insofar as it is emblematic of a pervasive instability of meaning in the novel, returns us to gender and law. We have already seen indeterminacy of meaning and the power it lends associated with antinomianism and with the feminine by Charles Chauncy during the Great Awakening. In *The Scarlet Letter* the power of those who unfix meaning and thus generate dissent and lawlessness is reasserted and literalized in the figure of a woman.

Still, all interpretation is not the same in *The Scarlet Letter.* Meaning may be subjective, reflecting psychological truth rather than objective reality, but Hawthorne distinguishes between those meanings propounded by the community and those uncovered by individuals. The nature of this difference is intimated from the start by the double vision of the opening scene of the novel. The townspeople look up at Hester on the scaffold and, instructed by those on the meetinghouse balcony, find in her a living symbol of sin; at the same time, Hester, regarding them from the singular "point of view" of the scaffold, reinterprets her past and present life in light of her crime. What the town sees is neither more nor less "true" than what Hester sees; nonetheless, some vision, if not privileged by the author, is at least more fully empowered than others. The shared interpretation of the townspeople, although it is no more legitimate in some ultimate sense than the vision of the individual, has far greater force in shaping the world. Hester is on the scaffold in the first place, after all, because the Puritans have attributed sinfulness to what might in another time or place be regarded as a "natural" act.

My point is that Hawthorne marks a difference between remarkable providences and private revelations. Regarding the world as fraught with meaning, the Puritans, Hawthorne explains, searched for evidence "that their infant commonwealth was under a celestial guardianship of peculiar intimacy and strictness" (*SL,* 252). So prone were they, in fact, to find supernatural significance in natural events that, as the narrator suggests with typical irony, it is unlikely that "any marked event, for good or evil, ever befell New England, from its settlement down to Revolutionary times, of which the inhabitants had not been previously warned by some spectacle" (*SL,* 251). The exag-

geration is ironic, but the problem is posed in perfect serious-
ness. Meaning originates in the individual imagination, but
communities, too, interpret events, and social institutions are
authorized not merely to interpret but to exact conformity to
their interpretations. These public interpretations serve a crucial social function: the "majestic idea" of a revealed collective
destiny is majestic indeed insofar as it enables community.

Nonetheless, to attribute public significance to private acts is
a problematic venture. Communities, the narrator concedes,
must judge their members, but, not being infallible, their judgments may be unduly harsh, as in Hester's case, or may even
result in outright injustice of the kind Hawthorne attributes to
his colonial ancestors in "The Custom-House." The Puritan impulse toward interpretation, the tendency to attribute providential meaning to any unusual event, is, of course, precisely
what is recorded in the Puritan accounts of Anne Hutchinson.
Hawthorne's Puritans reveal their arrogance by representing
themselves as an elect nation, but arrogance yields to danger in
the individual who interprets the world with reference only to
himself. The Puritans may have "misinterpreted" if not Anne
Hutchinson then at least Hester Prynne, but the antinomian's
claim to private revelations wreaks havoc.

As Dimmesdale stands on the scaffold at midnight and looks
up at the comet crossing the night sky, he sees projected there
the letter that signifies his guilt. He finds "a revelation, addressed to himself alone" (*SL*, 252). As Hawthorne points out,
this "could only be the symptom of a highly disordered mental
state, when a man, rendered morbidly self-contemplative by
long, intense, and secret pain, had extended his egotism over
the whole expanse of nature, until the firmament itself should
appear no more than a fitting page for his soul's history and
fate" (*SL*, 252). But the ironic resemblance between Dimmesdale's "diseased eye" that sees his private guilt written across
the sky and the Puritans who find their providence written
"in . . . awful hieroglyphics, on the cope of heaven" (*SL*, 252)
only emphasizes the orthodoxy of Dimmesdale's method. Good
Puritan that he is, Dimmesdale assumes that the comet is meant
as a sign from God to New England; moreover, he believes that
inner states find outward manifestation in the world. His read-

ing of the *A* is, in this sense, a perfectly orthodox attempt to establish a correspondence between the visible and the invisible worlds. But reading the heavens as his private scroll, he inflates his importance beyond all reason.

The disparity between social and individual interpretation, like the disparity between inner and outer selves, which is another version of the same, is likewise a figure for isolation in *The Scarlet Letter*. The individual and the community similarly project their hopes and fears out into the world and find there symbolic representation of their condition. But if the available symbols repeatedly yield different or antithetical meanings to the self and the community, then the chain of relation is severed, and the individual suffers a solitude so profound that he can see nothing but himself. This is Dimmesdale's plight on the scaffold, and it is Hester's punishment. So focused are they both on the scarlet letter and their adultery—on their private revelation, as it were—that they exist apart from the rest of humanity. As Hawthorne knew, this was the end result of Hutchinson's antinomianism; her claim to a truth not only different from the one accepted by her community but wholly self-referential finalized her banishment, a banishment accomplished metaphorically for Hester and Dimmesdale by the image of the "magic circle."

The town is, then, a social unit authorized to demand conformity to its vision of the world. It stands for an interpretive consensus based on the external authority of the Bible, a consensus Hawthorne regards as a prerequisite to order. This consensus legitimizes prisons, or at least makes them inevitable. The ideal society, as Emerson had already suggested, would be one in which individual and social judgments were perfectly coincident, a society in which prisons would vanish. *The Scarlet Letter,* despite its opening, turns finally to an image of perfect consensus as the only solution to the problem it so carefully lays out. Having explored the interaction between the community and the lawless individual, Hawthorne must bring these apparently irreconcilable extremes together in a workable vision of society.

Neither the social nor the aesthetic solution to the problem of *The Scarlet Letter,* however, is immediately apparent. Hester's seven years of ignominy, the narrator explains, were but "preparation" for her meeting with Dimmesdale in the forest. Having viewed Hester on the scaffold, at her needle, in cottage and mansion, town and forest, the reader too is prepared for the long-deferred action of the book. But that action turns out to be a reenactment of the adultery, and we are back where we began. And necessarily so, for insofar as Hester's history is "preparation" for conversion, that conversion is long since accomplished by sin.

Hester's "preparation" goes awry not just novelistically but theologically. In the Puritan morphologies of conversion, the sinful life of the "natural" man is followed by a period of preparation prior to the saint's assurance of salvation. This phase of the progress of the elect is characterized by attendance upon the Word, submission to the moral law, awareness of sin, and fear of its consequences.[9] Outwardly conforming to this pattern, Hester's intellectual progress inverts this scheme point for point. She has, during her period of "preparation," learned to reject both Word and Law and, rather than developing a heightened fear of the consequences of sin, she has learned a reckless courage. But, as usual, Hawthorne's irony carries an extra twist. Hester's preparation inverts the morphology of conversion in fact, but, to all appearances, Hester is moving through its phases with the most promising of Puritans. Only invisibly does she reverse its terms. We may deplore Hester as a hypocrite, but we are asked also to question the wisdom of relying on visible signs of sanctity as evidence of grace. We are asked, in other words, by the very structure of Hawthorne's language, to consider the merits of antinomianism and, less directly, Transcendentalism. Not surprisingly, then, Hester's "assurance"—the stage following "preparation" in the orthodox scheme—takes a form quite the opposite of that of the Puritan saint. Rather than grief, doubt, faith, and dependence, Hester experiences her conversion as a liberation of the self that for seven years has remained hidden behind a pious exterior. In the simplest terms Hester finally says aloud what she has been thinking all those years and thus makes herself "true," though we come to wonder whether this is the virtue we once thought it. In the lawless region of the forest, she proposes that the deed society condemns, nature may yet consecrate; she makes it clear that she arrogantly supposes her alliance with Dimmesdale to be justified. Insisting, moreover, on their freedom to "leave this wreck and ruin here where it hath happened" and "begin all anew" (*SL*, 288), she articulates an Emersonian optimism that we, as readers, are directed to find illusory. She and Dimmesdale can do and be whatever they choose, Hester insists, if they will only interpret themselves rather than rely on the judgment of the community that condemns them. The future is before them, in the wilderness or in Europe, and "the past is gone" (*SL*, 292). In a self-conscious attempt to give symbolic form to this newfound freedom, Hester alters her clothing once again. Discarding the symbol of the past, the scarlet letter, she recalls "her sex, her youth, and the whole richness of her beauty" from the "irrevocable past" (*SL*, 293). And as if heaven favored them, "forth burst[s] the sunshine" on this optimistic scene, and the "sad little brook" becomes a "mystery of joy" (*SL*, 293).

Everything that happens in the forest is false. Just as Hester's words misrepresent both past and future, so the sunshine is coincidental, if not imaginary: "Love . . . must always create a sunshine. . . . Had the forest still kept its gloom, it would have been bright in Hester's eyes, and bright in Arthur Dimmesdale's!" (*SL*, 293). The brook, we must assume, babbles as usual. But out of all this falsity we arrive at a kind of truth nonetheless. In the metaphorical Anne Hutchinson come to life, we discover the real error of the antinomian. Hester's conversion unmasks Hutchinson's language of dependence. The false front of self-abnegation—represented in Hester's case by her excessive generosity to the poor and her willingness to sacrifice herself to those in need and, in Hutchinson's, by the language of the self-in-Christ—is penetrated to reveal the radical assertion of self that stands behind it. Hester's "true" self is falser than her "false" one ever was. In her pride Hester, like Anne Hutchinson, makes a fatal error—in fact, the same error: she speaks out of her innermost self. Like Hutchinson, who in the very process of repenting her errors repeated them by claiming immediate revelation, Hester, when she finally speaks, by speaking repeats her crime.

Hester denies the validity of everything outside of herself: her sin is no longer sinful, the past is erased, the future is ready to be modeled to her will alone. Finding a "spiritual fact" in every "natural fact," she uncovers not herself as part of the universal harmony of the Transcendentalist but the world as an image of herself. Inverting Emersonian idealism—and in this way challenging its optimism—Hester's egotism redefines the world. Her assertion that the adultery is consecrated supplants divine providence with private revelation and reverses the process of both Puritan exegesis and Emersonian revelation. The effect of this is to catapult Hester into action. But at this critical juncture when the novel might finally happen, its ideological and its formal imperatives are so thoroughly at odds that Hawthorne calls action to a halt by invoking gender.

Pearl—symbolically, the scarlet letter come to life and, psychologically, the child who is displaced by Dimmesdale and whose very existence is being denied along with the rest of the past—recalls Hester to her irrevocable femaleness, to motherhood and thus to the social world. Demanding that Hester retrieve the letter if she would have a daughter, Pearl plants herself firmly on the side of human community, social reality, and, more important, on the side of a Puritan understanding of the correspondence between the visible and the invisible. Sinful within, Hester must be chastened without. Private revelation, if it is to be credited, must support, not supplant, its public equivalent, divine providence.

In the freedom of the forest, Hester articulates the conclusions of her silent speculation. Dismissing civil and religious law, she dispenses as well with the laws of nature and probability. Instructed by "Shame, Despair, Solitude," she demonstrates that she has failed to learn their lesson and insists that the world works according to principles that the novel has already proven false. Herself an inhabitant of "desert places," her experience as "outlaw" leads her to believe in the possibility of complete freedom and in the existence of a "better part" in man, a feminine part kept in "bondage" by the "iron men" but only waiting to be emancipated. But rejecting the idea of this feminine part as the complement that completes man, she attempts instead to elevate it to the whole. A true enthusiast, Hester trusts the teachings of her female heart even when these run counter to the evidence of the world around her. Her faith in herself, requiring no evidence, neither the good works of the Puritans nor the universal harmony of the Transcendentalists, raises the threat of a world without law.

In Dimmesdale, who has indulged in no such independent thought but has clung instead to the law as his mainstay, the freedom of the forest accomplishes a veritable revolution. A different minister from the one who went there returns from the forest. Imbued with a new "sense of power," Dimmesdale is incited to do "strange, wild, wicked" things, "with a sense that [they] would be at once involuntary and intentional; in spite of himself, yet growing out of a profounder self" (*SL*, 306). He is tempted to speak blasphemously to his elderly deacon, to plant a "germ of evil" in the snowy bosom of a young virgin, to argue against the immortality of the soul to a "pious and exemplary old dame." "Nothing short of a total change of dynasty and moral code," Hawthorne tells us, ". . . was adequate to account for the impulses now communicated to the unfortunate and startled minister" (*SL*, 306). Dimmesdale has become an unwilling exemplar of the effects of antinomianism. Hester's lawlessness has lent him a power that expresses itself in impulses that are explicitly antisocial, and he suspects he has purchased happiness at the price of his soul. On the eve of his return, at work on the Election Sermon, which his pride will not allow him to leave unfinished, he writes "with such an impulsive flow of thought and emotion, that he fancied himself inspired; and only wondered that Heaven should see fit to transmit the grand and solemn music of its oracles through so foul an organ-pipe as he" (*SL*, 312).

With Dimmesdale wandering in a maze of ungovernable impulse, convinced that he is God's own oracle, and with Hester's errors fully exposed, Hawthorne's choices are limited. He can follow out the subversive implications of the lovers' lawlessness, or he can bring them back into the fold. Having empowered his characters, it would seem that he must either set them free to act in the world of the novel or strip them of their illicit power. But Hawthorne refuses to pose the town and its prison as an alternative to the red rose of the forest. Instead, he proposes them, once again, as doubles by extrapolating the higher "law" that governs both, a law that relates the public and the private. In the process he comes to sound like the Emerson who insists on a universal truth that unites individuals "in different streets and towns." True selfhood is defined as membership. Hawthorne, like Eliza Buckminster Lee, retreats from the implications of his character. Faithful as he has been to Hester up to this point, the final scenes of the novel insist that there is no fundamental conflict between the individual who is true to himself and the legitimately constituted community.

Thus, Dimmesdale's fall achieves exactly what is needed for his regeneration. He returns from the forest "wiser" as well as wicked, and when we see him next, on Election Day, there is "no feebleness of step . . . his frame [is] not bent; nor [does] his hand rest ominously upon his heart" (*SL,* 324). So altered is he that Hester hardly knows him and Pearl is prompted to ask whether he is "the same minister that kissed me by the brook?" (*SL,* 325). The answer, of course, is that he is not. Dimmesdale comes out of the "maze" spiritualized. His private revelation allows him to preach the public one. He rejoins the community not merely as a member but as the prophet of the new and better "dynasty" it will inevitably yield. In order to assume this place, however, he must abandon Hester, as she intuitively understands when, from the edge of the crowd, she sees him, "so unattainable in his worldly position, and still more so in that far vista of his unsympathizing thoughts" (*SL,* 325), making his way to the church.

The Election Sermon is our clue to Dimmesdale's altered state, and we are given two accounts of it. The first is the sermon as Hester hears it, devoid of content, consisting only of "tone and cadence." Its words are "indistinguishable" to her, trapped as she still is in a wholly private revelation, but its significance is made clear by its alternating tones, one of them "majestic," "high," and "commanding," filled with the authority of his office, and the other a "low undertone," "a cry of pain" that "touched a sensibility in every bosom" (*SL*, 328), a private voice of private sorrow. In his ability to speak "to the great heart of mankind" in words at once public and private, in this "profound and continual undertone," Dimmesdale's "Tongue of Flame" finds its "most appropriate power" (*SL*, 328). His art, in which private, feminine experience informs masculine public statement, is not, by this means, feminized but completed. Neither Puritan nor antinomian, it is instead perfect. By contrast, Hester's wholly private, and thus wholly feminine, art when it is translated from embodiment to enactment is incomplete and lawless.

The sermon, we learn in the second account, is a typical one of its kind, taking as its subject "the relation between the Deity and the communities of mankind, with a special reference to the New England they were here planting in the wilderness" (*SL*, 332). No Jeremiah, however, Dimmesdale prophesies "a high and glorious destiny for the newly gathered people of the Lord" (*SL*, 332–33). Yet Hester is not the only one to detect the "deep, sad undertone" in this optimistic pronouncement. All of Dimmesdale's auditors agree that beneath the "swelling waves" of his eloquence is a strain of pathos, which they, not having Hester's knowledge of its origin, interpret not as the speech of the secret heart but, in equally private terms, as "the natural regret of one soon to pass away" (*SL*, 333). Having showered his "golden truths" over them, their "angel" must return to heaven.

The two tones of the sermon suggest that Dimmesdale has found a way to reintegrate the private and the public selves. In his private journey from sin to repentance, he has discovered the history and fate of New England. Like Edward Johnson, he finds the glorious destiny of the community prefigured in the sufferings of the saint. His life has meaning not merely as a record of an individual's struggle but as it types forth the struggles of the New Israel. Dimmesdale has found his way out of the maze of guilt and heresy and returned, newly empowered, to orthodoxy and community. It remains for him only to mount the scaffold in the light of day and confess his sin for him to die triumphant. And doing this, he does what is best both for himself and for his community, as we learn from the dramatic effects of his conversion. The "wild infant" Pearl is humanized by grief; her first tears, shed on her dying father, are a "pledge" that, unlike her mother, she will "grow up amid human joy and sorrow, nor forever to do battle with the world, but be a woman in it" (*SL*, 339). Chillingworth, deprived of his "Devil's work," shrivels away. And Hester is cautioned to look to her sin. In this sense Dimmesdale's confession on the scaffold confirms the Puritans' judgment of the original crime and demonstrates, furthermore, that confession and penance yield true repentance, that penitence is the "victory" the Puritans claim it to be.

Dimmesdale's death on the scaffold seals the fate of all the characters except Hester, the one with whom we are most concerned. Chillingworth dies, leaving his fortune to Pearl; Pearl returns to the Old World, with which she has been associated throughout, and, to the best of our narrator's knowledge, fulfills her pledge to become a "woman"; but Hester has still to act. At this point in the novel, as others have observed, the heavy hand of the author intrudes into the narrative. Hester is shipped off with Pearl to Europe where, despite occasional "vague reports," her life is a mystery. Nevertheless, repent Hester must if the antinomian implications of the tale are to be countered, and repent she does. Returning after many years to her cottage, Hester resumes the scarlet letter "of her own free will" (*SL*, 344). Taking up her "long-forsaken shame" in earnest, she now embodies the perfect, if somewhat delayed, congruence of law and conscience.

Just as the resumption of the scarlet letter at Pearl's insistence in the forest recalls an unwilling Hester to her public obligations as mother and as "general symbol," so this final restoration of the letter returns her to the community wherein she has her "real life." But with a difference: no longer a "stigma," the scarlet letter symbolizes instead Hester's genuine penitence. Accepting her guilt and with it her past, she reverses her "conversion" and is very nearly restored to purity. She, like her letter, becomes "a type of something to be sorrowed over, and looked upon with awe, yet with reverence too" (*SL*, 344).

Humbled by the recognition of her guilt, Hester abandons the grandiose image of herself as prophetess of a new dispensation and settles down to a life in which neither "selfish ends" nor "her own profit and enjoyment" (*SL*, 344) have any part, to a life of disinterested virtue. And just as Dimmesdale's fall enables his rebirth as the most eloquent spokesman for the nation and lends him the power of prophecy, so Hester's renunciation of her sinful past, too, inspires a glorious vision of the future. As soon as she ceases to imagine herself—"stained with sin" and "bowed with shame" as she is—the "destined prophetess," she becomes *ipso facto* a prophetess. Forfeiting self, she gains the female power of divination. In her new role as counselor of women, she opens the promise of the future. She assures the victims of passion of the day when "a new truth" will be revealed "in order to establish the whole relation between man and woman on a surer ground of mutual happiness" (*SL*, 344). "The angel and apostle of the coming revelation," she explains, "must be a woman indeed," but not a woman burdened with sin like herself. "Lofty, pure, and beautiful; and wise, moreover, not through dusky grief, but the ethereal medium of joy," this prophetess will show "how sacred love should make us happy, by the truest test of a life successful to such an end!" (*SL*, 344–45).

This is Hawthorne's final play on the story of Anne Hutchinson. Hawthorne returns Hester to Hutchinson's original error and corrects it. And having corrected the error that set Hutchinson's whole history in motion, he can end Hester's without even starting it. Behind Hester's reappearance as feminine advisor stands the courtroom exchange between Hutchinson and Winthrop on the subject of women as teachers. While Hutchinson insisted on her right to instruct both men and women in matters of doctrine, Winthrop articulated the orthodox position, based on Titus, that older women might teach younger ones "about their business, to love their husbands and not make them clash." Hester becomes the teacher Hutchinson should have been. Sharing the wisdom of her sad experience with other women, she instructs them precisely "about their business," about matters of the heart. The aging Hester rejects the illicit intimacy of adultery and urges instead "sacred love," ethereal joy, and domestic bliss; she teaches according to the "rule" in Titus. The prophetess she imagines will, like Lee's Naomi, combine humility, beauty, and the virtues of home and hearth; in fact, the "angel of the coming revelation" will be the sentimental heroine. This is not irony but tragedy: but for the scarlet letter, Hester might have been this "angel."

The penultimate passage of *The Scarlet Letter* hinges, then, on a fine distinction. It is not the validity of prophecy or invisible witness per se that is at issue in Hawthorne's tale but rather the relationship between private revelation and public ideology. The apostle whose coming Hester predicts will, after all, preach a private truth. Nonetheless, she will differ profoundly from Hester. She will teach not passionate defiance and spiritual arrogance but sacred love, not alienation but affection and community. Moreover, her heart knowledge will prove itself by the "truest test," her life. In the simplest terms, her revelation will be trustworthy because her life will exemplify what her heart teaches. But this, of course, is too simple. We have already learned in the forest that to live what the heart teaches is not, in and of itself, meritorious. What really matters is what the heart teaches. The point then is not just that inner and outer selves will work in tandem to reveal a "new truth" but that the truth entrusted to the prophetess of the coming revelation will be "divine and mysterious" and will be revealed only "when the world should have grown ripe for it" (*SL,* 344). This truth, far from subverting order, instead awaits the improved social arrangements that will evolve in "Heaven's own time." The particulars of the new "relation" between men and women that Hester foresees are never stated, but this hardly matters. What she prophesies is the domestic equivalent of the rising glory of America enunciated by Dimmesdale from the pulpit on Election Day. Like him, she finds figured in her private grief the magnificent future of the nation of saints.

Hester's "prophecy" is crucial to the social statement of *The Scarlet Letter,* for it weaves together all the threads of the novel and offers a solution to the dilemma of individual autonomy. Hawthorne does not retract his initial estimate of the Puritans as iron men with no right to meddle in questions of the human heart or ally himself with Hester's antinomianism. Instead, he builds the reformation of the Puritan community on Hester's vision of a brighter future to come. The scarlet letter finally teaches Hester the truth: she learns that the past is irrevocable and that only by assuming responsibility for her sin can she move beyond it. Nonetheless, she cannot, like Pearl, move beyond it into plot. Rather than living as a woman in the world and at peace with it like her daughter, Hester moves beyond the world by dying as a woman. Silenced once and for all, her meaning fixed for eternity, Hester assumes her final costume.

Appropriately, the slate tombstone that bears Hester's letter brings together setting and dress. The public token of a private event, the tombstone is erected at Hester's death but serves to memorialize and thus complete Dimmesdale's as well. In this respect and in every other, it demonstrates that Hester has finally found her place. The two graves, side by side and sharing one marker but "with a space between," recall us to the adultery and to the first—and last—meaning of the scarlet letter. Singularity of every kind has been banished along with Nature, which is strangely absent from this graveyard; the tombstone restores the scarlet letter to simplicity. No fancywork adorns the stone, only a black escutcheon containing a red *A*. A somber ground and a straightforward letter, the tombstone is the costume in which Hester was meant to appear at the outset of the novel. Even its colors return us to the novel's opening. The black of the prison and the red of the rose are no longer side by side and thus potentially antithetical; instead, they bear the "appropriate" complementary relationship of the two tones of Dimmesdale's sermon—the red of the private and the feminine is at the center of and contained within the black. And so too the antinomian Hester is contained. The political problem of the novel is thus solved. Similarly, the solution to the formal problem of the novel is suggested by the heraldic language of Hawthorne's description: "On a field, sable, the letter A, gules" (*SL*, 345). The stylized art of the escutcheon is mirrored in the conventionalized language of heraldry, which, in turn, mirrors the conventionalized Hester of the conclusion of *The Scarlet Let-*

ter. By returning to convention, Hawthorne averts lawless action on the part of Hester and gives over her plot to Pearl, no longer a monster but a woman, whose tears, like Naomi's, seal her relation to a world of human joy and sorrow. Out of Woman as lawbreaker comes, both literally and figuratively, Woman as lawgiver. *The Scarlet Letter* represents one culmination of the story of Anne Hutchinson. *Uncle Tom's Cabin,* in which Harriet Beecher Stowe argues that Woman because she is lawgiver must break the law, represents the other.

8

Feel Right and Pray

In 1852 Harriet Beecher Stowe urged the readers of *Uncle Tom's Cabin* to "feel right" and to oppose slavery. As Stowe presents them, these are synonymous: to consult feeling is to discover Christian truth written upon the heart; to oppose the Fugitive Slave Act is to choose Christ and to repudiate the world. Although Stowe directed her appeal to men and women alike, *Uncle Tom's Cabin*—a novel governed by distinctions of race and gender and written at a moment when "woman's fiction" dominated the American literary marketplace—not surprisingly insists upon the moral superiority of women. By nature and circumstance, Stowe suggests, women are more likely to "feel right" and are, therefore, less willing than men to tolerate the legalized horrors of slavery. The most virtuous women in *Uncle Tom's Cabin* are those who rely most fully on the heart to guide them. Setting a private, unassailable, and deeply felt knowledge of God's truth against the cruelty and corruption of a world governed by men, these women hold the promise of a future without slavery.

Uncle Tom's Cabin brings both the story and the literary history of Anne Hutchinson full circle. The young Nathaniel Hawthorne sketched the problem of Anne Hutchinson in terms of the larger one of "public women" and, more especially, women writers. Claiming that, "as yet, the great body of American women are a domestic race," he envisioned a time when "ill-judged incitements shall have turned their hearts away from the fireside" (*TS*, 18) and toward the world of letters. Not until twenty years later would Hawthorne's dire prediction come true, but when at last the "ink-stained Amazons" conquered the literary field, they apparently shared Hawthorne's ambivalence about their venture.

"Woman," Hawthorne warned in his sketch of Hutchinson, "when she feels the impulse of genius like a command of Heaven within her, should be aware that she is relinquishing a part of the loveliness of her sex, and obey the inward voice with sorrowing reluctance, like the Arabian maid who bewailed the gift of Prophecy" (*TS*, 19). Just such reluctance was claimed by the women novelists themselves. Elizabeth Phelps Ward, for example, explained that she had written *The Gates Ajar* (1869) at the "bidding of an angel," while Harriet Beecher Stowe insisted that God had penned *Uncle Tom's Cabin*. While these extravagant claims undoubtedly express the profound discomfort the woman writer experienced as she ventured into the male literary market, they also suggest the paradoxical relationship of the woman writer to her work.[1] On the one hand, by casting herself as medium, the woman writer confirmed her femininity in precisely the terms used by writers like Emerson. On the other hand, by representing herself as God's scribe, she proposed her work as a new revelation. Like the angel and apostle of the coming revelation imagined by Hester, the woman author proved herself a fit prophetess by writing herself out of her book and thus showing herself a woman. But denying herself and invoking God, she could, like Anne Hutchinson, assert herself all the more vigorously.

The problem of gender shapes the content as well as the context of domestic fiction. The female domestic novelist must authorize her fiction by publicly asserting her femininity. At the same time, she must not betray her heroine by seeming to choose art over womanhood. One might hypothesize, in fact, that the recurrent plot of the domestic novel in which a young girl struggles to quell a rebellious, passionate self and emerges a model of Christian humility and feminine virtue reproduces the conflict experienced by its author. But if perfect domesticity and Christian self-abasement characterize the heroine of this genre, so too does she affirm, in the words of one critic, "moral principles . . . identical with those incorporated in the dominant value system of American society."[2] The domestic novel brings the Gerty Flints and the Ellen Montgomerys around, from rebelliousness to submission, from antagonism to harmony, from independence to marriage. In the process it idealizes the status quo.

By saying that the domestic novel idealizes the status quo, I do not mean that it simply ratifies what is. There is a middle term in the transformation of the domestic heroine: she comes to terms with the world around her by becoming a Christian. Reading her Bible, she discovers a private truth, witnessed by God and attested to by her heart. But that discovery, rather than pitting her against the world, transforms her into a model for its improvement. The feminine interior self reiterates ideal Christian values, which, in turn, replicate the highest principles of society, though not necessarily the principles we see at work there. The adherence of the domestic heroine to "established patterns of living and traditional beliefs" does, then, as one scholar has suggested, provide the means to effect "a radical transformation" of society, but only insofar as that heroine is ideally feminine and the transformation she implies an idealization of what is and not an alternative to it.[3]

The danger of a Hester Prynne, in other words, can be contained by returning to the gender conventions of domestic fiction because that fiction empowers Emerson's sequestered lady, not Hawthorne's artist. Its heroine attains a "religious height" that prompts her self-sacrifice, submission, and charity and, further, establishes her as a powerful example for those around her. In her trials and her victory, and more particularly in the home she invariably establishes at the end of the novel, we find prefigured the redemption of a fallen world. Since the evils of that world are explained not in secular terms as the corruption of a social system but in Christian ones as the effects of the Fall, reformation is appropriately figured in individual conversion, an experience not just proper to the sphere of Woman but dependent on it.

Uncle Tom's Cabin begins where *The Scarlet Letter* leaves off, and it begins as well at the end of the typical domestic plot. Stowe's women are, from the start, the humble, loving, domestic creatures imagined by Hester and anticipated in the newlywed who closes the domestic novel. Beginning at the end, the issue that engages Stowe's attention is not the interior struggle of Woman as public criminal or private rebel but the public efficacy of a private, feminine sensibility. Her heroines have already won their victories over self; the question of *Uncle Tom's Cabin* is whether they can emerge victorious in the world by bringing slavery to an end. The model woman is, in other words, moved into history with the explicit object of altering its course. The sentimentalism of domestic fiction is turned to the purpose not simply of individual conversion but of individual conversion as a mode of social reform.

"The object of these sketches," Stowe explains in the preface to *Uncle Tom's Cabin*, "is to awaken sympathy and feeling for the African race, as they exist among us; to show their wrongs and sorrows, under a system so necessarily cruel and unjust as to defeat . . . all that can be attempted for them . . . under it."[4] Once exposed, however, the injustice of slavery must necessarily be opposed. Pitting divine law, revealed as feeling, against civil law, Stowe argues, as did Jackson's eulogists, that to violate the law of the state—in this case, the Fugitive Slave Act—is to uphold the law of the feminine heart. "While politicians contend, and men are swerved this way and that by conflicting tides of interest and passion," she continues, "the great cause of human liberty" is in the hands of God. But in *Uncle Tom's Cabin*, God's earthly emissary is feminine. Not men, swayed as they are by interest, but disinterested women must enact God's will and "set judgement in the earth" (*UTC*, 2). Before the novel even begins, then, the assumptions about gender that will govern it are clear. And so, too, is its problem, the problem of how to empower the feminine to oppose the law without recreating Anne Hutchinson.

Paradoxically, *Uncle Tom's Cabin* lays claim to the ideological conventions of domestic fiction by violating them in its very first scene. The Shelby episode, which begins the novel, occurs precisely at the intersection of those two spheres dubbed the home and the world by nineteenth-century rhetoricians of domesticity. Interdependent—in fact, mutually sustaining—the home and the world were nonetheless taken to be distinct in their activities, in their actors, and, most especially, in the moral values they asserted and the human characteristics they called into play. As Mr. Shelby sits in his dining room sipping wine with the slave trader Haley and reluctantly negotiates the sale of Uncle Tom and the child, Harry, he permits the ruthlessness of the market to invade the sanctity of the home—his home, as well, of course, as the home of Tom and Harry. But it is not just the literal Shelby home that is violated by the slave trade. In a larger sense, the sale of the Shelby slaves suggests that the very locale marked out by the domestic novel as the repository of feminine virtue is itself in jeopardy. Stowe's first and her subtlest demonstration of the evil of slavery is accomplished by showing that slavery disrupts the scheme of the domestic novel; it threatens both the actual and the literary conditions that ensure the disinterested virtue of woman and, in this way, predicts the problem the novel must solve.

Nevertheless, Stowe uses the Shelby episode to draw the requisite distinction between men and women and to portray the slave trade as a white male enterprise. White women, she suggests, because they do not themselves engage in the slave trade, are exempt from its corrupting influence—are, in fact, its natural opponents. Mrs. Shelby is no party to the transaction between her husband and the slave trader. In fact, she immediately protests the sale of Uncle Tom and Harry. She is given to understand, however, that only her complete ignorance of the financial position of her family allows this altogether admirable indulgence of feeling. Virtuous because she is dependent and powerless in her virtue, Mrs. Shelby is "reverenced and respected" by her husband for her "religious character" (*UTC*, 14). But reverence is one thing and power quite another; the most Mrs. Shelby can do is to engage in a not-so-subtle obstructionism in order to gain time for the runaway Eliza.

The Shelby episode draws the lines of conflict between white men, morally compromised by their participation in the slave market, and their Christian wives. But it has another effect as well, namely, to show the involvement of the home and its keeper in the practice of slavery. The Shelby chapters introduce slavery as itself a domestic institution, an intrusion of the marketplace into the home not only when the trader is sitting in the dining room but when he is nowhere to be seen. Slaves, after all, both manage and reside in households like the Shelbys', and the appellations lent them by their "families"—Uncle Tom, Aunt Chloe, Mammy—falsify the crudely economic relation between owner and slave and suggest instead that this relation is domestic and familial. The use of kinship terms to designate slaves perverts those terms, and, likewise, domestic slavery calls into question the "disinterestedness" of women. For if the home is not a sphere separate from the market but is instead a microcosm of it, the moral distinction between men and women collapses. Moreover, if language connoting "sacred" family ties can be attached to people who are, in reality, commodities in the slave market, the family is desacralized. Stowe calls up a conventional picture of devout women at home—in fact, she rests her hopes for an end to slavery on just such women—but her subject works against her: the other side of Mrs. Shelby's moral aversion to slavery is, clearly, her complicity in it.

Stowe proposes nonetheless to supplant masculine authority with feminine nurture, to call on the maternal and the Christian in women to counteract the inhumanity of slavery. Her insistence on mothers, black and white, as archetypal victims and unyielding opponents of slavery suggests that in her novel, like others of its kind, the home stands neither as complement nor as alternative but rather as corrective to the world. The best white women in *Uncle Tom's Cabin* are characterized by a commendable but disabling submission to God and husband. They, like their creators, serve as "interpreters of the established ethos, its guardians, or even, where needed, its restorers,"[5] but these functions depend on their insulation from the market-world that feeds them. Deriving their public identities and their private support from men, these women represent a culture of dependence. Were they to compete with men as autonomous beings, they would forfeit the very qualities at stake in that competition—in fact, they would share in what Stowe understands to be the tragedy of slave women, the deprivation of home, family, and femininity.

Stowe, then, draws a world of misery, destitution, and injustice not, like her contemporaries, "to chronicle the 'trials and triumphs' . . . of a heroine who . . . finds within herself the qualities of intelligence, wit, resourcefulness and courage sufficient to overcome them"[6] but to urge its reform by the invisible force of feminine love. Her task in *Uncle Tom's Cabin* is to make feminine feeling adequate to the social task of the novel. The domestic sentimental scheme is, in these terms, both essential and problematic, for while the world may encroach on the home, the home cannot be moved into the world without forfeiting its special redemptive qualities. Ironically, then, men, not women, must carry feminine values out of the home. As we will see, Augustine St. Clare and Uncle Tom are alternative models of a feminized manhood; in them race and gender come together to redefine the meaning of power.

Despite all of this, the novel's vision of the world once reformed is clear. It will look like the home, or rather it will look like the matriarchal Quaker settlement, which, in its profound isolation from the marketplace and its perfect domesticity, is the home writ large. Only during our brief glimpse of the matriarch Rachel Halliday and the community of Friends over which she reigns in the paradise of Indiana do we escape the contradictions inherent in Stowe's appeal to feminine feeling to end slavery. Elsewhere, the pattern of conflict that characterizes Stowe's portrayal of the Shelbys is repeated with increasing force. In the chapter "In Which It Appears That a Senator is But a Man," for example, the coincidence of feminine virtue with feminine powerlessness narrowly circumscribes the influence of the devout Mrs. Bird. Horrified at her husband's support of the Fugitive Slave Act, Mrs. Bird invokes what is "right and Christian" in an effort to counter her husband's insistence that slavery is not a matter of "private feeling" but of "great public interests." Humanity and Christianity are, of course, on Mrs. Bird's side, but her virtue is explicitly represented as depending on her exclusion from the realm of public affairs. "I don't know anything about politics," she exclaims, "but I can read my Bible and there I see that I must feed the hungry, clothe the naked, and comfort the desolate, and that Bible I mean to follow" (*UTC*, 84).

Seen one way, the implication of this statement is that if she did know anything about politics, Biblical injunctions might be overridden by interest. Mrs. Bird's moral rectitude, as her husband points out, is, like Mrs. Shelby's, a luxury of dependence: she has no constituency to please, no bread to win. The moral purity of her stance is assured by her exclusion from the world of politics. In this sense, Mrs. Bird articulates her powerlessness, a powerlessness that becomes more striking as Stowe goes about resolving the clash between husband and wife. From a slightly different vantage point, however, Mrs. Bird's statement contains its own critique. The very grammar of the sentence makes clear the moral primacy of the Bible. It implies that Christianity and not interest ought to hold sway even in the political arena: "Obeying God," Mrs. Bird insists, "never brings on public evils" (*UTC*, 84). In other words, both the impossibility and the desirability of carrying Christian values out of the home and into the world are reflected in Mrs. Bird's impassioned defense of the fugitive slave. The same elements that obstruct the translation of private feminine sentiment into masculine public action allow for the invocation of an absolute standard of morality that, if all were right in the world, would apply equally in the home and the Senate. The problem is that if all were right in the world, the world would be one in which absolute standards of morality would, quite literally, have no place.

Whereas in the case of the Shelbys conflict is preempted by the finality of the sale of Tom and Harry, the Bird episode is designed to speak directly to the collision of private feeling and public action. Stowe addresses this conflict by drawing a distinction between Mr. Bird, the private man, and Senator Bird, the public official. Summoned to aid Eliza and Harry, Mr. Bird acts out of feeling and acquits himself admirably, restoring in the process his wife's faith in his humanity. But as far as we know, this act of private charity—which, not incidentally, violates the very law he has helped to enact—has no effect whatsoever on his public posture. At home, the man partakes of the virtues the home represents. Removed from public view, the domestic sphere fosters the best of the private self—by definition, a feminine self. But the actions of the senator are dictated by the "public interests" that hedge him in on all sides. By turning to Mr. Bird in her effort to resolve the seemingly irresolvable conflict between private and public values, Stowe rescues intact the separate spheres of men and women. More important, she establishes the existence of an inner, feminine self in men that makes them, like women, susceptible to moral suasion.

The problem in *Uncle Tom's Cabin* is neither in defining the attributes of gender nor in assigning membership in one sphere or the other. Instead, it lies in empowering those capable of sympathizing fully with the plight of the slave. So closely are opposition to slavery and feminine sensibility associated that when Stowe tries to make her argument against slavery by extending the implications of domestic sentimentalism, she is stymied by the very terms she has so carefully established. Sentimentalism requires the representation of the interior life as feminine and the exterior one as masculine. In this way it readily allows for the creation of "feminine" heroes and "masculine" heroines. What this scheme makes impossible, however, is the creation of a fully empowered character who carries feminine values into the public domain and pits them against the masculine values of the marketplace. To the extent that men are portrayed as combining the masculine and the feminine, these represent different and distinct aspects of their character and behavior. Sentimentalism lends Stowe a framework that supports the idea that women and blacks are, by virtue of their circumstances if not innately, more Christian, more affectionate, more sympathetic, and more just than white men. But at the same time that domestic sentimentalism attributes to women a peculiar capacity to sympathize with the oppressed— right feeling—it deprives them of the capacity to translate this feeling into action outside the home.

Examined in this context, the character and fate of Augustine St. Clare completes a pattern begun with the Shelbys. From the first, St. Clare, unlike Mr. Bird, is blatantly feminine. A "graceful, elegantly-formed young man," St. Clare resembles no one so much as his blue-eyed, golden-blonde daughter Eva. Physically frail and languid in manner, he seems at first the very type of poetic youth. But he is not simply this—or rather, since poetry is an outpouring of the feminine inner self,

St. Clare cannot be poetic without being feminized. Stowe continually recalls us to this equation, both by emphasizing St.
Clare's feminine traits and by offering us his masculine counterpart. Augustine, named after the early Christian mystic, is
one of a pair of twins; the other, tellingly, is named Alfred after
the Saxon warrior and king. As might be expected, Alfred follows in the footsteps of his planter father while Augustine
receives his whole inheritance from his "divine" mother. She
bequeaths him "an exceeding delicacy of constitution" and a
morbidly sensitive nature, "more akin to the softness of woman
than the ordinary hardness of his own sex" (*UTC*, 158). Beneath
the "rough bark of manhood," St. Clare suffers from an acute-
ness of feeling not unlike Eva's.

But if Augustine is his mother's son, so too is he for all practical purposes his daughter's mother. Banished from the family
plantation by his brother as a "womanish sentimentalist" better fit to write poetry than engage in business, St. Clare does
neither. The very shape of his life is characteristically female. He
has, as far as we know, no employment outside the home. His
time and attention are entirely absorbed in the care of Eva, his
mother's namesake. It is in St. Clare that Eva confides and from
him that comfort, sympathy, and affection are forthcoming. As
if to highlight St. Clare's maternal role, his wife is stripped of
her femininity. Marie St. Clare is not, Stowe insists, a "whole
woman"; in fact, she is scarcely a human being. As Stowe twice
repeats, she is a commodity purchased by St. Clare in despera-
tion—"a fine figure, a pair of splendid eyes, and a hundred
thousand dollars" (*UTC*, 160). Unlike those other human commodities, the slaves, however, Marie St. Clare is not dehuman-
ized so much as inhuman. A "woman with no heart," she is
incapable of giving her husband the love that would allow him
to lead a purposeful life, and this emotional failure is explicitly
linked to her support of slavery in its cruelest forms and to her
ignorance of the feminine arts. She is unable "to mend the broken threads of life, and weave them again into a tissue of bright-
ness."

What Marie St. Clare lacks in sensibility she makes up in
selfishness, and just as one is illustrated by her want of domes-

tic skill, the other is, predictably, associated with the self-interested practices of the market. No "easy creditor in the exchange of affection," Marie St. Clare typifies the "thoroughly selfish woman" than whom "there is not on earth a more merciless exactor of love from others. . . . The more unlovely she grows, the more jealously and scrupulously she exacts love, to the uttermost farthing" (*UTC*, 161). So rigidly does Stowe divide the universe of the book that self-denial belongs exclusively to the home, while self-aggrandizement, self-indulgence, can only be represented in the language of commerce. As we might expect, Marie St. Clare, not her husband, is ultimately responsible for the sale of Uncle Tom to Simon Legree.

Taken together, the two St. Clares illustrate Stowe's tendency to represent character through gender-associated language, but Augustine is a far more complex character than his wife. Prone though he is to the sick headaches of the sentimental heroine, he is neither wholly feminine nor entirely virtuous. A master of slaves, head of an opulent household, the scion of an aristocratic family, St. Clare is, on the one hand, aimless and lethargic and, on the other, capable of what is unquestionably the most sophisticated analysis of slavery the novel offers. He alone has the education, the intelligence, and the experience to propose an analogy between slavery in America and English "wage-slavery," to understand the "appropriation" of labor, and to see clearly both the interests that sustain slavery and the inevitability of its end. Convinced that slavery is the "essence of all abuse," he nurses a "chronic remorse" while despairing of any solution. Having early given up any illusion of himself as the liberator of slaves, he practices a benign neglect in relation to his dependents that he himself regards as contemptible. Instead of being an "actor and regenerator in society"—a role for which he is morally, intellectually, socially, and financially equipped—he is "a piece of driftwood . . . floating and eddying about" (*UTC*, 237). His life, as he is the first to admit, is a "non sequitur."

But because St. Clare is a man and not a woman, neither author nor reader is willing to leave him to a life of impotent self-reproach. By the time we meet him, the horrors of slavery have so multiplied that the reader is hard put to excuse St. Clare's unwillingness to confront so obvious an evil. Endowed with both a feminine sensibility and a masculine ability to negotiate the world of affairs, able to feel and to think, equally fluent in the language of religion and that of politics, it is not enough that he simply love Eva. For while this attachment gives symbolic testimony of his potential virtue, we want acts from him, not symbols. But the two sides of his character, one feminine, the other masculine, rather than working in tandem to produce the ideal reformer instead pull in opposite directions and immobilize him. His noblest ambitions are thwarted by an acute ethical sense. His knowledge reveals not solutions but still more problems. The sense of duty he admires and in part shares with his Northern cousin Ophelia is undermined by his Southern indolence.

As if sensing that he must nevertheless be brought to action, Stowe uses Eva's death as the occasion for St. Clare's transformation. While Eva lives, St. Clare's life has, if not a grand purpose, at least a focus of attention: "All the interests and hopes of St. Clare's life had . . . wound themselves around this child. It was for Eva that he had managed his property . . . and planned the disposal of his time . . . to buy, improve, alter, and arrange, or dispose something for her,—had been so long his habit, that now she was gone, there seemed . . . nothing to be done" (*UTC*, 311). In reproof of the private nature of this activity, the failing Eva offers her father both the solace of Christianity and a public mission: in memory of her, St. Clare is to free his slaves—or at least Uncle Tom—and "persuade people to do right" about slavery. Everything leads us to anticipate that St. Clare will take on this new interest wholeheartedly, if only for his daughter's sake. He becomes in his grief "another man" —one who reads the Bible "seriously and honestly," who soberly considers his treatment of his slaves, who begins the process of Tom's emancipation and undertakes to do his "duty . . . to the poor and lowly" (*UTC*, 312). In this guise St. Clare holds out the possibility of a fusion of Mr. Bird and Senator Bird. But no sooner has St. Clare been brought to the point of translating his better feelings into deeds than he is struck down in a café brawl. In the best sentimental tradition, he dies with the words "home" and "mother" on his lips. Even here, in the juxtaposition of the "masculine" brawl and the "feminine" deathbed scene, our attention is directed to St. Clare's divided self.

One must ask why Stowe so abruptly checks St. Clare's career as Christian reformer and why, having decided to kill him off, she strains so to relate his death to the deaths of Eva, who precedes him, and Uncle Tom, who follows him to heaven. Unlike her father, little Eva is a character disabled by both age and sex. Too good to grow into adulthood in a world where Christian love is defeated at every turn by the brutality of slavery, Eva dies not of disease but of an excess of feeling. In her fatal empathy as in other respects, her virtues magnify and perfect those of the other women in the novel: too young to be a mother, Eva's dealings with Topsy nonetheless mimic the best of mothering; like the model Mrs. Bird, she abhors violence of any sort; with Mrs. Shelby, she longs to protect the weak and the helpless. Loyal, generous, self-denying, and faithful, Eva would if she could grow up to become the exemplary wife and mother. In fact, one proof of the evil of slavery is that it requires the sacrifice of Eva, at once a female Christ and a new Eve.

As others have shown, Eva's feminine virtue and her spotless death are repeated, in color, one might say, in Uncle Tom. She dies, pale and peaceful, in her lily-white bed while he is beaten to death in Legree's shed. All spirit, she embodies the New Testament while he is, on the contrary, "all the moral and Christian virtues bound in black morocco complete." She is allegory; he is realism. Yet "the old child and the young one" share the essential qualities of the heroine of domestic fiction: they are pious, submissive, self-sacrificing, and affectionate.[7] Insofar as the novel's assumptions about gender are equally assumptions about the effects of dependence, these necessarily implicate slave characters as well as women. In fact, the domestic scheme that structures *Uncle Tom's Cabin* is responsible for the feminization of Uncle Tom. His "femininity" is secondary to his blackness, which is, in turn, the mark of his dependent status. Deprived by slavery of the masculine prerogative of action in the world, Tom is relegated to the other sphere, the home. There, permitted to feel but not to act, he becomes womanlike. And womanlike, he dons the robes of the Christian martyr and becomes, as well, white.[8] Allied by their powerlessness and their virtue, Tom and Eva are, of course, the most powerful characters in the novel. Evangelists both, bringing the good news of mankind's redemption through Christ, their deaths finalize the opposition between slavery and domestic Christianity and hold out hope for the future.

Stowe was hardly alone in associating women and slaves. Both abolitionist and proslavery writers insisted on their likeness. In one case the likeness of black slaves to white women argued for their emancipation; in the other the analogy to female weakness was used to demonstrate the unfitness of blacks for freedom. Lydia Maria Child, author of *An Appeal in favor of that class of Americans called Africans,* outlined the similarity concisely: "The comparison between women and the colored race is striking. Both are characterized by affection more than by intellect; both have a strong development of the religious sentiment; both are exceedingly adhesive in their attachments; both, comparatively speaking, have a tendency to submission; and hence, both have been kept in subjection by physical force, and considered in the light of property, than as individuals."[9] For some women abolitionism therefore pointed directly to feminism, but this was not the case for Stowe.

In *Uncle Tom's Cabin* racial categories are subsumed by those of gender. As others have noticed, Stowe is very careful to distinguish black from white, mulatto from quadroon. These distinctions are central to her understanding of the relationship between race and gender. One scholar has suggested that the presence of characters of mixed blood allows Stowe to speculate on the "probable effects of an infusion of white blood into Southern slaves." He sees her use of characters like the runaway George Harris, "restive and rebellious mulattoes," as calling into question the "totality of [Stowe's] commitment . . . to the submissive virtues attributed to the full-blooded Negro."[10] But these characters function in another and, I would argue, more important way. They allow for the clear association of whiteness with maleness and blackness with femininity. In raising the possibility of active resistance to slavery, Stowe carefully uses mulatto characters whose empowerment comes directly from their white paternity: "Sons of white fathers . . . will rise," Augustine St. Clare predicts, "and raise with them their mother's race" (*UTC*, 274). Throughout *Uncle Tom's Cabin* relative blackness is associated with the augmented virtue and diminished power of mothers while relative whiteness betokens access to the privileges, the power, and the "haughty feelings" of fathers. This paradigm, central to Stowe's method of characterization in the novel, helps to account for the difficulty inherent in an Augustine St. Clare.

The deaths of Eva and Tom illustrate the final victory of the faithful over the injustice of this world. But if their deaths seal their meaning and bring converts to the cause of Christianity and, therefore, abolition, the death of St. Clare seems by contrast both gratuitous and discordant. Even in his newly regenerate state after the death of Eva, St. Clare partakes neither of the piety nor of the submissiveness of the Christian martyr. His death, unlike Uncle Tom's, is thus a "Reunion," not a "Victory." St. Clare is reunited with mother and daughter in heaven, but his life does not merit our particular respect nor his death set in motion a process of redemption.

It is tempting to argue that St. Clare dies because Tom's emancipation would short-circuit the plot of the novel, or because Stowe finds the transformation of a planter's son into an emancipator of slaves unlikely, or because, as Southern abolitionist, St. Clare is doomed from the start. Given Stowe's skillful management of plot elsewhere in the novel and her apparent lack of concern with the probable, however, none of these explanations are convincing. A more fruitful one lies in the impact St. Clare's new purposefulness would have on the embedded structure of *Uncle Tom's Cabin*. Augustine St. Clare is the only white character in the novel in whom masculine and feminine attributes are conjoined, and, oddly enough, for this very reason he endangers the terms of the novel. Combining virtue and power as he does, he could presumably translate private feeling into public action. He could, that is, both feel and compete. But to send St. Clare out into the world as "actor and regenerator" would be to rewrite the book.

In *Uncle Tom's Cabin* men pass in and out of the home, finding there respite from the business of the world and sometimes suffering a brief renewal of their faith and humanity. But the home can function as refuge, and women as moral arbiters, only if the home and the world are understood as separate but interdependent realms. In this scheme women maintain their disinterested virtue at the expense of their autonomy; they have influence but not power over the men on whose ability and willingness to compete they rely for their support. Disrupt this—create a character who can cross the boundary at will— and gender loses its moral valence: the Mrs. Birds and the Mrs. Shelbys lose their special capacity for right feeling, the state of a kitchen no longer symbolizes the moral worth of the family it feeds, and domesticity becomes indistinguishable from competition. If dependence is to account for the virtue of women and maternity for their superior emotional development, then the symbolic structure of *Uncle Tom's Cabin* must be governed by traditional distinctions between men and women. Were St. Clare to act rather than die, he would in the process dissolve this distinction. It has been proposed that in fiction "androgyny . . . is a male trait enabling men to act from their male side and feel from their female side."[11] Literary androgyny, in other words, does not dissolve but rather reiterates the "radical dualism" of the sexes. Were St. Clare to act from his female side, he might become the ideal "completed" being imagined by Fuller and Emerson or he might become Anne Hutchinson. Either way, he would disrupt the gender politics of the novel.

Stowe attempts to avert this danger by dissociating St. Clare from the women in the novel. His virtue, for example, is a legacy, not a sign of dependence. His morbid sensitivity is part and parcel of his poetic temperament. He adopts the role of mother because his wife has defaulted on her maternity. Nevertheless, the sentimental scheme that governs the novel and its representation of femininity as the highest good override these distinctions, and Stowe is unable to extricate St. Clare from the domestic rhetoric that signifies approval in the novel. The very language that makes him empathic, generous, affectionate, and fair has the secondary effect of "feminizing" him. St. Clare must be sacrificed, then, to secure the connection between powerlessness and redemptive faith, a connection crucial to Stowe's literary enterprise as well as her political one.

Stowe's argument against slavery depends on her ability to write Uncle Tom as a full-fledged character. Profoundly dispossessed of self, the slave cannot be drawn in the same way as the autonomous, white male hero of the novel. He can, however, be "humanized," and thus brought to life as a character, if he is created according to the principles which customarily govern the creation of female characters. Thus feminized, the slave can, moreover, be represented as partaking of a female virtue the very presence of which proves the injustice of his enslavement. But women, literal or metaphoric, if they are autonomous participants in the same individualistic competition as men, are morally compromised to the same degree. To pit the home against the world is to pit a dependent culture against the dominant one from which it takes its shape, and the equality implied by such a competition redefines the dependent culture as independent, thereby stripping it of whatever special qualities and prerogatives it claims by virtue of its dependence. *Uncle Tom's Cabin* requires femininity as a virtue not *in* the corrupt world inhabited by Augustine St. Clare but *of* that eternal home in which slaves, women, and children alike achieve freedom and equality.

I do not mean to imply that Stowe is conscious of the implications of St. Clare in precisely this way. I do, however, want to suggest that the problem of dependence is, necessarily, played out on every level of the novel. Stowe, like other domestic novelists, takes as axiomatic the idea that the dependence of women facilitates their virtue. In its broadest form her argument goes something like this: slaves are fully human, and it is, therefore, a sin to "own" them. We know of their humanity through their likeness to women—through their capacity for Christian faith and the depth of their "maternal" feelings. Women (and, by extension, slaves) are good and affectionate creatures whose dependence insulates them from the competitive, self-aggrandizing spirit of the marketplace. Naturally virtuous, swayed by neither politics nor profit, they feel more keenly than white men the evils of the world. Slaves and women, however, are empowered as examples, not as actors. They realize themselves by coming into the public roles of wife, mother, or martyr, not by asserting themselves as individuals in the world. Their public selves, in other words, are fundamentally private. This being so, they cannot remove their opposition to slavery from the private to the public arena without losing the moral force lent them by their domesticity.

Stowe's argument does not, of course, end with Augustine St. Clare. With his death Stowe turns her attention to reestablishing the merits of the feminine, this time not through the positive example of white women but through the confrontation between two men, the black Uncle Tom and the white Simon Legree. Interestingly, white women disappear from the novel once Marie St. Clare liquidates the family business and returns to her father's plantation. From this point on we travel through slave warehouse and swamp with Tom, only to arrive at Legree's plantation—a place not merely lacking the feminine touch but actively opposed to all forms of domesticity. There is no kitchen in Legree's house, no order, no peace, and no morality; there is only power. Legree himself has spurned with violence the mother who "clung to him, and sought, with passionate prayers and entreaties, to win him from a life of sin" (*UTC,* 381). The closest thing to a wife in Legree's life is the slave woman Cassy, whom he keeps as his mistress by sheer force. Cassy's history of use and abuse by white men serves as a counterpoint to events on the Legree plantation. One effect of the Legree episode is to emphasize by its absence the superior ethos of the home; the other is to invert the power relations of master and slave.

In the first half of *Uncle Tom's Cabin* we move in an orderly progress from one domestic setting to another—from the Shelbys to the Birds to the Hallidays—building toward the false hope of an Augustine St. Clare. With St. Clare's death we are left desolate in the wilderness with Tom, the most completely powerless and, as we learn, for that reason the most powerful character in the novel. Unlike the frail, pale St. Clare, Uncle Tom is a "large, broad-chested, powerfully made man of a full glossy black" (*UTC*, 26), capable of picking a double-weight of cotton to relieve his fellow slave. In him, femininity is a wholly interior attribute, signified by his extreme blackness and variously expressed as empathy, affection, domesticity, and humility. Tom's femininity, unlike St. Clare's, is bound not to poetic temperament but to religious faith. Feminized and disempowered by slavery, Tom cannot, of course, act. What he can do, as he tells Legree, is die and, by dying, reenact Christ's sacrifice.

Faced with the choice of betraying the fugitive slaves, Cassy and Emmeline, or submitting to what he knows will be a fatal beating, Tom goes willingly to his death and, in the process, redefines love as power. Bidding "farewell to every fear," in the words of his hymn, and "smil[ing] at Satan's rage" (*UTC*, 404), Tom achieves in death freedom from slavery, victory over Legree, and the redemptive power of Christ. The thorns of his crown become, like those of Christ in his vision, "rays of glory" (*UTC*, 401), bringing "tears of . . . repentance" to the Judas-like heathens, Quimbo and Sambo, returning feeling to the embittered Cassy, and striking terror in the impenitent heart of Simon Legree. More important than the tears of repentance that flow at Tom's death, however, is its dramatic impact on the young white slaveholder, George Shelby, who arrives at the Legree plantation to rescue Tom just in time to witness his death.

George Shelby, about whose character we know nothing beyond his adolescent attachment to Tom, is reborn at Tom's graveside as the liberator St. Clare once imagined himself. Filled with guilt and righteous anger, he calls on God to "witness, that, from this hour, I will do *what one man can* to drive out this curse of slavery from my land!" (*UTC*, 431). What he can do, of course, is free his slaves, and he returns immediately to Kentucky to do just that. But the slaves, as if to prove beyond any doubt their altogether feminine virtue, "tender back their free papers," saying "We don't want to be no freer than we are. We's allers had all we wanted" (*UTC*, 450). Only when George explains that their lives will remain essentially unchanged do they accept, with "thanks unto the Lord," their freedom. George's words of

reassurance to his slaves so closely resemble in their paternal-
ism those of the male mentor to the girl-heroine of the domestic
novel—"I expect you to be good and willing to learn; and I trust
in God that I shall be faithful, and willing to teach" (*UTC*, 451)
—that they suggest that, emancipated, the status of the blacks
will change only from that of slaves to that of women.

What one white man can do, then, is facilitate the feminine
virtue of the slaves by resolving that "nobody . . . should ever
run the risk of being parted from home and friends" (*UTC*, 451).
George Shelby, in other words, corrects the errors of his father:
the elder Shelby brought slavery into the home, the younger
one banishes it. Explicitly identified as "the liberator"—a title
that would seem to propel him into the public sphere—and
speaking as only the white man, fully autonomous and able to
act at will, can in *Uncle Tom's Cabin*, he nonetheless acts purely
privately, engaging neither in lawless opposition to slavery nor
in political action of any kind. As liberator he is, and must
be, dissociated from the possibility of antinomianism as completely as his black double, George Harris, who is no Nat Turner
but, on the contrary, a mulatto George Washington. George
Shelby's function is to fix and, thus, propagate the meaning of
the martyred Uncle Tom, and this he does by creating, like the
narrator in *The Scarlet Letter*, a tombstone. Uncle Tom's cabin,
Shelby tells his newly liberated slaves, is to be "a memorial to
put you all in mind to follow in his steps, and be as honest and
faithful and Christian as he was" (*UTC*, 451). Just as Tom himself is no longer victimized slave but instead victorious martyr,
so, after his death, his cabin no longer signifies slavery but instead Christianity. It alludes to that new and benevolent Master
who will insure that, even in freedom, the black will remain the
submissive, obedient, loyal creature he was in slavery. The liberation of the slave is accomplished without danger, disorder, or
even change as the black, freed by one master, is put into the
keeping of another.

Stowe contains the antinomian possibilities of "life among the
lowly" by replacing an earthly master with a heavenly one. In
life an insurrectionist like Nat Turner might authorize his re-

bellion by invoking "the spirit that spoke to the prophets in former days,"[12] but in *Uncle Tom's Cabin* that spirit is the exclusive possession of the feminine and the submissive. Confirming the feminine interior self as the repository of Christian virtue, Stowe supplants masculine actors with feminine exempla. The reformation of the fallen world lies with Christ, whose death redeems the sacrifice of the feminine in the deaths of Eva and Tom and inspires the slaveholder to "repentance, justice and mercy" (*UTC*, 460). Ultimately, then, the domestic ideology that underlies *Uncle Tom's Cabin* cannot translate feminine feeling into masculine deed. Consequently, the solution to slavery the novel offers is not social but individual, not political but spiritual, not public but private. Insisting on the moral superiority of the disempowered—wives, mothers, and slaves—*Uncle Tom's Cabin* moves, as it must, beyond the home wherein the powerless are guaranteed their virtue and the virtuous their lack of power. But it moves not out to the world of men but up to heaven, the perfect and eternal home.

It is, of course, only in heaven that the feminine can safely and completely supplant the masculine, but the fact that Stowe abandons the social for the religious does not mean that the novel's strategy fails in political terms. In fact, the tremendous impact of *Uncle Tom's Cabin* is bound to its substitution of the language of gender for that of politics. Removing the problem of slavery from the public to the private sphere, transforming it from a problem of state to one of individual faith, this substitution allows women—in fact, Stowe herself—to recall the nation to its own ideals and transforms the novel into a Jeremiad. On the one hand, enlisting the ideological conventions of the domestic novel in opposition to slavery, Stowe demonstrates that its terms prohibit the move from private feeling to public forms of redress and, thus, contains the lawlessness potential in opposition to slavery. On the other hand, empowering the domestic virtue of women, she calls America not to rebellion but to Christ. Addressing her reader out of the shared experience of maternity—"And oh!, mother that reads this, has there never been in your house a drawer . . . the opening of which has been to you like the opening . . . of a little grave?"—she appeals as a woman to other women to "feel right" and pray. Stowe rewrites Anne Hutchinson's defiance as not lawlessness but piety. No longer a monster, she is instead a mother. And as a mother, she finds her type not in Jezebel but in Mary, who repudiates both art and prophecy for perfect maternity:

> We see a woman in whom the genius and fire of the poet and prophetess is tempered by a calm and equable balance of the intellect. . . . Hers are the powers which might . . . have had a public mission, but they are all concentrated in the nobler, yet secret, mission of the mother. . . . Mary never seems to have sought to present herself as a public teacher; and in the one instance when she sought her son in public, it was from the tremulous anxiety of a mother's affection rather than the self-assertion of a mother's pride. In short, Mary is presented to us as the mother, and the mother alone, seeking no other sphere. Like a true mother she passed out of self into her son, and the life that she lived was in him, and in this sacred self-abnegation she must forever remain, the one ideal type of motherhood.[13]

The woman who "passes" out of herself into her child, a child not satanic but divine, the woman who chooses not self-assertion but self-abnegation, who is not real but ideal, Mary inverts the story of the American Jezebel. And this inversion, this rewriting of the story of Woman, empowers Stowe as author. Speaking in the voice of the mother, Stowe can speak with the authority of a prophet, not despite being a woman but because she is a woman: "Not surer is the eternal law by which the millstone sinks in the ocean, than that stronger law, by which injustice and cruelty shall bring on nations the wrath of Almighty God" (*UTC*, 460).

Epilogue

On the lawn of the gold-domed State House in Boston, opposite Saint-Gauden's famous frieze of General Shaw and his black regiment and far from the statues of Daniel Webster and Horace Mann, stands a bronze memorial to Anne Hutchinson. This statue portrays a demure young woman in colonial garb, her eyes fixed firmly on heaven, one hand clasping a Bible to her heart while the other wraps protectively around a little girl. You have to leave the sidewalk and cross the lawn in order to read the plaque on its base commemorating Hutchinson as a "courageous exponent of civil liberty and religious toleration." Beyond this, the plaque records only the date of Hutchinson's baptism in England and the fact of her death at the hands of Indians in East Chester, New York.

The State House statue was given to the Commonwealth by the federated Women's Clubs of Massachusetts in June of 1920, just two months before the ratification of the Nineteenth Amendment granted women full citizenship. It was not, however, formally accepted by the Massachusetts legislature until 1923 and has apparently never been dedicated. The statue is the product of a period in which assumptions about Woman's nature had clear political import. Its ambiguity—the ambiguity of a statue named Anne Hutchinson but picturing a mother, and a foremother at that—echoes the tension that characterized the debate over female suffrage. One legislator, when asked by a reporter for the *Boston Globe* in 1922 to explain the Commonwealth's reluctance to accept the memorial, captured this ambiguity, pointing out that the statue represents Hutchinson "as an idealist while many think she was aggressive."

His point, of course, was that the State House statue is a fiction. And so it is, in every sense. No portrait exists of Hutchinson, and, despite her many children, the only little girl who figures in her story is a daughter captured by the Indians in the East Chester raid. A fictitious representation, then, the State House statue also tells a story. In fact, it tells the same story told by Hawthorne and Stowe. The American Jezebel, arch-dissenter and mother of monsters, is here, as she is elsewhere, domesticated. And not merely domesticated, but idealized in bronze. The representation of Hutchinson as farsighted visionary and heroic mother requires, of course, the elision of the very history that made her famous, but the elision of that history highlights the tension between heretic and mother.

Thus, the State House statue stands as visual, visible reassurance that Woman, even dissenting woman and so certainly voting woman, holds no danger. Its message is repeated in a book appropriately entitled *Dames and Daughters of Colonial Days* (1900), written in the same period—a book that, without irony, claims Hutchinson as the "founder of the first Woman's Club in America." Hutchinson's life, its author tells us, "may be regarded as a prophecy of that larger liberty for which America has stood for generations."[1] The image of the statue, like the language of the book, rewrites the story of Anne Hutchinson— a story of Woman out of place—as the story of Woman in place, as a story of colonial dames and their daughters. The monsters, it reminds us, were really just children and Hutchinson herself not prophetess but prophecy.

Notes

1. Introduction

1. Nathaniel Hawthorne, *Tales and Sketches* (New York: Library of America, 1982), 18. Additional references to this edition will be cited in the text and identified by the abbreviation *TS* followed by the page number.

2. The most thorough exploration of the role of merchants in the antinomian controversy can be found in Emory Battis, *Saints and Sectaries: Anne Hutchinson and the Antinomian Controversy in the Massachusetts Bay Colony* (Chapel Hill: University of North Carolina Press, 1962). Other versions of this argument appear in Bernard Bailyn, *The New England Merchant in the Seventeenth Century* (New York: Harper and Row, 1955), and Larzer Ziff, *Puritanism in America: New Culture in a New World* (New York: Viking, 1973).

3. Lyle Koehler, *A Search for Power: The "Weaker Sex" in Seventeenth-Century New England* (Chicago: University of Illinois Press, 1980), 221.

4. Quoted in Gertrude Huehns, *Antinomianism in English History* (London: Cresset Press, 1951), 44.

5. Quoted in Huehns, *Antinomianism*, 93.

6. The biblical text most generally cited is Romans 6. For a discussion of the history of antinomianism as a term, see Ronald A. Knox, *Enthusiasm* (New York: Oxford University Press, 1950), and Huehns, *Antinomianism*.

7. George Bancroft, *History of the United States of America*, (Boston: Little, Brown, 1879), 6 vols., 1:298, 296.

8. David D. Hall, ed., *The Antinomian Controversy, 1636–1638: A Documentary History* (Middletown, Conn.: Wesleyan University Press, 1968), 213–14. All additional references to this volume, here and in subsequent chapters, will be cited in the text and identified by the abbreviation *AC* followed by the page number.

9. Huehns, *Antinomianism*, 169.

2. Disturber in Israel

1. Charles Francis Adams, *Three Episodes of Massachusetts History* (Boston: Houghton Mifflin, 1892), 2 vols., 2:367. Two years later, Ad-

ams published the documents of the controversy in a volume entitled *Antinomianism in the Colony of Massachusetts Bay* (Boston: Prince Society, 1894).

2. Adams, *Three Episodes*, 2:567–68.

3. The extent of division in the Puritan community is only now coming to light in such works as Philip F. Gura's *A Glimpse of Sion's Glory: Puritan Radicalism in New England, 1620–1660* (Middletown, Conn.: Wesleyan University Press, 1984).

4. Sacvan Bercovitch, "The Rites of Assent: Rhetoric, Ritual, and the Ideology of American Consensus," in *The American Self: Myth, Ideology, and Popular Culture*, ed. Sam B. Girgus (Albuquerque: University of New Mexico Press, 1981), 5–43.

5. Kai T. Erikson has explored the question of deviance in the antinomian controversy in sociological terms in his *Wayward Puritans: A Study in the Sociology of Deviance* (New York: John Wiley, 1966).

6. Cotton Mather, *Magnalia Christi Americana* (New York: Russell and Russell, 1967), 2 vols., 2:188.

7. Mather, *Magnalia*, 2:190.

8. The objective conditions of life in early Massachusetts were ideal for the enactment of such a theology. Settlements were small—in 1636 Boston, the largest town, had a population of less than one thousand, of whom approximately half were children—and the colony was remarkably homogeneous. Most of the original settlers came from east-central or southeastern England, and new colonists were recruited from among their friends and relatives. The open proprietary system of the early years meant that most newcomers were granted land and admitted to the full privileges of citizenship. Prospective settlers were carefully questioned, and only those intending permanent residence and of good character were permitted to stay. The majority of the colonists were engaged in agricultural activity; in 1634 only about one-third were merchants or craftsmen. Racial differences scarcely existed, and disparities in wealth were not, as yet, widespread or conspicuous enough to provoke serious division. Laws requiring church attendance extended the church's supervision to the community at large. Unlawful or unseemly behavior was brought quickly, by all accounts, to the attention of the appropriate authorities and was disciplined. The leaders of the Bay quite reasonably assumed substantial agreement on matters of morality and on questions of proper comportment, deference to authority, family roles and relations, and economic responsibilities. Without this configuration, "visible sainthood" would have been an empty concept.

9. Perry Miller and Thomas H. Johnson, eds., *The Puritans* (New York: Harper and Row, 1938), 2 vols., 1:316.

10. J. Franklin Jameson, ed., *Johnson's Wonder-working Providence, 1628–51*, in *Original Narratives of Early American History* (New York: Scribners, 1910), 19 vols., 9:127.

11. Ronald A. Knox, *Enthusiasm* (New York: Oxford University Press, 1950), 125.

12. Alan Heimert and Perry Miller, eds., *The Great Awakening: Documents Illustrating the Crisis and Its Consequences* (New York: Bobbs Merrill, 1967), li.

13. David D. Hall, *Faithful Shepherd: A History of the New England Ministry in the Seventeenth Century* (Chapel Hill: University of North Carolina Press, 1970), 113. For another discussion of the problems the Puritan minister faced in maintaining his evangelical role, see Darrett Rutman, *American Puritanism* (New York: Lippincott, 1970).

14. Thomas Shepard, *Works* (Boston, 1853), 3 vols., 1:139.

15. John Winthrop, "A Modell of Christian Charity," in *Colonial American Writing*, ed. Roy Harvey Pearce (New York: Holt, Rinehart, and Winston, 1950), 125.

16. Winthrop, "Modell," 130.

17. Winthrop, "Modell," 130–31.

18. See Cecelia Tichi, "Spiritual Biography and the 'Lords Remembrancers,'" in *The American Puritan Imagination: Essays in Revaluation*, ed. Sacvan Bercovitch (New York: Cambridge University Press, 1974), and Sacvan Bercovitch, *The Puritan Origins of the American Self* (New Haven: Yale University Press, 1975).

19. Miller and Johnson, *Puritans*, 1:246.

20. Harry S. Stout, "Word and Order in Colonial New England," in *The Bible in America: Essays in Cultural History*, ed. Nathan O. Hatch and Mark A. Noll (New York: Oxford University Press, 1982), 26.

21. Stout, "Word and Order," 28–29. Stout goes on to point out that "the Puritans' separatist 'Pilgrim' neighbors . . . retained the original message of free grace uncontaminated by notions of special errand or national covenant. Not surprisingly, the Geneva Bible remained the preferred version in Plymouth Colony. But as Plymouth itself revealed, such doctrinal purity provided no cultural glue for a world-redeeming mission. It was a view that led ultimately to withdrawal and separation."

22. Stout, "Word and Order," 31.

23. Winthrop, "Modell," 116–17.

24. Mather, *Magnalia*, 1:127.

25. The most recent and thorough study of the status of colonial women is Laurel Thatcher Ulrich's *Good Wives: Image and Reality in the Lives of Women in Northern New England, 1650–1750* (New York: Knopf, 1982). Both John Demos, *Entertaining Satan: Witchcraft and the Culture of Early New England* (New York: Oxford University Press, 1982), and Ann Kibbey, "Mutations of the Supernatural: Witchcraft, Remarkable Providences, and the Power of Puritan Men," *American Quarterly* 34 (Summer 1982):125–48, shed new light on gender relations in the colonies.

26. Lyle Koehler, *A Search for Power: The "Weaker Sex" in Seventeenth-*

Century New England (Chicago: University of Illinois Press, 1980), 216–37. Koehler's portrait of Hutchinson as protofeminist seems to me too simple. He fails to see the paradoxical combination of passivity and arrogance inherent in Hutchinson's stance. As a result, his account of the appeal of antinomianism is less convincing than it might be. Further, Koehler's evidence of "feminist" consciousness, however primitive, is weak. By portraying women as victims, he fails, moreover, to account for the large number of men aligned with Hutchinson. Nonetheless, Koehler at least acknowledges the special role of women in the antinomian controversy, an acknowledgment rare among historians of the crisis. For a critique of Koehler's argument, see Sidney Hart and John Putre's letter to the editor in *William and Mary Quarterly* 31 (1):164–69.

27. For contemporary responses to Familism, see William Wilkinson, "A Confutation of Certain Articles delivered unto the Family of Love" (London, 1579); John Knewstub, "A Confutation of Monstrous and Horrible Heresies" (London, 1579); and anon., "Sweet Singers of Israel" (London, 1678). For a modern historian's view, see Alastair Hamilton, *The Family of Love* (New York: Cambridge University Press, 1981).

28. Shepard, *Works,* 1:42.

29. Bercovitch, *Puritan Origins,* 93.

30. Larzer Ziff, "The Literary Consequences of Puritanism," in Bercovitch, *American Puritan Imagination,* 34.

31. Peter Bulkeley, *The Gospel Covenant; or The Covenant of Grace Opened* (London, 1651), 83.

32. Bulkeley, *Gospel Covenant,* 93.

33. Bulkeley, *Gospel Covenant,* 74.

34. Raymond Williams, *Marxism and Literature* (New York: Oxford University Press, 1977), 122.

35. Shepard, *Works,* 1:31–32.

36. For a consideration of the problem of denotation in the language of Hutchinson's examination, see Patricia Caldwell, "The Antinomian Language Controversy," *Harvard Theological Review* 69 (July–October 1976):345–67. For a lengthier discussion of the problem of Puritan expression, see Caldwell, *The Puritan Conversion Narrative: The Beginnings of American Expression* (New York: Cambridge University Press, 1983).

37. Joshua Scottow, *A Narrative of the Planting of the Massachusetts Colony* (Boston, 1694), 30.

3. A Masterpiece of Women's Wit

1. *A Short Story* went through four editions between 1644 and 1692; only the first lacked Welde's preface.

2. Christopher Hill, *The World Turned Upside Down: Radical Ideas During the English Revolution* (New York: Viking, 1972), 12, 130.

3. See Emory Battis, *Saints and Sectaries: Anne Hutchinson and the Antinomian Controversy in the Massachusetts Bay Colony* (Chapel Hill: University of North Carolina Press, 1962), 346–48, for a modern medical diagnosis of the monstrous "births."

4. Ann Kibbey, "Mutations of the Supernatural: Witchcraft, Remarkable Providences, and the Power of Puritan Men," *American Quarterly* 34 (Summer 1982):125–48.

5. For further discussion of this point, see Ross J. Pudaloff, "Sign and Subject: Antinomianism in the Massachusetts Bay," *Semiotica* 54 1/2 (1985), 147–63.

6. John Wheelwright, "Mercurius Americanus," in *Writings* (1876; repr. New York: Burt Franklin, 1968), 197.

7. Sacvan Bercovitch, *The Puritan Origins of the American Self* (New Haven: Yale University Press, 1975), 109.

8. J. Franklin Jameson, ed., *Johnson's Wonder-working Providence, 1628–51*, in *Original Narratives of Early American History* (New York: Scribner's, 1910), 19 vols., 9:25, 52. Subsequent references to this volume will appear in the text, identified by the abbreviation *WWP* followed by the page number.

9. Bercovitch, *Puritan Origins*, 114.

10. Norman Grabo, "The Veiled Vision: The Role of Aesthetics in Early American Intellectual History," in *The American Puritan Imagination: Essays in Revaluation,* ed. Sacvan Bercovitch (New York: Cambridge University Press, 1974), 27.

11. One would expect, for example, to find the story of Anne Hutchinson told in works like Thomas Lechford's *Plain Dealing, or Newes from New England* (London, 1642), Thomas Underhill's *Newes from New England* (London, 1638), or John Palmer's *An Impartial Account of the State of New England* (London, 1690). In fact, these, like Underhill's *A Lamentable Representation of the Effects of the Present Toleration* (London, 1656) and, later, John White's *New England's Lamentations* (Boston, 1734), while they recount the early days of the colony, make no mention of the controversy. Other works, like Thomas Morton's *New England Canaan* (Amsterdam, 1637), John Norton's biography of Cotton entitled *Abel Being Dead Yet Speaketh* (London, 1658), Nathaniel Morton's *New Englands Memoriall* (Cambridge, 1669), Thomas Shepard's *Journal* (1640–44), and Daniel Neal's *History of New England* (London, 1720) make brief or indirect reference to the Hutchinsonians. The topographical histories like Samuel Clarke's *New England Described* (London, 1670) and John Josselyn's *An Account of Two Voyages to New England* (London, 1674) quite naturally make no mention of the antinomians. Other major chronicles—Francis Higginson's *New England's Plantation* (London, 1630), Mourt's *Relation* (London, 1622), John White's *Brief Relation of the Occassion of Planting this Colony* (Lon-

don, 1630), and Thomas Prince's *Chronological History of New England* (Boston, 1736–55)—were written or end their accounts too early to treat the controversy.

12. See, for example, Perry Miller and Thomas H. Johnson, eds., *The Puritans* (New York: Harper and Row, 1938), 2 vols., 1:82, or Michael Kraus, *The Writing of American History* (Norman: University of Oklahoma Press, 1953), 29. For a discussion of this charge, see Cecelia Tichi, "Spiritual Biography and the 'Lord's Remembrances,'" in Bercovitch, *American Puritan Imagination*, 56–76.

13. Tichi, "Spiritual Biography," 70.

14. See, for example, Peter Gay, *The Loss of Mastery* (Berkeley: University of California Press, 1966); J. Franklin Jameson, *The History of Historical Writing in America* (Boston, 1891); Miller and Johnson, *Puritans*, 1.

15. Cotton Mather, *Magnalia Christi Americana* (Hartford, 1853), 2 vols., 2:508.

16. Mather, *Magnalia*, 2:512–13.

17. Mather, *Magnalia*, 2:509.

18. Mather, *Magnalia*, 2:517.

19. It is significant that the association of the antinomian character type with dissent, almost regardless of its form or content, persists into the twentieth century. Many cultural analysts employed the term *antinomian* to describe the New Left of the 1960s, among them Nathan Adler, "The Antinomian Personality: The Hippie Character Type," *Psychiatry* 31 (November 1968), 325–38; Perry E. Gianakos, "New Left Millennialism and American Culture," *Thought* 49 (December 1974), 397–418; Edward Shils, "Plenitude and Scarcity," *Encounter* (May 1969), 37–57; Richard King, *The Party of Eros: Radical Social Thought and the Realm of Freedom* (Chapel Hill: University of North Carolina Press, 1972).

20. John F. Berens, *Providence and Patriotism in Early America, 1640–1815* (Charlottesville: University of Virginia Press, 1978), 32.

21. Sacvan Bercovitch, *The American Jeremiad* (Madison: University of Wisconsin Press, 1978), 67.

22. Thomas Hutchinson, *The History of the Colony and Province of Massachusetts Bay* (1765; repr. New York: Kraus, 1970), 3 vols., 1:62–63.

4. A Flood of Errors

1. Alan Heimert and Perry Miller, eds., *The Great Awakening: Documents Illustrating the Crisis and Its Consequences* (New York: Bobbs Merrill, 1967), 184–85.

2. Richard Bushman, ed., *The Great Awakening: Documents on the Revival of Religion, 1740–45* (New York: Atheneum, 1970), 58–59.

3. As late as 1812, William Emerson points out that *Seasonable Thoughts* "is in the library of almost every American divine; and, even now, perused with pleasure and improvement by all the lovers of rational religion" (*An Historical Account of the First Church in Boston from its Formation to the Present Period* [Boston, 1812], 194).

4. The problem of antinomianism among the revivalists did not escape the notice of observers other than Chauncy, and concern about the heresy did not end in the 1740s. See, for example, from the 1740s, Jonathan Dickinson, "A Display of God's Special Grace" (Boston, 1742); Andrew Croswell, "Mr. Croswell's reply to a book lately published, entitled 'A Display. . . .'" (Boston, 1743); Andrew Croswell, "Heaven Shut Against all Arminians and Antinomians" (Boston, 1747). From the 1760s, see Joseph Bellamy, "A Blow at the Root of the Refined Antinomianism of the Present Day" (Boston, 1763); John Beach, "A Familiar Conference upon some Antinomian Tenets" (New York, 1764); David Judson, "Remarks upon a Familiar Conference. . . ." (New Haven, 1765); John Beach, "A Second Familiar Conference. . . ." (New York, 1765); John Beach, "A Defense of the Second Familiar Conference. . . ." (New York, 1766).

5. Charles Chauncy, *Seasonable Thoughts on the State of Religion in New England* (Boston, 1743), xxvi. Subsequent references to this edition will be cited in the text, identified by the abbreviation *STS* followed by the page number.

6. Charles Chauncy, "Ministers Exhorted and Encouraged to take Heed to themselves, and to their Doctrine" (Boston, 1714), 17.

7. Charles Chauncy, *Enthusiasm Described and Cautioned Against* (Boston, 1742), 5.

8. Charles Chauncy, "Ministers Cautioned against the Occasions of Contempt" (Boston, 1744), 20.

9. Chauncy, *Enthusiasm*, v.

10. Chauncy, *Enthusiasm*, v.

11. Jonathan Edwards, "God the best portion of the Christian," in *The Works of President Edwards* (New York, 1843), 4 vols., 4:545. Subsequent references to this edition will appear in the text, identified by the abbreviation *WE* followed by the volume and page number.

12. For a view of Edwards as conservative, see, for example, Edwin Gaustad, *The Great Awakening in New England* (New York: Harper and Row, 1957), 153–66. Among those who argue for Edwards's modernity, though with qualifications, is Perry Miller, *Errand into the Wilderness* (New York: Harper and Row, 1956), 153–66.

13. Jonathan Edwards, *Some Thoughts Concerning the Revival of Religion*, in *The Great Awakening*, ed. C. C. Goen, vol. 4 of *Works of Jonathan Edwards* (New Haven: Yale University Press, 1957–), 358. Subsequent references to this volume will appear in the text, identified by the abbreviation *ST* followed by the page number.

14. Cushing Strout, *The New Heavens and New Earth* (New York: Harper and Row, 1974), 151.

15. Jonathan Edwards, *A History of the Work of Redemption,* in Heimert and Miller, *Great Awakening,* 24.

16. Charles Chauncy, "The Idle-Poor secluded from the Bread of Charity By the Christian Law" (Boston, 1752), 22.

17. For a discussion of Chauncy's and Edwards's respective positions on charity, see Alan Heimert, *Religion and the American Mind* (Cambridge: Harvard University Press, 1966), 246–53.

18. Chauncy, "Idle-Poor," 14.

19. Chauncy, "Idle-Poor," 6.

20. Chauncy, "Idle-Poor," 15.

21. Benjamin Franklin makes a strikingly similar case in a letter to Richard Jackson, Philadelphia, May 5, 1753, in *Writings of Benjamin Franklin,* ed. Albert Henry Smyth (New York: MacMillan, 1905), 10 vols., 3:133–41. Here, Franklin speculates that the "order of God and Nature" has perhaps "appointed want and misery as the proper punishments for, and cautions against, idleness and extravagance." Defending the notion of a "natural" social ecology, he goes on: "Whenever we attempt to amend the scheme of Providence, and to interfere with the government of the world, we had need be very circumspect, lest we do more harm than good."

22. Edwin Gaustad claims quite convincingly that *Religious Commotions* was more probably written by Chauncy's classmate William Rand than by Chauncy himself. While he does not offer an author for *The Wonderful Narrative,* Gaustad denies that Chauncy wrote it. Both of these assertions are convincing given the extreme difference in style between these and Chauncy's established works. For a discussion of authorship, see Edwin B. Gaustad, "Charles Chauncy and the Great Awakening: A Survey and Bibliography," *Papers of the Biographical Society of America,* vol. 45, 2d quarter (1951).

23. Letter from Chauncy to Ezra Stiles, quoted in Gaustad, *Great Awakening,* 153: "I wrote and printed in that day more than 2 volumes in octavo. A vast number of pieces were published also as written by others; but there was scarce a piece against the times but was sent to me, and I had labour sometimes of preparing it for the press, and always correcting it for the press. I had also hundreds of letters to write, in answer to letters received from all parts of the country."

24. Letter from Chauncy to Nathaniel Chauncy, quoted in Gaustad, *Great Awakening,* 90.

25. The connection between Familist and antinomian doctrine is obvious; more striking is the fact that Familism (as defined by its critics, at least) looks so much like a logical extension of the radical New Light position. The Familists' claims that the learned are unable to preach truly, that none but the sinless can convey the truth, that those

who have the Spirit know all, that any true child of God can show his "pedigree," and that men are capable of perfect obedience to God are like a distant echo of those eighteenth-century American exhorters who professed the "key to knowledge."

26. C. C. Goen in his introduction to *ST*, 82; Donald Weber, "Joshua and the Fathers: The Rhetoric of Generational Conflict in the Great Awakening" (unpublished paper).

27. See Patricia Caldwell, "The Antinomian Language Controversy," *Harvard Theological Review* 69 (July–October 1976):345–67.

28. Edwards did, however, believe that it was not unreasonable to think that God would work according to a logic like that of the morphologies of conversion. See *Religious Affections*, in *Works of Jonathan Edwards*, vol. 1, ed. John E. Smith (New Haven: Yale University Press, 1957–), 151.

29. Daniel B. Shea, Jr., "The Art and Instruction of Jonathan Edwards' *Personal Narrative*," in *The American Puritan Imagination: Essays in Revaluation*, ed. Sacvan Bercovitch (New York: Cambridge University Press, 1974), 166.

30. See Gerald F. Moran, "Conditions of Religious Conversion in the First Society of Norwich, Connecticut, 1718–44," *Journal of Social History* 5 (Spring 1972):331–43, and "The Puritan Saint: Religious Experience, Church Membership, and Piety in Connecticut, 1636–76" (Ph.D. diss., Rutgers, 1974), and Cedric B. Cowing, "Sex and Preaching in the Great Awakening," *American Quarterly* 20 (Fall 1968):624–44, for the first point; Richard Bushman, *From Puritan to Yankee* (New York: Norton, 1967), 194; J. M. Bumstead, "Religion, Finance, and Democracy: The Town of Norton as a Case Study," *Journal of American History* 57 (March 1971):830–31; Philip Greven, *Four Generations: Population, Land, and Family in Colonial Andover* (Ithaca, N.Y.: Cornell University Press, 1970), 279; James Henretta,"The Morphology of New England Society in the Colonial Period," *Journal of Interdisciplinary History* 2 (Autumn 1971):379–98.

31. Barbara Eaton, "Women, Religion, and the Family: Revivalism as an Indicator of Social Change in Early New England," (Ph.D. diss., Berkeley, 1975), and Philip Greven, *The Protestant Temperament* (New York: Meridian, 1977), 124–40.

5. EMERSON AND THE AGE OF THE FIRST PERSON SINGULAR

1. Quoted in Henry May, *The Enlightenment in America* (New York: Oxford University Press, 1976), 129.

2. John Adams, "Thoughts on Government," in *The American Enlightenment*, ed. Adrienne Koch (New York: Braziller, 1965), 246.

3. John Adams, "Dissertation on the Canon and the Feudal Law," in Koch, *American Enlightenment*, 236 (italics mine).

4. For a version of this argument, see Myra Jehlen, *American Incarnation* (Harvard University Press, forthcoming), chap. 4.

5. Ralph Lerner, "Commerce and Character: The Anglo-American as New-Model Man," *William and Mary Quarterly* 36 (January 1979):13. Lerner argues that this view was shared by men as otherwise diverse as Adams, Franklin, Benjamin Rush, and, less obviously, Jefferson.

6. C. B. MacPherson, *The Political Theory of Possessive Individualism: Hobbes to Locke* (New York: Oxford University Press, 1962), 3.

7. George Washington, quoted in Koch, *American Enlightenment*, 24.

8. Alexander Hamilton, et al., *The Federalist Papers*, ed. Clinton Rossiter (New York: New American Library, 1961), 33.

9. William Emerson, *An Historical Sketch of the First Church of Boston from its Formation to the Present Period* (Boston, 1812), 28. Subsequent references to this edition will be cited in the text, identified by the abbreviation *HS* followed by the page number.

10. Mary K. Cayton, "'Sympathy's Electric Chain' and the American Democracy," *New England Quarterly* 55 (March 1982):12. For a consideration of Emerson with special emphasis on his attitude toward the new commercial age and the social organicism of the Federalists, see Cayton, "Society and Solitude: The Social Roots of Emerson's Romanticism" (Ph.D. diss., Brown University, 1981).

11. Joel Porte, *Representative Man: Ralph Waldo Emerson in His Time* (New York: Oxford University Press, 1979), 103.

12. John William Ward, *Andrew Jackson: Symbol for an Age* (New York: Oxford University Press, 1962), 200.

13. Quoted in Ralph L. Rusk, *The Life of Ralph Waldo Emerson* (New York: Scribner, 1949), 284.

14. Roy Harvey Pearce, *The Continuity of American Poetry* (Princeton: Princeton University Press, 1961), 189. For the association of Emerson with an antinomian strain in American literature, see Quentin Anderson, *The Imperial Self: An Essay in American Literary and Cultural History* (New York: Random House, 1971); Stephen Whicher, *Freedom and Fate* (Philadelphia: University of Pennsylvania Press, 1971); Larzer Ziff, *Puritanism in America* (New York: Viking, 1973); Joel Porte, *Representative Man*. For a consideration of antinomianism in Emerson's sermons, see Wesley T. Mott, "Emerson and Antinomianism: The Legacy of the Sermons," *American Literature* 50 (November 1978):369–97.

15. Robert E. Spiller and Alfred R. Ferguson et al., eds., *The Collected Works of Ralph Waldo Emerson* (Cambridge: Belknap of Harvard University Press, 1971–), 1:204. Subsequent references to this edition will be cited in the text, identified by the abbreviation *CW* followed by volume and page numbers.

16. See Perry Miller, *The Life of the Mind in America* (New York: Har-

court Brace and World, 1965), 3–35. The complicated influence of Mary Moody Emerson on her nephew is only now receiving substantial attention but will undoubtedly prove important in this regard. See Phyllis Cole, "The Advantage of Loneliness: Mary Moody Emerson's Almanacks, 1802–55," in *Emerson: Prospect and Retrospect,* ed. Joel Porte (Cambridge: Harvard University Press, 1982), and Evelyn Barish, "Emerson and the Angel of Midnight: The Legacy of Mary Moody Emerson," in *Mothering the Mind,* ed. Ruth Perry and Martine Brownley (New York: Holmes and Meier, 1984).

17. Quentin Anderson, *Imperial Self,* 14.

18. William H. Gilman et al., eds., *Journals and Miscellaneous Notebooks of Ralph Waldo Emerson* (Cambridge: Belknap of Harvard University Press, 1960–82), 16 vols., 4:79, 83. Subsequent references to this edition will be cited in the text, identified by the abbreviation *JMN* followed by volume and page numbers.

19. *Complete Works of Ralph Waldo Emerson* (Boston: Houghton-Mifflin, 1883), 14 vols., 6:23–24.

20. Letter to Thomas Carlyle, Dec. 31, 1844, quoted in *Selections from Ralph Waldo Emerson,* ed. Stephen Whicher (Boston: Houghton-Mifflin, 1957), 329.

21. Myra Jehlen, "New World Epics: The Novel and the Middle Class in America," *Salmagundi* 36 (Winter 1977):55.

22. Michael T. Gilmore, "Emerson and the Persistence of Commodity," in *Emerson: Prospect and Retrospect,* ed. Joel Porte (Cambridge: Harvard University Press, 1982), 70. For examples of "revisionist" histories of the Jacksonian period, see Edward Pessen, *Jacksonian America: Society, Personality, and Politics* (Homewood, Ill.: Dorsey Press, 1969), and "The Egalitarian Myth and American Social Reality: Wealth, Mobility, and Equality in the 'Era of the Common Man,'" in *The Many-Faceted Jacksonian Era,* ed. Edward Pessen (Westport, Conn.: Greenwood Press, 1977); Marvin Meyers, *The Jacksonian Persuasion* (Stanford: Stanford University Press, 1957).

23. Anne C. Rose, *Transcendentalism as a Social Movement, 1830–50* (New Haven: Yale University Press, 1981), 70.

24. See Jesse Bier, "Weberism, Franklin, and the Transcendental Style," *New England Quarterly* 43 (June 1970):179–90.

25. See Len Gougen, "Abolition, the Emersons, and 1837," *New England Quarterly* 54 (September 1981):345–65.

26. *Complete Works of Ralph Waldo Emerson* (Boston: Houghton-Mifflin, 1883), 6:16.

6. The Lady or the President

1. "Woman," in *Complete Works of Ralph Waldo Emerson* (Cambridge: Riverside Press, 1884), 14 vols., 11:339. Subsequent references to this

essay will be cited in the text, identified by the abbreviation W followed by the page number.

2. Margaret Fuller, *Woman in the Nineteenth Century* (New York: W. W. Norton, 1971), 23–24.

3. Fuller, *Woman*, 115.

4. Russel B. Nye, *George Bancroft: Brahmin Rebel* (New York: Knopf, 1944), 99.

5. Not only were earlier histories reprinted in the nineteenth century (Alexander Young's *Chronicles of the First Planter*, for example, was published in Boston in 1846) but the story of the antinomian controversy was recounted anew by both church historians and the new "modern" historians. See, for example, Isaac Backus, *Church History of New England from 1620–1804* (Philadelphia, 1844), and William Hubbard, *General History of New England* (Boston, 1848)—both of these written earlier—as well as T. A. L. V. I. Robinson, *Talvi's History of America* (London, 1851); Joseph Felt, *The Ecclesiastical History of New England* (Boston, 1855–62); John Adams Vinton, *The Antinomian Controversy of 1636* (Boston, 1873); Arthur B. Ellis, *A History of the First Church in Boston, 1630–1880* (Boston, 1881); and George E. Ellis, *The Puritan Age and Rule in the Colony of Massachusetts Bay, 1629–85* (Boston, 1888). Hutchinson's story was repeated as well in works such as Edith Deen's *Great Women of the Christian Faith* (New York, 1817) and James L. Kingsley's *The Lives of Ezra Stiles . . . and Anne Hutchinson* (Boston, 1834).

6. George Bancroft, *History of the United States of America* (Boston: Little, Brown, 1879), 6 vols., 1:305. Subsequent references to this edition will be cited in the text, identified by the abbreviation *US* followed by volume and page numbers.

7. B. M. Dusenbery, ed., *Monument to the Memory of General Andrew Jackson* (Philadelphia, 1846), 42.

8. Quoted in John William Ward, *Andrew Jackson: Symbol for an Age* (New York: Oxford University Press, 1962), 63.

9. Quoted in Ward, *Andrew Jackson*, 56; see also Dusenbery, *Monument*, 124–25, 158–59.

10. Dusenbery, *Monument*, 206.

11. See, for example, Ward, *Andrew Jackson*, 192–200.

12. Dusenbery, *Monument*, 35.

13. Dusenbery, *Monument*, 50.

14. Harriet V. Cheney, *A Peep at the Pilgrims* (Boston, 1850), 38.

15. Cheney, *Peep*, 134.

16. Cheney, *Peep*, 331.

17. Michael Davitt Bell, *Hawthorne and the Historical Romance of New England* (Princeton: Princeton University Press, 1971), 104. For an account of the romancers' view of colonial history in general, see 17–102.

18. John Neal, *Rachel Dyer: A North American Story* (Portland, 1828), 37–38.

19. Eliza Buckminster Lee, *Naomi, or Boston, Two Hundred Years Ago* (Boston, 1848), 43. Subsequent references to this edition will be cited in the text, identified by the abbreviation *N* followed by the page number.

20. Bell, *Hawthorne*, 182.

7. AN AMERICAN JEZEBEL:
HAWTHORNE AND *THE SCARLET LETTER*

1. Ian Watt, *The Rise of the Novel* (Berkeley: University of California Press, 1957), 13.

2. Watt, *Novel*, 12.

3. Nathaniel Hawthorne, *The Scarlet Letter* (New York: Library of America, 1983), 158. Subsequent references to this edition will be cited in the text, identified by the abbreviation *SL* followed by the page number.

4. Michael Colacurcio, "Footsteps of Anne Hutchinson: The Context of *The Scarlet Letter*," *ELH* 39 (September 1972):477.

5. It is interesting that Hawthorne does not employ the language of adultery in his historical sketch of Mrs. Hutchinson. Preeminently the "Woman" and passionate in her spiritual pride, his Hutchinson is nonetheless free of all suggestion of sexual misconduct. He alludes indirectly to the "monstrous births" but with no intention of repeating this portion of the "old and homely narrative." It is almost as if Hawthorne, understanding the births as metaphor and himself as historian, strips away the layers of figurative language that had accrued to Hutchinson's story in order to get at the "real" heretic—and, in a sense, to make room for his own metaphors. Hutchinson's crimes, as he represents them in the sketch, while they are intimately associated with her gender, are not sexual crimes per se.

6. Michael T. Gilmore has discussed the significance of the number seven in *The Scarlet Letter*. As he points out, Hester has broken the seventh commandment, the action of the novel covers a period of seven years from 1642 to 1649, seven years is the term of the indentured servant in the colonies and the number of the Sabbatism. See Gilmore, *The Middle Way: Puritanism and Ideology in American Romantic Fiction* (New Brunswick, N.J.: Rutgers University Press, 1977), 87, 108.

7. Michael Colacurcio has convincingly argued that Hutchinson's most committed follower, Mary Dyer, who was later hanged as a Quaker, serves as one of the models for Catherine in "The Gentle Boy." See Colacurcio, "Footsteps," 473.

8. For one portrait of the "feminized" minister of the nineteenth century, see Ann Douglas, *The Feminization of American Culture* (New York: Knopf, 1977).

9. For a discussion of Puritan preparationism, see Perry Miller,

"'Preparation for Salvation' in Seventeenth Century New England," *Nature's Nation* (Cambridge: Harvard University Press, 1967), 50–77; Norman Pettit, *The Heart Prepared: Grace and Conversion in Puritan Spiritual Life* (New Haven: Yale University Press, 1966); and Darrett Rutman, *American Puritanism: Faith and Practice* (New York: Lippincott, 1970).

8. Feel Right and Pray

1. The complex relationship between the female author and her work has been a central concern of feminist literary criticism. The first systematic and sustained treatment of the problem of female literary authority was Sandra M. Gilbert and Susan Gubar, *The Madwoman in the Attic: The Woman Writer and the Nineteenth-Century Literary Imagination* (New Haven: Yale University Press, 1979); the most recent treatment of this problem in relation to American domestic novelists is Mary Kelley, *Private Woman, Public Stage: Literary Domesticity in Nineteenth-Century America* (New York: Oxford University Press, 1984).

2. Henry Nash Smith, *Democracy and the Novel: Popular Resistance to Classic American Writers* (New York: Oxford University Press, 1978), 15.

3. Jane Tompkins, *Sensational Designs: The Cultural Work of American Fiction, 1790–1860* (New York: Oxford University Press, 1985), 145. My argument diverges from that of Tompkins most sharply on the question of the origins and the impact of the empowered domestic heroine in *Uncle Tom's Cabin*. Tompkins locates the radical thrust of Stowe's novel in its representation of the home, governed by Christian love and ruled by women. The conservatism of Stowe's domestic ideology, she argues, reconstitutes the home as a revolutionary alternative to the world of men: *Uncle Tom's Cabin* "puts the central affirmations of a culture into the service of a vision that would destroy the present economic and social institutions" (145). It is my contention that the home, a contingent sphere defined vis-à-vis a dominant male one, cannot destroy or supplant the world but only recall it to its own avowed ideals. And this is because the destruction (as opposed to the reformation) of existing economic and social institutions would, willy nilly, strip the home of the very virtues that Stowe admires in it. For a discussion of domestic economy and its force in *Uncle Tom's Cabin*, see Gillian Brown, "Getting in the Kitchen with Dinah: Domestic Politics in *Uncle Tom's Cabin*," *American Quarterly* 36 (Fall 1984):503–24. For the range of argument about the significance of the conservatism of domestic fiction, see Henry Nash Smith, "The Scribbling Women and the Cosmic Success Story," *Critical Inquiry* 1 (September 1974):49–70; Nina Baym, *Woman's Fiction: A Guide to Novels by and About Women* (Ithaca, N.Y.: Cornell University Press, 1978).

4. Harriet Beecher Stowe, *Uncle Tom's Cabin or, Life Among the Lowly*

(Cambridge: Harvard University Press, 1962), 1. All subsequent references to this edition will be cited in the text and identified by the abbreviation *UTC* followed by the page number.

5. Myra Jehlen, "Archimedes and the Paradox of Feminist Criticism," in *Feminist Theory: A Critique of Ideology*, ed. Nannerl O. Keohane, Michelle Z. Rosaldo, and Barbara C. Gelpi (Chicago: University of Chicago Press, 1981), 207.

6. Nina Baym, *Woman's Fiction*, 22.

7. For a discussion of Uncle Tom as heroine, see Elizabeth Ammons, "Heroines in *Uncle Tom's Cabin*," in *Critical Essays on Harriet Beecher Stowe*, ed. Elizabeth Ammons (Boston: G. K. Hall, 1980), 152–65.

8. This argument is made most emphatically (though not exclusively) by James Baldwin in *Notes of a Native Son* (New York: Bantam, 1964), 12–13.

9. Lydia Maria Child, *An Appeal in favor of that class of Americans called Africans* (Boston, 1833).

10. George Frederickson, *The Black Image in the White Mind* (New York: Harper and Row, 1971), 118.

11. Jehlen, "Archimedes," 210.

12. "The Confessions of Nat Turner" (1831), in *William Styron's Nat Turner: Ten Black Writers Respond*, ed. John Henrik Clarke (Boston: Beacon Press, 1968), 101. Nat Turner was, of course, the prototype for Dred, the prophet-hero of Stowe's next novel. Although *Dred: A Tale of the Great Dismal Swamp* (1865) conjures up the possibility of slave insurrections by its allusions to Turner, it, like *Uncle Tom's Cabin*, rejects violent rebellion as a subject, and Dred remains prophet, not actor, to the end. Nonetheless, *Dred* does record Stowe's shift away from the colonization movement and toward abolitionism.

13. Harriet Beecher Stowe, *Woman in Sacred History* (New York, 1874), unpaginated.

EPILOGUE

1. Geraldine Brooks, *Dames and Daughters of Colonial Days* (New York: Thomas Crowell, 1900), 3, 28.

Index

also Antinomianism; Hutchin-
son, Anne; Individualism
Finney, Charles Grandison, 117
Franklin, Benjamin, 89n.21, 107–108
Fugitive Slave Act, 193, 196
Fuller, Margaret: *Woman in the Nine-
teenth Century*, 140–41; men-
tioned, 145, 152, 170

Gender: and antinomianism, 10, 14,
102–106, 145, 165–66, 179, 189–90;
and dissent, 103–106, 135, 145,
160, 179; in Great Awakening,
103–106; and individualism, 138,
162. *See also* Individualism; Woman; Women
Geneva Bible, 37, 48, 49, 50
Gorton, Samuel, 65
Great Awakening: in America, 72–
74; class and gender in, 102–106;
compared to antinomian controversy, 75, 93–106; in Europe, 72;
and individualism, 97; itinerancy
during, 73–74; lay exhortation
during, 73–74; social composition of, 104. *See also* Chauncy,
Charles; Edwards, Jonathan
Groome, Samuel, 64

Halfway Covenant, 70, 72
Hawkins, Jane, 56
Hawthorne, Nathaniel: "The
Custom House," 162, 166, 180;
"The Gentle Boy," 173; "Mrs.
Hutchinson," 1–4, 11–13, 161–64;
The Scarlet Letter, 161–92, 195;
mentioned, 136, 193, 194, 216
Hogg, James: *Confessions of a Justified
Sinner*, 8
Hooker, Thomas, 25
Hutchinson, Anne: as American
Jezebel, 9, 17, 41, 43, 58–59, 64,
67, 68, 143, 145, 174, 216; George
Bancroft's account of, 146–48;
and charges of Familism, 43–44,
45–46; claim to revelations, 27,
40, 63; in colonial chronicles, 52–
71; on covenant of grace, 19–20,
32; on covenant of works, 20–21;

and Ralph Waldo Emerson, 148–
49; William Emerson's account
of, 112–14; as Eve, 55–56, 57, 58–
59, 64, 67, 138–39, 145; as fanatic,
111–12, 146–47, 154; and female
autonomy, 41–46, 70; in "Mrs.
Hutchinson," 1–4, 11–13, 161–64;
as Hydra, 65, 67, 68; and Mary,
170–71, 174, 214; as "masculine,"
158, 161; as mother of "monsters," 56–58, 63, 67, 135; on
problem of assurance, 26–27; as
prophetess, 2, 27, 40, 63, 68,
138–39, 143, 144, 155, 189–91, 194,
214–16; on role of ministers, 21–
22; in *The Scarlet Letter*, 165–66,
172, 180, 183, 189–90, 192; as seductress, 55–56; and sexual misconduct, 43, 45–46, 166; as
Transcendentalist, 15; use of Geneva Bible, 37, 48, 49, 50; and
Roger Williams, 148–49; as woman, 1–4, 11–14, 41–46, 63, 70, 161–
92; and women writers, 1–4, 13,
155–64, 193–96. *See also* Antinomianism; Antinomian Controversy; Woman
Hutchinson, Lucy, 142
Hutchinson, Thomas, 71, 107
Hutchinson, William, 4

Individualism: and antinomianism,
14, 35–36, 47–48, 49–50, 70,
92–93, 97–98, 111, 116–17, 118–19,
121–22, 134, 153–54; economic,
115–16; eighteenth century, 108–
11; Emerson on, 118–34; and fiction, 161–63; and free enterprise,
126, 127–30; and Great Awakening, 87–98; and Puritanism, 47–
49, 50; in *The Scarlet Letter*, 161–
92; in *Uncle Tom's Cabin*, 193–214

Jackson, Andrew: America of, 127;
as antinomian, 150–52; eulogies
of, 150–53; and feminine virtue,
152; and law, 151; as self-reliant
man, 150–51; mentioned, 196
Jacksonians, 128, 130

Compositor: Harrington-Young Typography & Design
Text: 10/12 Palatino
Display: Palatino
Printer: Braun-Brumfield
Binder: Braun-Brumfield